Henry Plantagenet

RICHARD BARBER

THE BOYDELL PRESS

First published 1964
The Boydell Press, Ipswich
Reissued 1972

New edition 2001
Reprinted in paperback 2003

ISBN 0 85115 824 2 hardback
ISBN 0 85115 993 1 paperback

The Boydell Press is an imprint of Boydell & Brewer Ltd
PO Box 9, Woodbridge, Suffolk IP12 3DF, UK
and of Boydell & Brewer Inc.
PO Box 41026, Rochester, NY 14604–4126, USA
website: www.boydell.co.uk

A catalogue record for this title is available
from the British Library

Library of Congress Cataloging-in-Publication data
Barber, Richard W.
 Henry Plantagenet / Richard Barber. – New ed.
  p. cm.
 Includes bibliographical references and index.
 ISBN 0–85115–824–2 (acid-free paper)
 1. Henry II, King of England, 1133–1189. 2. Great Britain
– History – Henry II, 1154–1189. 3. Great Britain – Kings and
rulers Biography. I. Title.
DA20   –068063
 942

CONTENTS

ILLUSTRATIONS

Colour illustrations
Following page 102

Black and white illustrations

Plate 6: Radio Times Hulton Picture Library
Plates 2 and 3: British Museum
Plates 4, 5 and 7: Archives Photographiques, Paris

HENRY PLANTAGENET

The earth goeth on the earth
    Glistening like gold;
The earth goeth to the earth
    Sooner then it wold.

The earth buildeth on the earth
    Castles and towers;
The earth saith to the earth:
    'All shall be ours!'

From an epitaph at Melrose Abbey.

Prologue

EIGHT centuries separate us from the age of Henry II. With each year's passing our links with the Plantagenet's times grow fewer and more slender, and the obstacles to understanding the thoughts and ways of a man living in his circumstances becomes correspondingly greater. Nor are the scattered remnants of his legacy sure guides; for if we still honour the system of trial by jury, the modern jurymen are not witnesses but assessors, and if we still count in pennies, a penny is no longer a day's wage. The institution of monarchy itself and the figure of the king have a wholly different aura: the royal personage in Henry's days had an element of the divine, a relic of the days not long before, when the king was magical in his power, priest as well as ruler, and on occasions the sacrifice for his people's well-being. Attitudes of mind are yet harder to recapture, and here lies the greatest difference of all; for logic, to a twelfth-century statesman, was a scholar's technical term, and cold reasoning was apt to be called craft. Instinct and emotion played a much more obvious part in men's deeds and decisions, and the specious excuses with which acts of doubtful legality are now invested were only just beginning to play a part in international politics.

Even those elements of life that seem easiest to comprehend at such a distance may well elude us. When in some remote part of England's countryside, the scene seems changeless under an unchanging sky, the sense of timelessness is false. Both the English weather and the English landscape have changed. In Henry's day, the winters were harsher, the summers drier; when the Thames at Oxford was frozen in the first days of December of 1142, none of the chroniclers noted the frosts as exceptionally early or severe. Droughts figure more sharply and frequently in the annals than we would expect, although this is partly because a dry season in a community dependent on the land was an overwhelming disaster and not, as now, a mere inconvenience.

The familiar patchwork of England's landscape—its alternating squares of corn, pasture and roots, even its broad grazing lands flecked with sheep—would have been strange to twelfth-century eyes. Only the wild places, moor and forest, have remained the same, and their extent is greatly diminished. Forests which were vast reserves for the game which the Norman kings loved to hunt covered much of southern England; their fragments can be seen in the New Forest and in Epping Forest. In them, he who dared to fell trees to make a clearing, to take game—whether deer, or hare, or lesser fry—was liable to the harsh penalties of the special forest law designed to protect the royal pastime. Outside the wild and forbidding confines of the forest, where the occasional wolf and the fugitive from justice lurked alike, the countryside was divided into minute patterns by the village lands, farmed by lord and villein alike on the strip principle. Huge unfenced fields were divided into lengths, each no more than twenty or thirty yards wide, and varying numbers of these strips were allotted to each farmer. A narrow grass balk, or more often only an open drain, divided the holdings, and one man's strips were usually scattered around the village lands. The whole of each field was surrounded by movable hurdles to keep wild beasts and stray cattle off the crops, and once in every two or three years, the field would be left to lie fallow. After harvest, the animals of the village would be put to graze on it for a short while. In some parts of the country—notably the south-east, which had been tilled and enclosed long before the manor and village came to play so great a part in society, and the wilder west and north—other systems prevailed; but the feudal law of service and bond which made the serf's life proverbially hard was universal.

Relief from the day's work, from the endless succession of toil from dawn to sunset, was as rare for many of the lesser lords as for their serfs. Only the great men of the realm journeyed to any extent, along the rough tracks and remains of Roman roads which were the only means of communication. Movement from place to place was slow; an express courier on royal business, able to change horses as and when required, might cover forty to fifty miles a day in good country. At one of the most dramatic moments of Henry II's reign, a courier rode from Alnwick to London in five days and four nights with the news of the capture of the king of Scotland. Where the land was wild, or many streams had to be forded—bridges were few and far between—life was correspondingly more isolated and travel slower. The pattern of villages across the face of England was much as we know it now; but those little hamlets of a few rough wattle houses lacked the network of connecting paths and roads which have slowly developed in the intervening centuries.

In sharp contrast to the static nature of the society he ruled, the king was a quicksilver figure, without a permanent base. A number of royal residences were the nearest to a home that he knew; Clarendon, Woodstock, Westminster and Winchester were Henry's favourites. Most often he was a guest in some baron's hall, and if travel proved difficult, he might find himself at nightfall in such shelter as he could find, while his court fought over the possession of a hovel unfit for pigs. All his requirements, from the chancery where the royal documents were written out, to the royal chapel, had to have a place in the train of carts which followed him on his travels, even if they had permanent bases elsewhere. The Norman king was no stranger to discomfort and even danger; but they were different from the hardships of his people's everyday life, oppression, injustice and endless toil.

Nor did the cities offer any escape from the less pleasant aspects of the countryman's existence. Their narrow streets were busy, trade flourished, but their buildings were for the most part of timber, their roads fetid with refuse in summer, miry and treacherous in winter. The citizens enjoyed a little freedom, but were suspected by the lords as a result, and the king kept a strict control on any organisations within the towns which might challenge his authority in the least degree. The rise of the urban centres was a slow one, hampered by many setbacks: Henry II himself was no friend to London, whose charter he suspended for the latter years of his reign. Only when Richard I found himself in need of money for the Crusade were the citizens able to regain it, by making a large contribution to the treasury. Nevertheless, the London of those days, as portrayed by a biographer of Thomas Becket in about

1172, may still sound to modern ears a paradise of simplicity and spaciousness:

'Among the noble cities of the world that are celebrated by fame, the city of London, seat of the monarchy of England, is one that spreads its fame wider, sends its wealth and wares further, and lifts its head higher than all others. It is blest in the wholesomeness of its air, in its reverence for the christian faith, in the strength of its bulwarks, the nature of its situation, the honour of its citizens, and the chastity of its matrons. It is likewise most merry in its sports and fruitful of noble men. . . . On the east stands the Tower, exceeding great and strong, whose walls and bailey rise from very deep foundations, their mortar being mixed with the blood of beasts. On the west are two strongly fortified castles, while from them there runs a great continuous wall, very high, with seven double gates, and towers at intervals along its north side. On the south, London once had similar walls and towers; but the Thames, that mighty river teeming with fish, which runs on that side and ebbs and flows with the sea, has in the passage of time washed those bulwarks away, undermining them and bringing them down. Upstream, to the west, the royal palace rises high above the river, an incomparable building ringed by an outwork and bastions, two miles from the city and joined to it by a populous suburb.

'On all sides, beyond the houses, lie the gardens of the citizens that live in the suburbs, planted with trees, spacious and fair, laid out beside each other.

'To the north are pasture lands and pleasant open spaces of level meadow, intersected by running waters, which turn mill-wheels with a cheerful sound. Nearby lies a great forest with wooded glades full of lairs of wild beasts, red and fallow deer, boars and bulls. The corn-fields are no barren gravel, but rich Asian plains such as "make glad the crops" and fill the barns of their farmers "with sheaves of Ceres' stalk".

'There are also around London in its suburbs excellent wells, with sweet, wholesome and clear water, whose "runnels ripple amid pebbles bright". Among these Holywell, Clerkenwell and St Clement's Well are most famous and are visited by thicker throngs and greater multitudes of students from the schools and of the young men of the city, who go out on summer evenings to take the air. This is indeed a good city, when it has a good lord!'

The writer, William Fitzstephen, goes on to describe several lively scenes from the life of the city, of which the most vivid are the scholars' debates, the throng at the public cook-shop, and the citizens' sports at Smithfield.

'On holy days the masters of the schools assemble their pupils at the churches whose feast day it is. The scholars dispute, some in demonstrative rhetoric, others in dialectic. . . . Sophists who produce fictitious arguments are accounted happy in the profusion and deluge of their words; others seek to trick their opponents by the use of fallacies. Some speakers occasionally try to make persuasive harangues in rhetorical style, taking pains to observe the precepts of their art and to omit nothing concerned with it. Boys of different schools compete in verse or argue the principles of the art of grammar or the rules about the past and future tenses. There are others who employ the old wit of the cross-roads in epigrams, rhymes and metre; with "Fescennine license", they lacerate their comrades in outspoken lines, though no names are mentioned; they hurl abuse and gibes, ridicule the foibles of their comrades, perchance even of their elders. . . .

'Moreover there is in London on the river-bank, amid the wine sold from ships and wine-cellars, a public cook-shop. There daily you can find the seasonal foods, dishes roast, fried and boiled, fish of every size, coarse meat for the poor and delicate for the rich, such as venison and various kinds of birds. If travel-weary friends should suddenly call on any of the citizens, and do not wish to wait until fresh food is bought and cooked and "till servants bring water for hands and bread", they hasten to the river-bank, where everything that they could want is ready and waiting. . . . Those who desire to fare delicately need not search to find sturgeon or guinea-fowl or Ionian francolin, since every sort of delicacy is set out for them here.

'Every Sunday in Lent after dinner a "fresh swarm of young gentlemen" goes forth on war-horses, "steeds skilled in the contest", . . . armed with lance and shield, the younger with shafts forked at the end and blunted. "They wake war's semblance" and in mimic contest exercise their skill at arms. Many courtiers come too, when the king is in residence; and from the households of earls and barons come young men not yet knights, to compete there. Each is fired with the hope of victory. The fierce horses neigh, their limbs tremble; champing the bit, impatient of delay, they cannot stand still. When at length the "hooves of trampling steeds career along", the young riders divide their hosts, some pursuing those that take flight, unable to overtake them; others unhorse their comrades and gallop on.

'At Easter, they make sport with tournaments on the river. A shield is firmly tied to a stout pole in midstream, and a small boat, rowed with the current by many oarsmen, carries a young man standing in the bows, who has to strike the shield with his lance. His object is to break the lance by striking the shield and keeping his footing. But if he strikes it and does not splinter the lance, he falls into the river, and the boat goes on without him.

'When the great marsh along the northern walls of the city is frozen, crowds of young men go out to amuse themselves on the ice. Some run to gather speed, and slide along the ice with feet apart, covering great distances. Others make seats of ice shaped like millstones and get a group of others who run in front of them holding hands to drag them along. Sometimes they go too fast, and all fall flat on their faces. Others more skilled in ice-sports fit the shin-bones of beasts to their feet, lashing them to their ankles, and use an iron shod pole to propel themselves, pushing against the ice; they are borne along as swiftly as a bird in flight or a bolt from a mangonel. Many of the citizens delight in taking their sport with birds of the air, merlins and falcons and such-like, and with hunting dogs. The inhabitants of the city have the special privilege of hunting in Middlesex, Hertfordshire, the Chilterns, and in Kent as far as the river Cray.'[1]

Against such a background as this the people of London lived and worked. But what were the larger configurations of race and tradition in which they shared? When Henry II came to the throne, it was eighty-eight years since the Norman invaders had overthrown the Saxon dynasty and ruling class, and Normans had figured among the great men of the country for almost a century. How sharp the division between Norman and Saxon was immediately after the Conquest is almost impossible to determine. But by the mid-twelfth century, the line had become blurred to a great extent. True, Saxon names figure rarely among the lords; so much so that a French historian of the nineteenth century could portray Becket as champion of the Saxons against the Norman invaders. It would be nearer the mark to see the question as one of property. If Saxons had managed to retain their lands, they would probably have intermarried with the newcomers, and their names would have become Anglo-French; if they had been deprived of their inheritance, they would have sunk to the level of serfs. Because the higher stratum of society was chiefly Norman, and the lower stratum predominantly Saxon, this did not make *ipso facto* for dissensions. Society's order was part of God's natural order, and a Norman lord was hardly distinguishable from a Saxon one after a century.

On the European level, nationality and language were not problems of the same magnitude as they are today. The contrast lay between the local, uneducated communities, and the international group of men who could speak Anglo-French (and hence feel at home on both sides of the English Channel), or Latin, which was understood from one end of western Christendom to the other. Even the few signs of national feeling were curiously local in flavour: more reminiscent of the tales told about the men of one region by the inhabitants of another than of the heat of rival loyalties. The picture of English students as hearty drinkers, lovers, and eaters, in the poem *Burnel the Ass*, and the story that Englishmen had tails, do not sound like the insults hurled by one nation at another, but smack of local legend and gossip. Only with the rise of the popular languages to the status of Latin, which meant that the literature and business dealings of different peoples were no longer mutually understood, and with the weakening of the feudal structure of society in favour of an embryonic State, did a man's birthplace come to acquire a new importance. Even the Jews were no exception to this international attitude, for their French origins made them share the attitudes of the Anglo-Norman barons and clergy. Their society stood somewhat apart, but their different customs were viewed with tolerance, and only their skill in finance aroused envy.

B

This unity was in the main due to the great institution of
the Roman Church, and the great system of feudalism. Both were
ubiquitous, albeit in varying forms, in western Europe. The
church's universality was plain for all to see. The pope's decree
ran almost as widely as that of the Roman emperor before him. In
the Church, a man could rise from English monk to French abbot,
and thence to pope by way of an Italian archbishopric and an
embassy to Sweden, as Adrian IV had done. A traveller could go
into any church in Latin Christendom, from Jerusalem to Glas-
gow, and find essentially the same service in use. And the pope
could curb a defiant monarch to his will by excommunicating his
servants or laying an interdict on his domains. These weapons, so
deadly in their time, seem strange to us now, when the two swords
of spiritual and temporal power are entirely separated and heresy
is more orthodox than orthodoxy itself. To be put beyond the pale
of the faith was as fierce a penalty as outlawry. No good christian
was supposed to have truck with the excommunicate, whether in
everyday life, in matters of state, or in personal contact. However,
the Church could not impose its sentence as zealously as the royal
officers, and in practice, excommunication did not make life impossible: the members of the king's household so sentenced by
Becket were able to carry out their tasks efficiently. Interdict was
another matter: a general ban on all church services affected everyone in so devout an age. And if those who paid only lip-service
found this no hardship in the ordinary way, the withdrawal of all
sacraments included baptisms, marriages and funerals. The mere
threat of interdict was enough to turn the most obstinate king
aside; yet it was not the pope's last weapon. The sovereign himself
could be excommunicated and his subjects released from their oaths
to him: an authorised incitement to revolt. Although only recognised as a legitimate procedure in the previous century, the interdict was no mere threat, but a reality: it was used in Scotland in
1181, France in 1200, and England in 1209.

Feudalism worked in a less positive way towards an international attitude. Instead of a basis of territorial sovereignty, a
lordship over land which could be changed only by conquest or
gift, feudalism gave the medieval state a structure which made the
king more responsible to his subjects, and which, by dual allegi-

ances, rendered borders less hard and fast. The feudal bond could be dissolved, at least in theory, if the lord to whom allegiance was rendered failed to do justice to his vassal or to protect him adequately. Nor—again in theory—was allegiance passed from father to son by inheritance. Hence the lands of any one man, be he emperor or minor baron, were linked only by a series of personal agreements subject to definite provisos. From this foundation, no ruler could hope to build a permanent state, and hence certain vital areas, notably in eastern and southern France, remained permanent buffers between the personal ambitions of neighbouring princes. Militant nationalism could not emerge while such conditions prevailed, and it was only when the kings of France and England had discovered how to render the feudal element in their states unimportant by exploiting to the full royal prerogatives and privileges, especially in legal and fiscal matters, that the first modern states emerged.

The corollary of this was that kings fought not to aggrandise their countries, but to enlarge the power of their dynasty. Henry Plantagenet fought to build an empire for himself and his sons; and his dealings with the latter have a double irony as a result. Philip Augustus opposed Henry, not as ruler of France against the ruler of England and Normandy, but in order to break down the Angevin walls which enclosed the Capetians' personal ambitions. The politics of the age were manoeuvres restricted by very few but very powerful vested interests, aimed at securing largely personal ends.

In these circumstances, Henry's genuine concern for his subjects' welfare is at once praiseworthy and a hallmark of his farsightedness. Royal government relied on two rather ambiguous positions: the king as the most powerful of all barons, and the king as a leader and special delegate of God. The main revenue came from the first element: the vast royal estates; and the main expenditure went on the second: the administration of law and the maintenance of internal and external order. This may seem oversimplified as, in tracing the course of Henry's career, the sophistication of much of his governmental machinery becomes apparent; yet beneath the new-found efficiency and formality, the old bases of power remain.

The means by which the twelfth-century ruler attained his ends varied from the very subtle to the brutal. In the absence of a standing army, the baronial feudal host was a substitute of limited usefulness. Liable by feudal law to serve for only forty days, the barons were reluctant to undertake great expeditions overseas or far from their own lands; and for each occasion that they were persuaded to oblige the king, there was another when they either refused outright or made difficulties. As a result, the suppression of local revolts within his own domains was a major problem for Henry. While he could unite his vassals against a common enemy, internal troubles might mean that the only troops available were in fact the barons who were in revolt. He solved this difficulty at a very early stage by the extensive use of mercenary troops; but even these never constituted anything approaching a permanent army. As for naval forces, these were non-existent. He could call on the men of the Cinque Ports to provide service in the form of fifty-seven ships for forty days, but these were used as transports only. For his Irish expedition, he had to hire or commandeer merchant vessels from the south and west coasts. The royal navy consisted in effect of Henry's personal galley, the *Esnecca* or 'Sea-snake'—probably a long, low craft designed for swift crossings of the channel—which was kept at Southampton. It was not until John's reign that the navy was formed, and, almost at once, won its first great victory against the French at Damme.

The armed forces were of little help in an expansive and aggressive policy: the defenders had a better chance of success in wars in which geography played so large a part. So the ambitious prince had to turn to other means. Marriage alliances were his foremost weapon: a procedure that now seems totally alien to us. The basic difference between royal marriages then and now was the dowry. Today, a royal princess can expect much less in the way of settlement than a millionaire's daughter. Then a king might give several counties with his daughter's hand if the suitor seemed likely to prove a valuable ally. The counts of Anjou were past masters at this game, and often secured the richest of all prizes: the sole heiress. Such was Matilda of England, Henry's mother; such was to be Eleanor of Aquitaine, his wife. By their scheming, their house grew within three centuries from an unimportant domain

around Angers to a central power, both geographically and politically, in France. Maine was added to Anjou in the early twelfth
century, and the union of the house with that of Normandy made
them partners in an alliance which dominated the lordship of the
king of France. The decisive point in Louis' relations with Henry
was to come when the French sovereign divorced Eleanor of
Aquitaine and left her wide lands at the mercy of the man who
succeeded in gaining her hand. Only with the advent of Philip
Augustus, a king prepared to exploit any weakness and to prefer
force to the letter of the law, was the Angevin stranglehold
broken.

These methods of diplomacy were subtle, the rules which governed
international politics intricate: and in many ways this was a reflec-
tion of the mood of the twelfth century. The chivalrous, empty
heroics of the later medieval period, the underlying brutishness of
the earlier centuries, were absent; instead, men's minds probed the
practical applications of their new-found intellectual powers. More
than any other century in western civilisation, this was the age of
the mind; crude though the achievements may seem, both art and
thought created in this time masterpieces of unsurpassed beauty, as
in the great Romanesque churches and cathedrals and the epic
romances, and also laid the seeds which yielded a rich harvest in
future generations. It was a time of fervour and activity; and if it
has bequeathed fewer great names to grace our records than later
centuries, the unknown masters and artists paved the way for the
soaring majesty of Gothic art; for the rise of the universities; for
the rich flowering of medieval philosophy with Albert and Aquinas;
for the new legal and scientific learning—all of which came to full
splendour in the next century. From humbler beginnings, the
language of the people attained an expressiveness which Latin had
not known for five centuries.

    In some measure, this came about because the christian
lands were for the first time free from the threat of barbarian incur-
sions. The Vikings had become peaceable and accepted settlers, the
Magyars no longer disturbed Germany's eastern borders, and the
only challenge to the existing order was that of another civilisation:
Islam. The Saracens and Turks of later legend might be uncouth

and savage, but in reality their way of life was far more refined
than that of the Christian west.

The rivalry with Islam found its sharpest expression in the
circumstances of the Crusades. To the Mohammedan princes, the
Holy Land was a useful political asset and they were rarely interested
in hindering travellers from the west: to the Christian warriors
it was sacred terrain, not to be sullied by infidel rule, even if these
infidels sometimes permitted the free passage of pilgrims. Hence
when Jerusalem fell into the hands of the Seljuk Turks in 1076,
it was not long before Christendom was roused to action. But,
suffering from all the disadvantages of a hard-pressed outpost
which was difficult to garrison and supply, the Kingdom of
Jerusalem did not last long. Passing from Godfrey de Bouillon 'that
illustrious hero whose kingly rule seems to have corresponded with
the very ideal of perfection in the social order', to his descendants
and thence to the house of Anjou, the kingdom slowly diminished.
Saladin's attacks and the faults and difficulties of its defenders led
in 1187 to the second capture of Jerusalem, an event foreseen
throughout the previous decade. Help came too late; and the later
crusades failed in their declared object.

In the process, however, the Christian knights and rulers
who fought in Palestine were made aware of two things: the fact
that Christendom was a political and limited entity, and that the
culture and virtues of Islam were not dissimilar from their own.
If the main importance of the crusades in Henry's day was their
role as a political issue and a distraction from local affairs, this
level must also be recognised. Furthermore, the crusading armies
were the only sign of Christian feudalism acting in common purpose and allegiance. It was the Church's first taming of the knight's
innate ferocity, evidence of the new value set on high ideas and
deeds, which, if it existed side by side with atrocious barbarism
and lawlessness, was nonetheless playing a greater part in men's
lives.

Now that the preoccupation of mere existence had vanished,
scholarship flourished at the beginning of the century. The settled
schools of the cloister, narrow in outlook and restricted in their
contact with the outside world, were overshadowed by the
cathedral teachers. These secular clergy knew the hard realities of

political life, and their pupils came from among the townsfolk as well as from those intending to enter the church. A new audience coincided with fresh discoveries in the field of Greek learning; and the two fused to produce a school of radical thinkers who were prepared to use the new logical arguments to discuss theological questions. For logic, a commonplace to us today, was then a dramatic new concept, as far-reaching for the Church as the theory of relativity for scientists today. Since the Church was the largest and most powerful organisation in western Europe, this was no rarified academic diatribe, but an argument which threatened the established authority on which society's structure rested. Abelard, when he discussed the Trinity in terms of dialectic, was almost a political agitator, and his enthusiastic, devoted and unruly following of students were a danger to the peace. In eastern Christendom, wars had been fought over differing doctrines of the Trinity, and this could yet happen in the west. But the authority of the Church had quickly overawed the individual conscience, and the dissensions had been healed before the middle of the twelfth century.

The intellectual energy which impelled the new learning and its great leaders was turned into safer, more constructive channels in the latter half of the century. The universities of Paris, Bologna, Salerno and Oxford took shape. At Bologna, jurisprudence was studied again, and the lawbooks of Rome were eagerly sought out, examined and discussed, to lay the foundations of modern legal science. Until now, the real basis of law had been practical rather than theoretical, a constant revision of traditional methods of punishing the criminal and of keeping the peace. The abstract concepts of justice, citizenship and law were forgotten; and when the ancient laws proved inadequate, it was the ruler's task to 'interpret' them and provide a new means to the new end. Much of Henry's work was of this nature; and always at those moments when his methods were most controversial, his insistence on the hallowed authority behind them was loudest. The more we learn of the preceding decades, the more this claim becomes justified; but that it had to be made at all shows how different the twelfth century's ideas about the true basis of laws were from ours today. Henry was only slightly influenced by the new work on Justinian's great code, and the effect was restricted to questions

of church law. His attitude was strictly practical; he sought to
dispense justice to his subjects, preferably adding to his revenue
while doing so. The only real new development in which he was
involved came about more by chance than from conscious design.
This was the arbitration between the kings of Castile and Navarre
in 1177. Such settlements of international disputes by outside
authority were to grow in frequency in the succeeding centuries,
but this early and successful instance was settled by nothing more
than Henry's personal opinion. There was no recourse to principles
of Roman or christian law; nor was the concept of papal superiority to monarchs, as used in later years, invoked.

   Another source of the new learning of these times was the
Mohammedan civilisation. Through the many translations from
Arabic made during the century, much of its intellectual wealth
came to the west, particularly its heritage from Greece. In the Latin
west, Greek had been almost forgotten, and the great masters of
the schools were only partially known. The Fathers of the Church
were the dominant figures in philosophy; and philosophy was in
turn limited to a narrow theological field. With the rediscovery of
Greek learning through Arabic translations of its literature, scholars
in the twelfth century were able to continue in a Christian con-
text the work of the schools of Athens. Spain was the centre of this
commerce of the intellect; here the conflict of Moor and Christian
brought Arabic and Latin into contact.

   From this there sprang a revival of science. Observation and
experiment allied to logic were used to explore the physical world
again, in a way unknown since Aristotle's time. The wonders of
the universe were no longer a magnificent but unfathomable display of God's power, but a machine whose workings could be ex-
plored and reduced to comprehensible terms. Such was the next
insidious threat to the Church's supremacy in matters of belief
that began to develop during these years. It was not until 1210
that Aristotle's work was first attacked, the provincial synod of
Paris putting them under ban as tending to heresy. The suspect
texts were not Aristotle's own, but had been mingled with the
commentaries of Avicenna, whose Islamic doctrine it was that
caused the trouble. Greek science had therefore this added taint
of pagan theology acquired by its transmission through Arabic

scholars, which made its assimilation into western culture yet more difficult.

A less spectacular but more vital development was taking place between the realms of high philosophy and high fantasy: the emergence of an educated class active in lay affairs, owing their pre-eminence neither to rank nor to clerical preferment, although the latter was often their reward. No better illustration of their attitude and pretensions to learning can be found than in Richard Fitz-Neale's introduction to his account of the workings of the exchequer. He relates how 'in the twenty-third year of the reign of king Henry II, as I was sitting at a turret window overlooking the Thames' (presumably in the palace of Westminster), a fellow-official had come to him and suggested that he write a treatise on the royal exchequer. He demurred at first, saying that he was not a literary man, and that such things were too commonplace for a literary work. The other replied:

> 'Writers on the liberal arts have compiled large treatises and wrapped them up in obscure language, to conceal their ignorance and to make the arts more difficult. You are not undertaking a book on philosophy, but on the customs and laws of the exchequer, a commonplace subject, in which you must use appropriate and therefore commonplace language. Moreover, though it is generally permissible to invent new terms, I beg you not to be ashamed to employ the common and conventional words for the objects described, so that no additional difficulty may be created by the unusual language.' [2]

This new class of men were essentially practical in outlook, knowing such book-craft as was necessary to their occupation, but skilled in everyday problems rather than in the by-ways of dialectic and rhetoric. Scholarship *per se* was not for them. Although some of them became churchmen or scholars, their distinctive feature as a class was that they did not hold their positions as a result of training for other professions, but had their own particular culture and outlook, tempered by the fact that the Church had a monopoly of education. Richard Fitz-Neale is a case in point: he served in the king's entourage from 1158 until 1184 without rising higher in the church hierarchy than archdeacon. If in his later years, from

1189–98, he was bishop of London, this was a reward for, rather than a cause or corollary of, his success.

At the opposite pole of learning, the languages of the common people were developing into literary media throughout Europe. Only the insular Saxons had made their tongue a real vehicle for poetic thought, and their efforts had vanished into obscurity with the Norman conquest. Now poets appeared in every country of Europe who could not only, like their forebears, compose vast epics, but could also write them down for posterity, and give them some sort of literary shape. This flowering was rapid; for example, the earliest recorded fragments of Arthurian poetry in French of about 1130 are separated from the great cycles of romance by less than a century. Henry's wife, Eleanor of Aquitaine, seems to have had connections with this development, and Henry himself showed great interest in both Arthur's legends and the work of the new poets.

Hence the intellectual background of Henry's lifetime was one of turmoil, of new beginnings and of disturbing challenges to the existing order. Of this, little reached the king except the new alertness of men's minds, and a new respect for order and system. The practical effects of the new learning did, however, cast some reflections in his ambit. As Gratian had summed up the laws of the Roman Church in his *Decretum* of 1151, so Glanville, albeit less critically, was to record the practice of the English courts in a systematic work on English law. Both Henry and his adversary, Thomas Becket, were to find use for the *Decretum* in their arguments over the way the English church should be governed. Even in the king's pastimes, learning had a place, for a treatise on falconry, one of the first to contain something more than inherited lore, was dedicated to Henry.

What problems confronted Henry in this multifarious age? Most of them stemmed from his early winning of a great kingdom and a greater empire. He had to impose his authority on most of France and all of England, and to maintain his lands in peace and justice against his enemies, both within and without. Nor was this a matter of routine government. Over much of his lands, the machinery by which the king or lord ruled was either in decay or had never existed, or was only newly re-established. He had to weld the disparate elements of his realms into some sort of unity and conformity to a manageable ideal; nor was this an idealist's self-appointed task for posterity's benefit, but a stark necessity. For Henry was only twenty-one when he came into this vast power, and even by the short-lived standards of his time, he could expect to rule for a quarter or even half-century. Hence it was in his own direct interest to seek solutions of wider range and implication than those used by statesmen who only achieved such mighty heights towards their lives' ends.

Henry's authority in his various realms depended on varying titles and different statuses. In England, he was undisputed king. Across the Channel, in Normandy, he was duke; in Anjou and Maine, count; in Aquitaine duke by virtue of his marriage: for all these French domains he owed homage to the king of France. Hence he himself benefited from the inherent strength of two of the three ruling orders of the time: the monarchy and the baronage. If he undermined the English barons, to a limited extent he undermined his own position in France; if he defied the French king, he set a bad example for his English barons. Only in his opposition to the Church's claims to temporal power could he be—and was—consistent and resolute in his stand.

Once the first stage of establishing his authority was accomplished, he was confronted by the task of maintaining it, a task in his days more unusual, for brief power and rapid decline were commonplace. This was typefied in the literary image of the Wheel of Fortune, on which in twelve great chairs sat the rulers of the world, rising slowly to the top of the circle, only to be dashed from their seats just as they topped the height of their ambition. Merely to maintain his position, Henry had to carry out an immense series of diplomatic manoeuvres throughout his life. Everywhere he was faced by forces which, whether secretly or openly, were opposed to his power. The barons resented their loss of independence under his strong hand; the king of France was made suspicious and uneasy by his powerful vassal; his own sons were eager for greater power and chafed under his harsh bit. Henry never embarked on a policy aimed directly at curbing the power of the barons or at breaking that of the king of France, for he was too dependent on both in various ways; at best he obtained fruitful co-operation against a common enemy, at worst an uneasy *modus vivendi* degenerating on occasions into open revolt. On the other hand, he was quite prepared, where his sons were concerned, to 'chastise them with scorpions'. All of them had grounds for complaint in their father's treatment of them, save John; yet each of them in turn had provoked Henry into action. The Angevin family were genuinely fond of each other, but family ties were subordinated to their fierce individual pride and ambition. It was on this rock that Henry's fortunes finally foundered. He could not understand or tolerate in others that which was all too plainly his own ruling trait: love of power. It was not something inherited from his father, who had yielded Normandy to him without a murmur: and it was perhaps only the insistence of his eldest son on claiming his birth-right that made Henry so stubborn—not because he refused to yield, but because he was too proud to seem to yield.

In one sphere Henry never reached the position he desired: in his relations with the Church; and his undoubted involvement in the events leading to Becket's murder rendered him unable to dictate his own terms of settlement afterwards. He was first faced by an opponent whose resolution outstripped even his own, Thomas Becket. Henry's demands were not unreasonable, and in the event defeat was not so very different in its results from victory. The development of the episode to cataclysmic proportions was less due to the opposition of two unrelenting men of principle than to the tensions resulting from a duel between two powerful characters. Henry was expert at picking hardworking and loyal servants for himself, but he was inclined to underestimate his opponents: thus he refused to see in their true light not only Becket and Philip Augustus of France, but also his own sons.

So Henry's problems were partly created by his own character: on the one hand his ambition led him to become ruler of wide realms, and to desire the greatest possible power within them, while on the other he failed to appreciate the resistance he had aroused. But he had also inherited a still greater number of difficulties from his predecessors arising from the dramatic events which form the prelude to Henry's reign, the background to our sixty years' story.

1

The Troubled Land

ON DECEMBER 1, 1135, a small group of the most illustrious men of England and Normandy gathered at a hunting-
lodge in the forest of Lyons, not far from the Norman capital,
Rouen. Grave and anxious, they awaited there a great event: the
passing of a king. Henry I, master of wide lands on both sides of
the Channel, had been taken ill a week earlier, as he pursued his
favourite sport in the beech-woods above the Seine valley.[1] Feeling
the approach of death, he had sent for the archbishop of Rouen,
and his bastard son, the earl of Gloucester, stood at his side. For
three days now they had been there, and the end was not far
off.

As Henry lay there, he could look back on a peaceful reign
of thirty-four years in England. The common people might call
him tyrant; but law and order reigned throughout the land, and it
was said that a man might carry a sack of gold the length and
breadth of it without being molested. If he had oppressed them
with his strict enforcement of forest laws, he had protected them
from the harsher lawlessness of barons great and small. In Normandy too, since the death of his brother, Duke Robert, and his
nephew, William Clito, the only serious rival to his power, the
government had been secure and prosperous. Yet present peace and
prosperity were overshadowed by a future that held no such
promise. Since the tragic and untimely death of Henry's only son
and heir, Prince William, in the disastrous sinking of the *White
Ship* fifteen years earlier, the internal politics of the realm had been
dominated by one problem: who would succeed to the throne?

William's twin sister,[2] Matilda, survived him. But she was the wife of the German emperor, Henry V, and it was unlikely that either the German or English barons would accept a ruler who united the two realms, or that the empress of Germany should become queen of England. So, although the possibility of such a union had to be considered in Henry's policy, he preferred to marry again and hope for a new heir. Unfortunately, his match with Adela, daughter of the count of Louvain, had proved child-less; and when the German emperor died in 1125, Henry I sum-moned Matilda to the homeland she had not seen since her child-hood, and over which he intended her to rule. She came, reluc-tantly: German by education and adoption, she had made herself beloved in Germany, and the German people are said to have begged her to remain. In December of that year, she reached Normandy and joined her father for Christmas. On New Year's Day of 1127, the barons of England swore a solemn oath to recog-nise her claim to the throne as 'Lady of England'. Although she had been empress for fifteen years, she was only twenty-four, and there was little delay in finding a new husband for her. The choice was soon made: Henry arranged a match between her and the heir to the county of Anjou and Maine, Geoffrey Plantagenet. Geoffrey was betrothed to her at Rouen at the Whitsuntide of 1127, and the marriage took place a year later in Maine.[3] He was eleven years Matilda's junior; but this was far from unusual in political marriages of the time; her first husband had been many years older than her, and Geoffrey was, like his descendants, precocious for his age.

The following year, he was given the chance to prove his mettle; for his father, Fulk V, married the heiress to the kingdom of Jerusalem, and set out to claim his new land. He resigned Anjou to Geoffrey,[4] who was already experienced in the workings of a state and well used to subduing recalcitrant vassals. His skill was at once put to the test by the revolt of the lords of Amboise and Sablé, to whom his brother Hélie had allied himself; and war was to remain his chief occupation for the rest of his life. The very purpose of his father-in-law in arranging his marriage was likely to involve him in conflict, for Henry I needed an alliance with Normandy's traditional enemy in order to counter-balance the league which Louis VII of France had arranged with Flanders, and

GENEALOGY OF THE HOUSE OF ANJOU

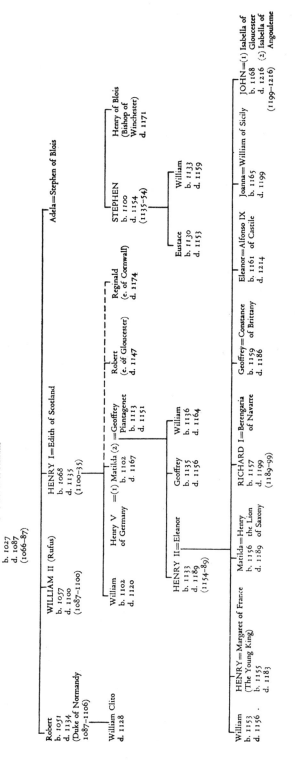

which supported the efforts of Henry's rebellious nephew, William Clito.

However, either from personal reasons, or because Geoffrey was preoccupied with suppressing the rebellion, the pair separated in July 1129, and Matilda went to Rouen leaving her husband to his own devices. Two years later, she crossed to England with her father, but Geoffrey, unwilling to let her become too involved elsewhere, demanded her return, and a council held by Henry on September 8, 1129, decided that she should be sent back to Anjou. Henry's desire for an heir from the match doubtless played some part in this decision; but he had to wait another eighteen months before his wish was fulfilled. The eldest son of Matilda and Geoffrey was born while his mother was at Le Mans, capital of Geoffrey's smaller domain, on March 5, 1133, and named after his Norman grandfather.

In an age of dramatic characters, the young prince Henry's ancestry had more than its share of them. Matilda, his mother, who had been mistress of the Holy Roman Empire at the age of nine, had hardly reconciled herself to being a mere countess, and retained the title of empress for the remainder of her life; her son was frequently called Fitzempress by his contemporaries. Hard and masterful, she must have been the dominant partner in the early years of their marriage. The birth of her three children and her preoccupation with England meant that she and her husband were later separated for long periods. Even after her final departure from her father's kingdom in 1147, and retirement from politics, she saw little of the count. She came from a line of warriors on both sides; on her father's side, both her father and grandfather had won their kingdoms by force of arms, and her great-grandfather on her mother's side, Edmund Ironside, had fought off the Danes with considerable success. So it was only natural that she should lead her own forces in England until her son was old enough to take affairs into his own hands. It seems that she regarded herself as guardian of Henry's rights rather than as fighting for her own, and that her partisans recognised Henry as the real heir. She never adopted the title of queen, but continued to call herself 'domina Angliae', partly because she was never formally crowned, and partly, perhaps, because of this feeling that she represented her son.

From the surviving, perhaps slightly conventional portrait, of Geoffrey Plantagenet,* Henry's father,[5] we can form some idea of the man: tall, fair and lean, with quick eyes, his appearance betrays to some extent the impetuous nature which written records reveal; fiercely energetic, always on horseback, and skilled from boyhood in the arts of war, he also shared with his father-in-law a reputation for learning unusual for their days. But while Henry I, as youngest of the Conqueror's three sons, had received a more than usually thorough education, being at one moment destined for the church, Geoffrey, possessor of a superb memory and fond of disputes and lawsuits, had a ready rather than a polished mind, most at home in the rough politics and diplomacy of the age. His forebears had created the state of Anjou by force and craft, starting with Fulk the Red's viscounty of Angers. From this town, rising black-stoned above the river Maine, five miles from its confluence with the Loire, the Angevins had built up their county by slowly extending their power eastwards along the Loire valley to include Tours and, to the south, the fortresses of Chinon, Loches and Montrichard, until further expansion would have led to conflict with the counts of Blois. To the north lay the county of Maine, caught between the enmity of the Normans and their new southern rivals; this land had been acquired by Geoffrey's father, Fulk the Black, as the dowry of Geoffrey's mother. Westwards, the Breton frontier remained unsettled until the beginning of Fulk's reign, when the Loire for some fifty miles from its mouth, as far as the castle of Montrelais, was acknowledged as Breton territory. The southern limit of Anjou was determined by the power of the counts of Poitou; and nowhere did the Angevin influence reach more than thirty miles south of the Loire.

But within these lands, over which the counts ruled as feudal suzerains, several magnates hardly inferior to the Angevin house held sway. The lord of Mayenne, whose relatives held wide lands in Brittany and Normandy, was the most powerful in Maine; while in Anjou itself, the lords of Sablé, Craon, Montreuil-

* He was reputedly known as 'Plantagenet' from the sprig of broom (planta genesta) which he wore when riding.

Bellay and Montsoreau (the last on the Loire) were all capable of causing considerable difficulties for the count, as well as barons who held land primarily from another lord, such as the masters of Parthenay in the south who owed allegiance to Poitou.[6] The count's power depended on little more than an efficient exploitation of his own resources, of which the chief were the demesne lands, which were directly under his control, and such use as he could make of his legal claim to suzerainty and the many benefits, both in terms of money and property, attached to it.

It had taken two hundred and fifty years of marriage alliances, ransoms and wars to assemble the domains over which Geoffrey Plantagenet ruled, and the early counts had receded into the mists of legend by his day. Epics had grown up around the figure of Geoffrey Greygown, his great-great-great-grandfather, and his son, Fulk Nerra, 'the Black', who was perhaps the most striking of the family. Fulk's mother, so it was said, had brought demon blood into the house of Anjou. Famed for her beauty, but of unknown race, the count of Anjou had married her solely for the fairness of her body. She came but rarely to mass, an unusual habit in an age when regular attendance was the chief yardstick of piety. Nor, when she came, did she pay much attention to the service, but always left after the gospel and before the elevation of the Host. The count, remarking this, one day ordered four men to hold her back when she made to leave the church. As usual, once the gospel had been read, she started to go, but the men seized her cloak to restrain her; on which she slipped out of her cloak and flew out of the window, never to be seen again.[7] From this mysterious ancestress the house of Anjou was said to have inherited its ferocious temper—which was certainly true of Fulk V, Geoffrey the Fair, and, as we shall see, Henry II himself—and its family turmoils, apparent in the revolt of Hélie against Geoffrey, and of which Henry was to have more than his fair share. Even though the idea of the count marrying for love rang false, since the Angevins were the greatest exponents of the art of dynastic marriage of their day, the traits of the demon countess were plain to see in her supposed descendants, and the legend enjoyed wide currency. Referring to this story, St Bernard once said of Henry Plantagenet and his race: 'From the devil they came, to the devil they will go', a grim prophecy which in Henry's latter years sometimes seemed very close to fulfilment.[8]

If the past of the young prince's family was fable, its future was dominated by harsh reality. Although Henry's succession seemed assured, for the oath sworn by the English barons to Matilda had specifically included any sons she might bear, there were other considerations. The death of William Clito, her cousin, in 1128, had not assured to her eldest child the inheritance of England, Normandy, Anjou and Maine, for one other rival to the Anglo-Norman share remained: Stephen, count of Blois, who had been the first to swear homage to Matilda in 1127. Grandson of the Conqueror, his claim derived through his mother; and if the law was doubtful in regard to his right of inheritance, it was no clearer in regard to Matilda's, for neither England nor Normandy had had a woman for their ruler. The problem was further complicated by the uncertainty of the method by which the heir could claim the throne. The usual practice was to ensure recognition of a successor, sometimes by coronation, before the previous ruler died; but the English monarchy retained vestiges of the Saxon elective system, and might tended to be the final arbiter. Henry I had only obtained the English throne by moving rapidly on the death of William Rufus; and Normandy had been won from Duke Robert, who in laying claim to England lost both territories to his youngest brother. Hence if Stephen kept his oath, there was no difficulty; but if he chose to break it, it would be easy enough to obtain a papal dispensation for having done so, once he had become *de facto* king. So, even though Matilda was the official heir, and another oath to her and to Prince Henry was exacted in 1133, those now standing around the old king's deathbed could not be certain to whom the prize would finally fall.

The Anglo-Norman domains offered rich prospects to their ruler. Wide in extent, the English realm was the more important of the two, being independent of any feudal overlordship, whereas Normandy's dukes had still to do homage to the king of France. Scotland was still friendly towards England, and the Scottish king did homage to the English ruler for his estates in England. Wales and Ireland remained unsubdued, in spite of Henry I's forays into the former: but the Welsh marches were peaceful compared with the endless petty warfare on the other side of the Channel. No barons had yet succeeded in amassing sufficient territorial power during the seventy years following the Conquest to constitute a serious challenge t⁻ the Crown, unless they could lay claim to the Crown itself. England was more firmly in the king's power than any lands outside the royal domain on the continent; for franchises, areas where the local lord enjoyed almost regal powers, were only beginning to develop. William I, in his original apportioning of England among his companions, had been careful to retain the strategic towns and castles in his own hands, and the royal lands formed a systematic group quite unlike the haphazard products of gradual accumulation abroad.

Normandy offered a less secure possession, at least on its boundaries, where France, Anjou-Maine, and Brittany were all to some degree hostile, with opposing territorial aims. Without natural frontiers, the marches of Normandy created perpetual problems. Within the duchy, which had been founded by the invasions of the Northmen two centuries earlier, the lands belonging directly to the duke were rivalled only by those of the Church, for both in the first nucleus of the duchy and in the later acquisitions to south and west, a large portion of lands had been retained by the duke. Only the barons closely related to the ducal house, and whose possessions lay chiefly on the borders, were of any real importance: these comprised the counts of Eu and Aumale to the east, and of Mortain to the west. Almost all the Norman barons held fiefs in England, which lent further stability to the Anglo-Norman realm, since except in the case of a general revolt, any trouble-making baron could easily be coerced into submission by the confiscation of his fiefs in one or other half of the realm.

But the young prince Henry was as yet unaware of these political complications which were to determine in so many ways the course of his life's work. He would have been more closely affected by the birth of his two younger brothers, Geoffrey in 1134, and William in 1136. The first years of his life were spent with his mother: in the spring of 1134 he was taken to Argentan with her, where his grandfather saw the long-awaited heir for the first time.

On June 1, Geoffrey was born there, a second surety for the Angevin and Norman line. But a quarrel between Matilda and her father led to Henry and his brother being moved south to Angers in the summer of 1135; their mother followed shortly afterwards, and it was probably at the Angevin capital that William, her youngest son, was born in the following August.

By then, the storm had broken: Henry I was dead, and Stephen of Blois had broken his oath, seizing the English crown. Matilda was faced by a long, hard struggle to regain her rights. It was not until 1139 that she departed for England, leaving Henry with his father. We know that Henry did not remain exclusively at Angers, but sometimes moved round his father's domains as the count and his entourage carried out the business of government; but which particular regions of his father's territories were the background of his childhood days remains unknown; only one charter specifically records his presence, at Carrouges on the Norman border, in 1138, when he was aged five.

We know more about his education. At some time during this period, the young prince was put in the charge of Peter of Saintes, his first teacher, a man renowned for his knowledge of poetry; and Henry and his brothers seem to have received a more than usually thorough education. Perhaps their father regretted the lost opportunities of his own youth; Matilda never showed any great interest in such matters, although both her father and half-brother, Earl Robert of Gloucester, were learned by the standards of the age. Under Peter's tuition Henry remained until 1142, learning the rudiments of Latin and of reading, and possibly also of writing, although the latter was regarded as a skill more appropriate to clerks and clergymen than to kings and princes.

Meanwhile, Henry's parents had both been active in defence of his rights. Matilda's departure had been occasioned by Earl Robert of Gloucester's repudiation of his oath to Stephen at the end of May 1138, and the formation of an Angevin party in open opposition to the king. Stephen did not improve his position by choosing this moment to attempt to rescind the liberties granted to the Church in 1136 at the council of Winchester. He also seized the castles of various barons whom he did not trust but whose loyalty he might otherwise have retained, when Matilda's impending arrival was rumoured in 1139. She came both as a claimant to the throne herself, and as guardian of her son's rights. Taking advantage of Stephen's excesses against the Church and his use of brutal mercenary troops, which had antagonised many of his erstwhile sympathisers, she rallied the forces of rebellion which Stephen had to some degree checked. The Scots had been defeated at the Battle of the Standard at Northallerton in 1138, and her uncle, David of Scotland, had been forced to withdraw from England; although he lent valuable support to his niece's cause, Scottish arms produced no decisive effect in the conflict after this reverse. A revolt in the fenlands had been suppressed by Stephen, and only Earl Robert held out for his half-sister at Bristol.

Within eighteen months, the situation had been dramatically reversed. At Christmas 1140, Stephen laid siege to Ranulf of Chester's castle at Lincoln, the latter having allied himself to Matilda. After a fruitless blockade until February 1141, he had to face the earl of Gloucester's relief force in a battle outside the town. His army, weary from the long winter siege, broke at the first charge of Robert's troops, superior in both numbers and condition; Stephen himself was captured and sent to be imprisoned at Bristol. Matilda found a favourable reception at Winchester on March 3; proceeding to London, whose citizens claimed to have elected Stephen to the throne, she was acclaimed in the capital as well. Even Stephen's brother, Henry, bishop of Winchester and the greatest of the lords of England, acknowledged her as ruler. The empress seemed to have secured the upper hand, and for some months ruled England as its uncrowned queen. But her arrogant ways fatally damaged her cause, arousing the temper of the Londoners against her. When she was expelled from the chief city of the realm, an angry mob at her heels, her fortunes declined once more. Henry of Winchester's uneasy allegiance was broken, and in a skirmish outside his cathedral city his troops captured Robert of Gloucester. Only at the price of the king's own liberty could the chief supporter of the Angevin cause be freed. Stephen's captivity had lasted a bare nine months when he was released.

Now that the civil war was plainly going to be a matter of years, not months, the accompanying lawlessness, already serious, rose to its full height. The monks, who are the only historians of these dark days, have left a grim picture of the ravages of war and famine, without parallel save in the days of the Black Death two centuries later. From the comparative peace of a monastery, the situation may have seemed little short of the days of Antichrist; yet there is no excess of exaggeration* in the chroniclers' words when they describe the stark realities of the hard world outside. The Fens suffered from a particularly ruthless and arrogant baronage. To them almost all the devastation there during Stephen's reign can be ascribed; and their cruelties, as depicted by the monks of Peterborough, have become classic in the annals of medieval warfare:

> For every powerful man built his castles . . . and they filled the country full of castles. When the castles were built, they filled them with devils and wicked men. Then, both by night and day, they took those people that they thought had any goods—men and women—and put them in prison and tortured them with indescribable tortures to extort gold and silver; for no martyrs were ever so tortured as they were. They were hung by the thumbs or by the head, and corselets were hung on their feet. Knotted ropes were put round their heads and twisted until they penetrated to the brains. They put them in prisons where there were adders and snakes and toads, and killed them like that. Some they put in a torture chamber—that is in a chest that was short, narrow and shallow, and they put sharp stones in it and pressed the man in it so that he had all his limbs broken. In many of the castles was a 'noose-and-trap'—consisting of chains of such a kind that two or three men had enough to do to carry one. It was so made that it was fastened to a beam, and they used to put a sharp iron around the man's throat and his neck, so that he could not in any direction either sit or lie or sleep, but had to carry all that iron. Many thousands they killed by starvation.

* Except in the implication that local conditions were universal, whereas only small areas were seriously affected; cf. the extract from the Peterborough Chronicle.

. . . When the wretched people had no more to give, they
robbed and burned all the villages, so that you could easily
go a whole day's journey and never find anyone occupying a
village, nor land tilled. Then corn was dear, and meat and
butter and cheese, because there was none in the country.
Wretched people died of starvation; some lived by begging
for alms, who had once been rich men; some fled the country.[9]

England was in desperate state, and likely to remain so for
some time as far as the Angevins were concerned. Matters were only
slightly better in Normandy. The position had been complicated
for Matilda from the outset, because her husband had had recourse
to arms in the autumn of 1135 in order to claim her dowry from
her father. This incursion had proved abortive, chiefly because the
Angevin invaders could not be restrained from wanton violence.
On the death of Henry I, the Norman barons had formed a kind
of regency, and only minor lords had recognised Matilda. For a
while, a project of inviting Theobald of Blois to become duke
was mooted, but this was abandoned on Stephen's accession to the
English throne; for many barons were inclined to favour his cause,
if only from fear of losing their English lands. Stephen was formally recognised on December 22, 1135, only three weeks after
Henry's death.[10]

Geoffrey thereupon began his efforts to conquer Normandy by
main force, which was to cost ten years' warfare. In this he acted
purely as his son's representative and never as an actual claimant.
The first raid was launched the following autumn at Michaelmas,
and although an initial success was scored with the capture of
Carrouges, he was forced to withdraw within a fortnight, and no
other lasting results were achieved. Stephen arrived in Normandy
in March 1137; and in May of that year, Eustace, Stephen's son,
did homage to Louis for Normandy: an act which meant that
Louis of France, Geoffrey's feudal overlord, would openly support the claims of the house of Blois. Nonetheless, civil disturbances continued within Normandy, without Geoffrey's intervention; neither these, nor four more minor raids by the Angevin
count in 1137–8, materially changed the situation. Geoffrey bided

his time, waiting for suitable opportunity; either an unpopular act of strong government or evidence of Stephen's incompetence would be equally favourable to his purpose. Throughout the next three years, it became apparent that Stephen had less of the Conqueror's blood in his veins than Matilda. When Stephen's slight attempts at government were entirely stopped by his capture at Lincoln, Geoffrey bestirred himself to action again. He issued a formal summons to the barons to surrender their castles to himself as representative of the rightful heir. A last appeal went to Theobald of Blois from the Norman barons; but none expected this move, of doubtful legality, to be successful, and by the end of 1141 all eastern Normandy, except Rouen, lay in the hands of the Angevin, including the important towns of Caen, Lisieux, Bayeux and Falaise, peacefully surrendered in face of inevitable conquest.

So far the two campaigns to win the lands that were one day to be Henry Plantagenet's had been conducted almost independently by his parents. Matilda and the Angevin party in England had suffered a sharp decline in their standing, and the high hopes of the spring of 1141 had vanished with the loss of not only her royal captive but London as well. It seemed to the empress that Geoffrey's recent and easily won success might allow him to send support to her, and to this end she sent the earl of Gloucester to ask his assistance. A more distinguished emissary could not have been chosen among her supporters; the most important of Matilda's English party, he had been largely responsible for her successes, while she had only herself to blame for most of her disasters. Earl Robert knew better than anyone what was needed from Normandy: a force large enough to end the strife in one swift, decisive campaign, and if possible, Geoffrey himself to lead it. The empress lacked both means and men, while Stephen was more likely to win a war of attrition, since he held the rich counties of the south-east. Matilda drew her support chiefly from Somerset, Gloucestershire, Herefordshire, Worcestershire and Monmouthshire: the area in which the war had been fought for the most part, and which even in peacetime was poorer in resources than her rival's territory.

When Robert arrived, about June 24, Geoffrey was busy

reducing such Norman castles as still resisted him. These lay chiefly in the west of Normandy, in the Bessin and Stephen's own county of Mortain. During the course of the summer of 1142, at least ten of them fell before his onslaughts, including the important strongholds of Vire, Tinchebray and Mortain itself. In this mood of activity and success he was not in the least inclined to abandon good prospects of a complete and rapid conquest of Normandy for uncertain hopes in England, and he needed all the men and money at his disposal for his own purposes. Yet he could not abandon Matilda, lest this should encourage her enemies to new attacks which she could ill withstand. By treating the problem as one of morale rather than financial or military need, Geoffrey found a ready solution which would not entail any reduction of his own resources, by sending the young prince with a small force. The presence of the boy regarded by many of Matilda's adherents as the rightful heir would both satisfy the empress, and discourage her enemies.

Thus it came about that one day in September 1142, Henry of Anjou, aged nine years and six months, landed in England for the first time. He disembarked on the Dorset coast near Wareham in the company of his uncle and a handful of knights. The voyage had been prosperous; and the earl of Gloucester immediately set about the siege of the neighbouring castles of Wareham, Portland and Lulworth, giving the young Henry his first taste of warfare. These were in his hands by the beginning of November. But meanwhile, Stephen had returned to the offensive. Within a month of the young prince's landing, he had succeeded in besieging Matilda in Oxford. Hence Robert, once he had achieved his immediate object and made the coast secure for a possible retreat, moved north to Cirencester with Henry, and assembled forces with which to march to the relief of Oxford. But Matilda decided that more urgent action was required, and took advantage of the onset of winter to make a dramatic escape with four soldiers through the snow and frost at the beginning of December. She was lowered from the walls in a basket and, going through the enemy lines in a white mantle, crossed the frozen Thames on foot. At Abingdon, the empress found horses, and rode to Wallingford. Although

Oxford, after a three months' siege was in urgent need of relief, the risks of defeat were considered too high for any attempt to be made, and the bad weather hindered military operations. On December 20 the city surrendered.

Robert and Henry had gone straight to Wallingford on hearing of the empress' flight, and there mother and son were reunited for the first time in more than three years. It was a brief meeting; soon afterwards, perhaps in the first weeks of 1143, Henry was sent to Bristol, where his uncle's court, similar to those of the lesser counts of France in scale, was established. It was distinguished by the men attached to it. Geoffrey of Monmouth might be found there, author of the *Historia Regum Britanniae*: the most popular of the mythical histories of the period, and a major landmark in the development of the legend of King Arthur, to delight future generations. Adelard of Bath was another man of great learning attached to this circle; he had been studying Islamic science since the first decade of the century, his chief interest being astronomy. His work *On the Astrolabe* was dedicated to the young Henry about the time that the prince was at Bristol.[11] Henry's actual teacher was Master Matthew, who may have been Matilda's chancellor, under whom he continued his education, with the earl of Gloucester's son Roger as his fellow-pupil. It was now that he laid the foundations of his great skill as a linguist in later years. He remained at Bristol for less than two years, but Master Matthew may have gone with him on his return to Normandy. He crossed the Channel again, perhaps in answer to a summons from his father, in 1144. Later, the English teacher was replaced by William of Conches, one of the most distinguished thinkers of the school of Chartres; and under his tutelage Henry completed his education.

During Henry's visit, the situation had changed little in England; the only major undertaking on either side had been an abortive attempt by Stephen to capture Lincoln. The power and depredations of the independent barons was steadily increasing; men like Geoffrey de Mandeville, earl of Essex, and William of Aumale, succeeded in doing much damage to the kingdom before they met the untimely deaths recorded with such heartfelt and pious moralisings by the chroniclers. In Normandy, however, the fall of the city of Rouen on January 20, 1144, and the surrender of its castle on April 23 meant that very little of Normandy remained outside Geoffrey's power, since Avranches and the south-west had been subdued in the previous year. The only evidence of Henry's presence on the continent at the time is a single charter which shows that he was at Angers in the early part of 1144,[12] but whether he arrived in time to see the end of the operations at Rouen, his father's greatest hour of triumph, is doubtful. He was probably with him when the last strongholds of the north-east were overthrown during the next two years. Driencourt, on the border, was taken with the help of a newly formed alliance with Louis VII of France and count Thierry of Flanders. Under the terms of this Geoffrey did homage for Normandy, and henceforward assumed the ducal title. With the fall of Arques the next year, none remained to dispute his rule. He had already begun the series of administrative reforms for which he and his son were to become famous, and had added to his new territories a precious piece of land on the French border known as the Vexin, comprising the towns of Gisors, Neaufles and Dangu, given to him by Louis under the treaty of 1144. The king of France was to have cause to regret this later, when Henry made of it a key position in the border strategy of Normandy against France.

During these years of exceptional activity, Henry was at an impressionable age. His father's work was one important element in the formation of his own ideas of the functions of a ruler. Geoffrey's entourage might lack models of piety or even men as expert at combining religion and statesmanship as Suger, abbot of St Denis, and Bernard of Cluny, later canonised, both of whom were to be found at the French court, but the Angevin household was no place for the indolent or luxury-loving. Geoffrey had given Anjou an efficient governmental machine,[13] and did much towards the establishment of a similar régime in Normandy during his six years as duke.[14]

In Anjou, he had established the power of the count's tribunal in such a way that it dealt not merely with cases that fell within the scope of the ordinary feudal overlord, but also dis-

pensed justice directly; any plaintiff with good cause could apply
to it for redress. Normandy had already enjoyed a system of ducal
courts, but these had lapsed in the years of anarchy, and had to be
revived. This was done under a new form, called the assize. Royal
justice had previously been dispensed by the king's agents, charged
equally with the administration of his lands and other aspects of
government, and whose titles and functions were varied and con-
fusing in the extreme. The other duties were now separated, and
justice was transferred to special courts held once or twice a year in
each of the twenty-two 'vicomtés'.

The finances of Normandy were also in disorder. Geoffrey
saw the need for a sound coinage, and to this end he seems to have
abolished the mint at Rouen, allowing only the Angevin coin and
the English sterling to be used, and issuing no new Norman currency. Efficient and direct administration was needed, and the old
divisions, 'vicomtés', were for this purpose largely superseded by
bailiwicks under the care of their officials, the bailiffs. It was left
to Henry in later years to define the exact functions of these
officers. As to the recovery of the many royal estates which had
been purloined, Geoffrey was too dependent on the barons' goodwill to undertake this necessary step towards restoring the ducal
authority.

Geoffrey might have accomplished the first part of his task by
1146, but Matilda was no nearer her goal. She asked for help
from Geoffrey once again at the end of the year. He offered little
more encouragement than on the previous occasion; her son, in
nominal command of a small force, arrived in England at the
beginning of 1147. In spite of wild rumours about the enormous
size of the force and the huge resources of treasure brought over by
the Angevin expedition, the small number of his band of knights
soon became known. Furthermore, these had been hired on a
promise of payment and not for ready cash: and when success
failed to materialise at the first castles that resisted them, at
Cricklade and Black Bourton, the prince's army soon abandoned
him, leaving him in such desperate straits that he had to appeal
to his mother for money. She, unfortunately, was in a like predicament, and left England about Lent, never to return. Henry was

now master of his own fortunes as far as claiming the English throne was concerned. For the moment, however, there was little he could do. He stayed on for some months, raising such funds as he could. The death of Robert of Gloucester, his uncle and the mainstay of the Angevin cause, was the final blow to his hopes;[15] for when he applied to the new earl of Gloucester, his request for money was met with a curt refusal. Surrender seemed dangerously near; but, as a last hope, knowing something of his opponent's temperament, Henry sent an envoy in secret to the very king whose throne he was attempting to claim, asking Stephen, as his kinsman, to relieve his plight. He was rewarded for his boldness with a sum sufficient to enable him to leave for France; nor do any conditions seem to have been attached. Arriving at Bec on Ascension Day, May 29, 1147, he was received by a solemn procession of clergy and people. His first attempt to claim his rightful kingdom had been a dismal failure; but Henry was only fourteen, and such a reverse did little to damp his youthful hopes.

2

The Winning of a Kingdom

TWO YEARS passed before Henry was allowed to make another attempt to invade England: years of peace on both sides of the Channel. In the meanwhile, his mother withdrew from an active part in political affairs—a decision perhaps taken before she returned from England. She was now forty-seven, and her remaining years were darkened by prolonged illness. Her husband showed no great interest in pressing her claim to the English throne, and Henry was left to look after his own fortunes. Before he could take any positive action and lead an army in his own right, he would have to become a knight; and it seems that his father may have even tried to discourage him, for he could quite well have performed the ceremony. Henry was obliged to seek this honour, the twelfth-century equivalent of coming of age, at the hands of his great-uncle, David of Scotland.[1]

Preparations for the expedition began in the spring of 1149, and were rapidly completed, for at the end of March, Henry landed on the south coast. By April 13 he was at Salisbury, where he issued a charter founding an abbey at Lockswell 'for the health and salvation of Geoffrey, duke of Normandy, and count of Anjou'. He then moved northwards by way of Gloucester, and reached Carlisle just before Whitsun in the company of Roger, earl of Hereford. Here he was received with great respect and sumptuous preparations by David, his cousin Henry of Huntingdon, and the earl of Chester. On the feast-day itself, May 22, the king of Scotland ceremonially dubbed Henry knight. The young Plantagenet could now claim his inheritance, and set out at once to do so. Stephen immediately replied to this piece of propaganda by arranging that his own son, Eustace, should be knighted.

David had brought with him a large army of Scots, and with this force he and Henry moved south, intending to besiege York and then join the earl of Chester at Lancaster.[2] This campaign came to little; the appearance of Stephen outside York with a well equipped force caused the invaders to abandon their designs on that city, and when Ranulf of Chester failed to arrive as planned at Lancaster, the Scots returned home. Henry, in little better case than on his previous expedition, was left to make his way to the counties which remained true to his cause, in the southwest of England. His companions were a small body of knights including the earl of Hereford; using wild and lonely paths, they avoided capture and arrived at Hereford exhausted but reasonably safe. Word of the Plantagenet's arrival there reached Stephen, and Eustace was sent to intercept Henry on his way to Bristol. However, Henry was warned of this, and by leaving Dursley castle at midnight, he stole a march on his would-be captors and succeeded in eluding them.

Although Henry had failed to achieve any great exploits on this expedition, this did not mean that his adherents were inactive or dispirited. Stephen himself was kept well occupied by the hostile movements of the earls of Chester and Norfolk, and by the garrison at Bedford. Henry now took advantage of Stephen's commitment elsewhere to enter Devon, where the latter's party were causing a considerable disturbance. The prince, with the support of a large force assembled by the earls of Gloucester and Hereford at Devizes, took the castle and town of Bridport.[3] This was his first personal military success, and although he was certainly helped by more experienced soldiers, the boldness of the undertaking bears the hallmark of Henry's own character. He then proceeded to ravage de Tracy's lands, but the latter withdrew to his castles, and before Henry could begin a siege, news came of an impending attack on Wiltshire by Eustace. He at once sent on a body of troops to reinforce the garrison of Devizes, and followed in good order with the remainder. But Stephen's son arrived before the reinforcements could get inside the castle, and pillaged the town. However, the garrison, encouraged by the arrival of their friends, put up a spirited resistance, and the attackers had to beat a hasty retreat to avoid serious losses.

In spite of these minor successes, it was nonetheless evident that the Angevin partisans had neither the resources nor the determination to bring matters to a head. Stephen's forces were well organised, and both the king and his son were commanders of some ability. So Henry decided to return to his father's lands, and there to raise a more imposing force of Normans and Angevins with which he could bring the conflict to a speedy and favourable end. He arrived in Normandy in January 1150, and rejoined his father in Anjou. Perhaps on the strength of reports of his prowess in England, but more probably as part of an arrangement made before the prince left in 1149, Geoffrey made over the duchy of Normandy in a ceremony at Rouen. Henry now assumed the title of 'dux Normannorum', duke of the Normans, which replaced his previous epithet, 'son of the duke of Normandy and count of Anjou' on all his official documents, which were issued on his authority in ever-increasing numbers. He also acquired his own chancellor, William de Vere, who had served his mother in this capacity.[4] For the most part, the men who had served and advised his father in the duchy remained in their places; and there is no evidence of changes in the inner circle of government. Reginald de St Valery, Robert de Courcy, Robert de Neufbourg and Richard de la Haye, who appear as seneschals, at the head of the local administration, are all known to have served Geoffrey. Some names occur for the first time: Humphrey de Bohun, Richard du Hommet, and Warin Fitzgerald; but the records of this period are so few that their earlier careers must remain a mystery.

It was a generous gesture on Geoffrey's part to surrender the duchy, having spent ten years and much energy on its conquest. Although his claim to Normandy as Matilda's husband was far from universally recognised, he had done homage for it to Louis, and was undisputedly its rightful ruler in feudal law; nor was he under any obligation to give it up to his son, unless this was an unrecorded condition made when he did homage. It may be that Louis had laid down that the duchy was to be transferred when Henry was knighted, which would explain Geoffrey's apparent reluctance to knight his son. But there is no trace of the rift between father and son which such a situation would imply. In the

D

event Henry was to prove less open-handed in similar circumstances than his father, to his own detriment.

Under feudal law, any new vassal coming into possession of
a fief was supposed to do homage to his lord as soon as possible;
but it suited both Henry and Geoffrey to take advantage of the
weakness of Louis VII, and delay the ceremony for as long as they
could, using it as a counter in their diplomatic manoeuvres. The
chief reason for this, from Geoffrey's point of view, was a quarrel
with one of the lords on the southern border of Anjou. The castle
and town of Montreuil-Bellay, between Saumur and Thouars, was
in the hands of the Berlai family, who had been particularly
troublesome vassals. Geoffrey decided to make an example of
them, and laid siege to the castle. Unfortunately, the fortress
proved its reputation for exceptional strength by withstanding
him for three years, by which time its lord had invoked the aid
of Louis. The latter, however, was in no hurry to intervene, and
it was only in 1151, after Geoffrey had at last taken Montreuil-
Bellay; that the French king invaded Normandy with the help of
Stephen's son, Eustace. Henry was besieging a rebellious lord at
Torigny, near Caen, but on Louis' appearance in the north-east, he
hastened to Arques, where, with a small army, he resisted the first
onslaught of the invaders. Meanwhile, Louis' brother took La
Nuë, belonging to an Angevin ally, only to have Geoffrey appear
and retake it. Louis then proceeded to burn Séez, but in August
was confronted by the Angevin army across the Seine before he
could do any more damage. Neither side was prepared to risk open
battle, for there was the risk of total defeat; and hence the intervention of the clergy to make peace was welcomed. By the terms
of the truce, Geoffrey and Henry were to go to Paris to submit to
the arbitration of Bernard of Clairvaux.

When in August 1151 Henry rode into Paris at his father's side,
it was his first visit to the chief city of Europe; for such was the
reputation enjoyed by the French capital. Distinguished intel-
lectually by the presence of the most famous thinkers of the day,
it was also the home of the greatest contemporary theologians; for
all philosophical thought at this time was aimed at the furtherance

of religion. Students flocked here from all western Christendom; and about this time, the first organised courses of higher education since Roman days were beginning. Paris was the arbiter of taste in other matters too; for even if Louis himself and his advisers were of a pious turn of mind, his queen, Eleanor of Aquitaine, was a champion of the new literature in the tongue of the common people which was coming to the fore in tales of chivalry and romance and in secular love-lyrics. What Paris lacked in wealth by comparison with London, it made up for by its cosmopolitan outlook and population. If Rome was the heart of Christendom, Paris was its head, containing all its intellectual ferment. All this could not fail to make a deep impression on Henry, and it was rumoured years later that he had fallen in love with Eleanor during this visit; but the chronicler was probably indulging in a little wisdom after the event.

The negotiations opened with Geoffrey in intransigent mood. At first, he refused to consider the release of Gerald Berlai. Braving threats of excommunication, he prayed instead that God would never pardon his sin,[5] following this by an abrupt withdrawal from the talks. However, he returned, and took a more conciliatory line; in this change, we may detect Henry's hand, for the younger Plantagenet was thinking of his projects against Stephen. For these, he needed peace in Normandy, even at a price. There were special reasons for haste, since the hard winter of 1150–1 had added greatly to the distress and discontent in England, and this advatage would be lost with the new harvest. As a result, Louis managed to extract a confirmation of the cession of Gisors on the Franco-Norman border,* and the addition to this of most of the rest of the Vexin. Henry had to perform a solemn ceremony of homage to Louis for Normandy.

Peace had been made; and if the price was high, Louis expected some reward for deserting his erstwhile ally Eustace by making the pact. Henry might not rejoice over the outcome of the negotiations, but he was now free to pursue his plans of conquest. Now that Geoffrey had at last settled the problem of his rebellious vassal, he may have been prepared to offer his son some assistance at last. The two retired to Maine on their departure from Paris,

* This reversed the terms of the treaty of 1144.

and went their separate ways, having sent orders into Normandy for an assembly of the barons at Lisieux on September 14, to take council about the projected invasion of England.

Stephen's position beyond the Channel was to remain unchallenged for another two years. As Geoffrey rode back with his entourage through the wooded hills of Maine, the heat of the late summer became intolerable, and he halted to bathe in a wayside pool on the road leading to Le Mans. But the cool inviting water proved fatal; for soon afterwards, on September 7, the count of Anjou died of a chill at the nearby castle of Chateau du Loir, aged only thirty-eight. Henry hastened south, to find the nobles and prelates awaiting his arrival before they took any steps to bury the body of his father. Geoffrey knew the ambitious temper of his eldest son, and had his own ideas as to the disposition of his lands among Henry and his brothers on his death. He had required his magnates to swear that they would not allow his body to be buried until Henry had promised to obey the provisions of his will, without its being read. Henry hesitated, naturally enough, to take an oath binding him to unknown provisions; but at the urgent insistence of his father's closest companions, he did so, albeit with bad grace. Then the count's body was taken north to Le Mans, twenty miles distant, where it was buried in the cathedral with all due honour.

Once the funeral was over, Henry hastened to discover the conditions to which he was bound. For the present, they were not as irksome as he might have feared; his brother Geoffrey was to have the three castles of Chinon, Loudun and Mirebeau, in the south-east of Anjou. These fortresses, a strategically important group not thirty miles apart, were given by Henry to his brother shortly afterwards. As to the second condition laid down by his father, he had no intention of complying with it, since it was in direct opposition to his own aims. By this clause, Geoffrey was to have Anjou and Maine, his father's lands, as soon as Henry was recognised as king of England, thus depriving Henry of half his continental domains. Perhaps Geoffrey had in mind the long-standing enmity of Angevin and Norman and felt that the dissensions that might arise from such a union would be to the advantage of neither land. He may not have expected Henry to regain England, or may have hoped to deter him from ventures beyond the Channel; or finally, he may have been concerned to prevent troublesome rivalry between brothers—all too frequent elsewhere at the time—by providing each with an adequate territory. If Henry ever contemplated carrying out the clause, he was to find further cogent reasons for not doing so before the time came to fulfil its terms.

For the moment, Henry made his way south from Le Mans to Angers, where he was formally recognised by the barons of Anjou as their rightful ruler. He spent the winter in Anjou and Normandy, presumably consolidating his position and making new arrangements for the attack on Stephen: a project he had by no means abandoned. A council was arranged at Lisieux, on April 6, 1152; but greater matters intervened yet again, of an even more unexpected nature.

In July 1137, when Henry was a mere four years old, Louis VII of France had married the orphan heiress of Aquitaine, the fifteen-year-old Duchess Eleanor. Eleanor's father had placed her in the ward of Louis VI; and since the latter was an astute politician, he had secured her vast inheritance in central and southern France for the royal house by marrying her to his son. Like so many political marriages, no account was taken of the temperaments of the pair. Eleanor belonged to a race of troubadours and warriors. Her grandfather, William IX, had been one of the first of the new southern poets. The Poitevin barons were renowned for their independent turn of mind, and peace was rare for their lords; even when at rare intervals their vassals were quiet, the dukes of Aquitaine devoted the respite to expansion rather than to internal affairs: crusades against the infidel in Spain, such as that undertaken by Eleanor's grandfather in 1120, or the conquest of new territory; William IX took the county of Toulouse, only to lose it again, leaving a long-standing claim which succeeding masters of his duchy tried to enforce.

The queen of France had inherited in full measure the character and energy of her predecessors, and perhaps their inclination for the sports of love as well. She made a remarkable impression on her contemporaries in days when queens appeared in history only at their marriages, at the birth of heirs, and at their pious deaths. Only Matilda enjoyed comparable attention, and then only for a much briefer period. Both were held up by rhetorical chroniclers as warning examples: Matilda for her insolent pride and Eleanor for her lasciviousness. Around the latter judgement a fierce controversy has raged; but since the evidence is little more than a series of opinions by men hardly qualified to judge, the verdict is now generally agreed to be one of acquittal for lack of adequate grounds. It is only in contrast with her husband, Louis, that she might fairly be called wanton; for Louis' gentle and pious nature was more suited to the religious than to the royal life. Eleanor's reputed reaction after fifteen years of boredom is perhaps just: 'I have married a monk, not a king!'[6] Her conduct had only once occasioned specific reproach: during her journey to Palestine with Louis on the Second Crusade, her intrigues with Raymond of Antioch, who wished to divert the French army to his own ends, had led to an accusation of misconduct with him. Since he was her uncle, and the indictment was made forty years later by a chronicler who disliked this prince, the foundation for the judgement is very slender. It can be explained by the natural pleasure of Eleanor at finding congenial company after two months of hardship on the journey from Constantinople, which may have led her to commit some slight indiscretion. Besides, her lack of high intent compared unfavourably with Louis' steadfast earnest. Other calumnies of this sort are counterbalanced by the testimony of John of Salisbury, who was at the papal court when the French king and queen passed through Tusculum on their return from the East on October 9 and 10, 1149.[7] He explicitly tells us that it was one of Eleanor's enemies who enjoyed the king's confidence and had been responsible for nurturing Louis' suspicions. Eleanor had deeply wounded the king by pointing out that they were related within the prohibited degrees for marriage, and that since there was no son it would be proper to dissolve the union. Louis was torn between his religious feelings and his undoubted love for his wife.[8] In spite of the pope's attempt to reconcile the pair, and his anathema against anyone who mentioned their relationship, religion prevailed over a passionate, 'almost childish', feeling for Eleanor in Louis' mind.

Politically the situation was more difficult still. After fifteen years, Eleanor had only produced two daughters, instead of the son that the king's councillors so urgently desired. Divorce, as the queen had perhaps suggested, was the proper remedy for this situation; but if she went her own way, more than half the French kingdom—her inheritance of Aquitaine—would have to be surrendered with her. Hence the decision was no easy one: on the one hand, the kingdom's future stability, on the other its very character and existence, were in the balance. Even if the king had had genuine cause to complain about the queen's behaviour on the crusade, his most trusted adviser, Suger, the abbot of St Denis, would certainly have refused to allow him to initiate the necessary proceedings.[9] But on Suger's death, in January 1151,[10] the counsels of Bernard of Clairvaux prevailed, and, chiefly on religious grounds, but relying also on dynastic and personal arguments, the king decided on separation. When the two Angevin rulers arrived in Paris in August of that year, Louis' mind may have been made up already; but the romantic accounts of Henry and Eleanor's first meeting have no other foundation than speculation. The possibility of their marriage could not have entered into the calculations of the most far-sighted political observer. Although they were two of the most fascinating figures of their age to their contemporaries, there is no reason why, a generation apart (Henry was eighteen and Eleanor twenty-nine), they should have been attracted to each other, and even less evidence of it in their subsequent career. The idea that Eleanor asked for the divorce,[11] whether to marry Henry or for any other reason, is equally a product of fantasy; she may not have been averse to the project, and may have taunted Louis with the suggestion, but the final decision remained entirely in Louis' hands.

So at the beginning of 1152, Louis left for Aquitaine with Eleanor, demolished the fortifications he had erected, and withdrew the officials he had sent from his own court to run Eleanor's lands as part of his domains.[12] On March 11, a solemn council of all the prelates of France assembled at Beaugency under the presidency of the archbishop of Sens. Having heard evidence as

to the relationship of Eleanor and Louis, which was proved to be
within the fourth degree according to canon law, this body pronounced the marriage null and void on March 21. The sentence
was of doubtful validity, 'arranged with much toil and by specious
oath'. Although no formal endorsement of the marriage had been
issued by the pope, strong verbal prohibitions had been laid by him
on any attempt to dissolve it.[13]

Eleanor left at once for Blois, intending to make her way to
Poitiers. But she was now a rich prize for any lord who could
capture her and marry her. Louis, by a fatal oversight, had failed
to make any definite arrangement by which he could retain control over her remarrying or over her lands, holding that the usual
right of feudal wardship would be adequate. She had to leave
Blois hurriedly when the attentions of count Theobald became too
pressing, and reached Tours in safety. Henry's younger brother,
Geoffrey heard of her arrival and decided to try his luck. Fortunately, Eleanor was warned of the ambush laid for her by the
seventeen-year-old adventurer; and instead of leaving on the usual
road southwards from the Porte des Piles, eluded him by going
another way. Avoiding Geoffrey's three castles, she covered the
last fifty miles to her capital, Poitiers, in safety.

Once she reached Poitou, she set about putting her domains
in order; but there could be no security until she had found a new
husband capable of maintaining her authority. Of the eligible
lords, one stood out above all others as a fitting match. His
domains bordered those of Aquitaine, and as a potential rival he
was more dangerous than any other. Although much younger than
herself, his skill in warfare and government were already well
known. It was these reasons, and not her personal emotions, which
made Henry, count of Anjou, duke of Normandy, and rightful
heir to England, the obvious choice for Eleanor's point of view.
An alliance in marriage with him would create a formidable
empire, in whose government Eleanor might expect to play a part.

If Henry had been inactive until now, and had not joined
in the attempts to waylay Eleanor, it was neither from ignorance
of the situation nor from collusion between him and the mistress
of Aquitaine. That she secretly sent messengers to him to offer

GENEALOGY OF THE HOUSE OF CAPET

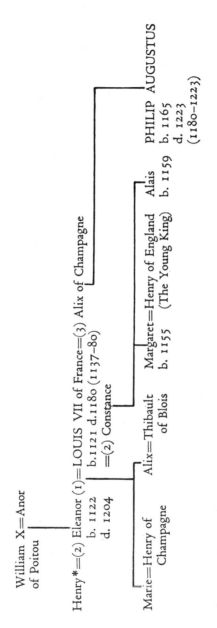

William X==Anor
of Poitou

Henry*==(2) Eleanor (1)==LOUIS VII of France==(3) Alix of Champagne
     b. 1122 b.1121 d.1180 (1137–80)
     d. 1204 ==(2) Constance

Marie==Henry of Alix==Thibault Margaret==Henry of England Alais PHILIP AUGUSTUS
Champagne   of Blois b. 1155 (The Young King) b. 1159 b. 1165
                          d. 1223
                          (1180–1223)

* See Genealogy of the House of Anjou

her hand to the duke of Normandy and count of Anjou, is most unlikely;[14] if such a mission arrived, it was almost certainly in order
to bring an acceptance of an offer made by him. As to his inaction:
he had been a hundred miles north of the duchess' route, and
could have done no good by a sudden pursuit. The council of
barons at Lisieux, originally intended to discuss military preparations, was now asked to approve the duke's scheme for marriage
instead. Arrangements were soon completed. Although in strict
feudal law, Louis' permission as overlord was needed, and in
strict canon law a papal dispensation because of their relationship
should have been obtained, no notice was taken of these potential
hindrances. The rule that vassals about to marry required the consent of their lord was respected more often in the breach than in
the observance, although Eleanor, who was an heiress and technically Louis' ward, was more open to criticism than Henry on this
point.[15] As for the papal dispensation: Louis had not troubled to
obtain one when he married Eleanor, and Henry stood in exactly
the same relationship to her as her former husband had done. A
project of marriage between Eleanor's daughter Marie and Henry
had been rejected in 1146, six years before, on precisely these
grounds; but Bernard of Clairvaux was responsible for this, and
he was particularly scrupulous over such matters. The other possible objection to the marriage was pure scandal: it was rumoured
that Geoffrey had prohibited his son from marrying Eleanor
because she had become his mistress while he was at the French
court as seneschal of France.[16] But the story assumes incredible
foresight on Geoffrey's part, and merely shows how ready the
chroniclers were to believe the worst of Eleanor.

The Norman duke hastened southwards to Poitiers, where
the marriage was celebrated on May 18, 1152. At a single stroke,
he had extended his sway southwards to the foot of the Pyrenees,
and westwards to the Atlantic coast—the edge of the known world;
and he could lay claim to the lands running down to the Mediter-
ranean shore: in all, an empire such as had not been seen in the
West since the death of Charlemagne three centuries before.
Besides this, one of the most celebrated beauties of the age, whose
charms he was more likely to appreciate than the monkish Louis,
was now his wife. A little of her loveliness survives in four por-

traits of her in stone and in glass that have come down to us; but she lives on more vividly in the troubadour's verses:

Waer diu werlt alliu min	*If all the lands were mine,*
von dem mere unz an den Rin,	*From sea's edge to the Rhine,*
des wolt ih mih darben,	*I'd gladly lose them all*
daz diu künegin von Engellant	*To have the queen of England*
læge an minen armen.	*Lying in my arms.*

There was only one cloud on the horizon: the immediate and active response of Louis to the situation. He summoned Henry to his court to answer for his disobedience, a command with which the Plantagenet could hardly be expected to comply. When his vassal failed to appear, Louis formed a coalition with Geoffrey (Henry's brother) and Theobald of Blois—Henry's unsuccessful rivals—and with a group of rebellious Angevin barons. When this news reached him, Henry was once more on the point of leaving for England; this time he had actually assembled his forces at Barfleur, and was about to embark.

Swift action was needed, and Henry provided it. He first marched to the relief of Neufmarché, on the eastern border of Normandy. This fortress surrendered before his arrival, and he turned south instead, ravaging the Vexin *en route*, to meet Louis, who had crossed the border fifty miles north of Paris and was threatening Pacy. On the appearance of the Norman troops, the French king retreated within his domains, to Mantes, and Henry, after invading Dreux and burning Moulins, garrisoned the Norman frontier. Feeling that the situation in the north was now safe enough for him to turn to the suppression of Geoffrey's revolt in Anjou, he first won over his brother's chief allies, who surrendered Chinon, Loudun and Mirebeau. He then took Montsoreau, where he captured many important rebels, including Geoffrey himself. This success dissolved the French coalition; Louis had fallen ill, and a truce was made soon afterwards, leaving Henry, who had spent barely two months in dealing with the rebels, free to turn to other affairs.[17]

He spent part of the winter making a progress through Aquitaine with Eleanor, of which only one incident has been recorded. While at Limoges, he demanded the maintenance customarily given to the ruler of Poitou when he visited the town by the monastery of St Martial. The monks refused, on the grounds that he was not resident in the castle, but living in a tent pitched outside the walls; whereupon, in a fit of Angevin temper, he gave orders that the outer walls, recently erected for the defence of monastery and town, should be thrown down. The rest of the journey was probably occupied by more constructive work, its aim being the establishment of a stable régime, loyal to Henry and Eleanor, among her notoriously independent vassals.

Journeying northwards once more, Henry arrived at Barfleur about the turn of the year, to resume his interrupted plans. The situation in England had in the interval become even more favourable to his cause. During the previous year, Stephen had attempted to obtain papal permission to have his son crowned during his own lifetime as heir to England; but the promise of Eustace's earlier years, when he and Henry had been rivals in military exploits, had not been fulfilled. The pope, perhaps influenced by an emissary from Theobald, archbishop of Canterbury, one Thomas Becket, who described Eustace's brutality and lack of statesmanship, refused to allow the coronation. Thus the pope tacitly favoured Henry's claims. Stephen's party were further disheartened by Henry's success abroad; his youth, energy and skill in war and politics contrasted sharply with the king's reputation.

Henry's host sailed from Barfleur in thirty-six ships, and landed in England somewhere on the Hampshire or Dorset coast on January 6, 1153.[18] His forces numbered perhaps 140 knights and ten times as many foot. The duke's first action was to enter a nearby chapel, where mass was being said, and the opening words of the lesson, it being Epiphany, gave him as favourable an augury as he could have wished: 'Behold the Lord our governor, and the kingdom in his hand.' His first objective was to besiege Malmesbury, which while it was held by Stephen's supporters threatened the communications between his two centres of support, Bristol and Gloucester. His troops soon took the surrounding town, but in so doing entered the church, which they pillaged, and, murdering several monks and priests, committed sacrilege. Henry, horrified by this and fearing possible reactions of opinion, at once sent the chief offenders back across the Channel; and their shipwreck was regarded as a divine judgement on their sin. Stephen had meanwhile heard of the predicament of his garrison, and hastened to their relief; he drew up his army outside the town in a fierce storm, which was blowing in the faces of his men, but before a pitched battle ensued, the terms of a truce were agreed by which the castle was to be demolished.[19] However, the agent sent by King Stephen to supervise the demolition decided that the duke's party offered better prospects, and in return for the restoration of his lands, handed over the castle intact. Stephen, discomfited, withdrew; and Henry's men, exhausted by the long siege, rested for a while before resuming the campaign.

Henry himself made a tour of the west, perhaps to obtain further support, visiting Devizes, Evesham and Gloucester, before he made renewed attempts on castles held by Stephen. He was successful in raising a small number of new followers, of whom the most important was Robert, earl of Leicester, whose thirty castles in the Midlands were a valuable asset, his support being won in return for a charter of rights. He then moved to the Midlands, where, after visiting Leicester on June 7, he laid siege to earl Ferrers' castle of Tutbury, on the advice of Robert of Leicester. This well-fortified stronghold withstood a long siege, but Henry brought it to a successful conclusion when the earl and his followers joined the Angevin party. Meanwhile, another force had taken Warwick, and his position in central England was almost unchallenged. Bedford was pillaged, but the castle still held out. Going on to Stamford, where he was encamped on August 31, Henry met with more success, taking town and castle; but at Nottingham, the castle garrison fired the town and he was forced to retreat.[20] The king was hampered during this time by Hugh Bigod, earl of Norfolk, who kept him under constant pressure, and hindered him from sending help to any of the castles which Henry besieged.

But the important fortress which the duke had intended to relieve after Malmesbury still remained under siege; this was the castle of Wallingford, commanding the Thames valley above Reading. Stephen had built Crowmarsh castle just across the river, with the object of preventing access and starving out the garrison, and it was this that Henry attacked. He was at first repulsed by Stephen's men, who kept themselves hidden until the last moment and succeeded in surprising their enemies; but gathering a large force, he returned, undeterred, to the attack. Stephen countered by sending an advance guard of 300 horse into Oxfordshire to harass the duke while the main royal army assembled, and at some time in October, the two armies faced each other in their encampments on opposite sides of the Thames. Stephen barricaded the bridge, but Henry, by an act of great daring, took this and pitched his tents less than half a mile from those of Stephen's troops. As usual in such circumstances, the consequences of a pitched battle seemed too fraught with danger for either side to risk its fortunes, and parleys were begun on the suggestion of the earl of Arundel. Henry and Stephen held a long private discussion alone on horseback in the plain between their armies, at the end of which a truce and the razing of Crowmarsh within a few days were ordered, and negotiations for a permanent peace begun. It was not until November 6, however, that Henry went to Winchester to meet Stephen, at the instigation of the archbishop of Canterbury and the bishop of Winchester. Here the parties concerned agreed on terms: terms which were greatly affected by events during the late summer and autumn. For Eustace had ravaged Cambridgeshire and the land round Bury St Edmunds at the beginning of August, committing fresh acts of sacrilege: in apparent retribution, he was stricken by a sudden illness which carried him off on the tenth of the month. The earl of Northampton and the earl of Chester, 'whose hand, like Ishmael's, was against every man', also died about this time; and prospects for a final peace were greatly improved thereby. William of Warenne, Stephen's illegitimate son, was neither interested in nor fitted for the crown, and hence Henry was now the only serious contender for his grandfather's inheritance.

The treaty of Winchester, agreed in November 1153, marked the end of eighteen years' sporadic warfare in which neither side had decisively defeated the other, in spite of circumstances which had strongly favoured Henry during the last months of the struggle. The result was a compromise, and not a particularly workable one at that, couched in general terms. No complete and reliable copy of its text survives, but its conditions can be reconstructed. Henry was accepted by Stephen as his heir, and Henry's heirs after him, and surety was given for the succession; in return for which the duke did homage to Stephen as king. Henry was to have some share in the government of England, although whether it was as adviser or as co-ruler remains doubtful. William of Warenne was to have the lands held by his father before he became king, which were very carefully specified, and to do homage to Henry for them. Stephen was to ensure that none of his castles or fortresses should be a hindrance to Henry's succession to the throne: a clause which perhaps included instructions for the demolition of all such strongholds erected since 1135. Mercenaries were to be expelled, the disinherited restored to their lands, the laws universally enforced, and ancient privileges renewed. Each of the articles was sound in itself, but no account was taken of possible obstacles and objections, nor were any tangible suggestions for their implementation included.[21] Barons on both sides would resist the destruction of their castles, and both king and duke would have difficulty in subjecting their faithful supporters to such terms, which would not seem the best reward for long service in the face of adversity, particularly when it came to depriving them of lands which, however wrongfully obtained, had been theirs for fifteen years.

Duke and king proceeded from Winchester to London together, where the terms were solemnly confirmed amid general rejoicing; and at a great council at Oxford about January 13, 1154, the barons did homage to Henry as their future king. Stephen and Henry returned to London. The difficulties which the treaty involved now became apparent: the country was still under two administrations, as it had been for so many years, and even the small efforts towards improving the situation envisaged at Winchester caused dissension. Soon afterwards, at Dunstable, an argument developed over the demolition of the 'adulterine' castles, which almost led to a renewed rupture in relations. Nonetheless, at the beginning of Lent the king and duke still went together to Canterbury and thence to Dover to meet count Thierry of Flanders. They finally parted company at Rochester. Unaware of plots by Flemish mercenaries, who had good reason to fear the peace that he might bring, Henry returned safely to Normandy after a visit to London, in April 1154.

In spite of raids on the Norman border by Louis in July 1152, who burnt Verneuil and unsuccessfully attacked Vernon, little had happened since Henry's departure for England. Louis was incapable of taking a properly garrisoned and provisioned castle, and Henry had made all the necessary defensive arrangements before crossing the Channel. Only one event of importance had occurred: Eleanor had borne Henry a son, William, on August 17 of the previous year (1153), thus ensuring the Plantagenet succession, and adding insult to Louis' injury, since in fifteen years she had given him only two daughters.

 Henry could now turn aside from military matters to the problem of securing his authority in Normandy. This he did by gradually revoking the grants made by his father, a matter for extreme caution and prudence, which he carried out without meeting serious resistance. He then suppressed a minor revolt in Aquitaine, and followed this by making peace with Louis; by this he regained Verneuil and Neufmarché for a cash payment, and obtained Louis' formal renunciation of the title of duke of Aquitaine, which he had continued to use after his divorce from Eleanor. At some time in September, Henry was forced by a serious illness to curb his activity, but he had recovered by October, when he helped Louis to suppress a revolt in the Vexin. The rift between Plantagenet and Capetian was always purely one of policy, and the two men seem to have liked each other, in spite of the great differences between their respective characters. When they parted, Henry went to deal with the rebellious lord of Torigny, whose castle he had besieged without success three years earlier; and it was here that the news of Stephen's death reached him.

 The last month of his rival's reign had been spent besieging and destroying castles in the north, the last being that of Drax in Yorkshire. He had then come south again to Dover for a second meeting with the count of Flanders, probably over a projected crusade. Not long after this, he caught a slight chill and died at Faversham on October 25, where he was buried. Messengers left at once to inform the archbishop of Canterbury, Theobald, and Henry. Thanks to the former, although 'England was without a king for almost six weeks . . . the peace was not disturbed, by God's grace, either for love or fear of the new ruler'.

Henry had waited to take the castle at Torigny before going to Barfleur, where contrary winds delayed him for a month. He landed in his new kingdom on December 8, 1154, accompanied by Eleanor and his brothers, Geoffrey and William, and hastened to London. There, on the Sunday before Christmas, December 19, he was crowned by Archbishop Theobald according to the ancient ritual of the realm. At twenty-one, Henry Plantagenet was king of England, duke of Normandy and Aquitaine, count of Anjou and Maine, and the greatest ruler in the western world.

E

3

A Prince Among Princes

THE SURVIVING portraits of Henry bear little resemblance in their conventional glibness to the striking figure preserved for us in the verbal descriptions of his contemporaries. A little over medium height, his stocky, well-built figure proclaimed his great physical strength, his slightly bowed legs his incessant journeying on horseback. His face, square and leonine, with a freckled complexion, flame-red hair and beard, and prominent grey eyes, reflected his rapidly changing moods and fierce energy; when in a good temper, his expression was soft and gentle, but in the storm of his quick anger, his eyes became bloodshot and his handsome features flushed dark red, his voice grew more harsh and cracked than usual. His clothes were always becoming. In his early years he never dressed extravagantly; it seems that towards the end of his reign, the sums spent on royal robes figured as a considerable item in the exchequer accounts.[1] He shunned the long hair and carefully kept hands of his more luxurious courtiers, wearing gloves only when hawking and keeping his head close-cropped, because, it was rumoured, he feared baldness.[2] Among his Anglo-Norman barons, he always wore the short Angevin cloak, which by contrast with their long robes earned him the nickname of Curtmantle.[3]

His habits were at once the wonder and despair of those around him. Frugal in both eating and drinking from fear of corpulence, he was no lover of comforts; restless to a fault, he never sat down except to eat—much to the annoyance of his courtiers, who had to stand also. He would hear state business even at mass, and was always travelling, 'moving in intolerable stages like a courier'. On one occasion, he rode sixteen miles through blinding rain at night across the mountains from St Davids to Pembroke;[4] and his followers made this their chief complaint against him. To the four things that Solomon called hard to discern—'the way of an eagle in the air, the way of a serpent upon a rock, the way of a ship in the midst of the sea, and the way of a man with a maid'—this age had added a fifth, or so they were accustomed to say: the way of king Henry on his journeyings.[5]

'If the king had promised to remain in a place for that day— and especially when he has announced his intention publicly by the mouth of a herald—he is sure to upset all the arrangements by departing early in the morning. As a result, you see men dashing around as if they were mad, beating their packhorses, running their carts into one another—in short, giving a lively imitation of Hell. If, on the other hand, the king orders an early start, he is certain to change his mind, and you can take it for granted that he will sleep until mid-day. Then you will see the packhorses loaded and waiting, the carts prepared, the courtiers dozing, traders fretting, and everyone grumbling. . . . When our couriers had gone ahead almost the whole day's ride, the king would turn aside to some other place where he had, it might be, just a single house with accommodation for himself and no one else. I hardly dare say it, but I believe that in truth he took a delight in seeing what a fix he put us in. After wandering some three or four miles in an unknown wood, and often in the dark, we thought ourselves lucky if we stumbled upon some filthy little hovel. There was often a sharp and bitter argument about a mere hut, and swords were drawn for possession of a lodging that pigs would have shunned.'[6]

Even his pleasures were active and energetic; hunting was his chief delight, and the only reason for which he would abandon affairs of state was for the enjoyment of the chase. For instance, when he was due to meet Thomas Becket at Northampton in the most dramatic of the many crises of his reign, he turned aside instead

to spend the day hawking on the rivers and streams that lay along
his route.[7] When he had planned a day's hunting, he would be
up and in the saddle at crack of dawn, riding across the wildest
terrain, over moor and waste land, through forest depths, into the
heart of mountain ranges, in pursuit of his quarry. His skill as
huntsman and falconer was renowned, and his name is connected
with one of the earliest scientific treatises on falcons, drawn from
older Norman and Anglo-Saxon lore on the subject.[8] Throughout his reign, the Exchequer accounts are full of records of hawks
and falcons bought for the king's use; on one occasion, Henry
spent over £56 on sending a ship to Norway to buy falcons there,
and some tenants paid for their lands at the rate of so many falcons
per year.[9] Men who wished to obtain a speedy hearing of their
lawsuits knew that a good falcon was the gift most acceptable to
the king.[10]

It was during his reign that the royal forests probably
reached their greatest extent, covering, according to one estimate,
one third of the whole country. Inside their boundaries, red and
fallow deer and boar were the chief game; roe deer were less
prized since they tended to drive away the other species. The
royal huntsmen used a mixed pack of hounds in the pursuit of their
quarry; liam hounds started the beast, greyhounds pursued it by
sight, and brachets followed its scent. When a boar was being
hunted, the object was to kill as quickly as possible; the hounds
would hold it at bay until it charged, when the hunter would
spear it, often a dangerous task since the spear had to be held
rigidly and at the correct angle if the beast's impetus was to be
stopped before the slashing tusks could reach the man. Then the
ritual of venery, the correct cutting of the carcass, would begin.
With deer, on the other hand, the quarry was run by the hounds
until they brought it down and the huntsman's falchion dispatched
it.

Hawking was a less energetic and more skilful pursuit, and
one in which ladies were allowed to join. Many kinds of birds of
prey were used; in later years, legislation was to reserve their use to
different ranks of men according to the esteem in which they were
held. The great jerfalcons of Greenland, Iceland and Norway were
reserved for royalty; and Henry certainly used these birds and

prized them highly. On one occasion, just before he crossed to
Ireland, his Norway falcon was set upon by a Welsh merlin and
killed, an event which aroused some ominous comment. The more
common peregrine was, under the same statute, deemed appropriate for earls, the goshawk for the yeoman, the sparrow-hawk for
priests. Merlins were allotted to knights, being between the falcons and hawks in size and power. Whichever bird was used, it
had to be carefully trained and cared for; but the time spent on
this was repaid by superb sport. The usual practice was to either
fly the bird 'out of the hood', that is, take off its hood and release
it from the wrist when the game was sighted, or to make it 'wait
on', hovering above its master until beaters or dogs on the ground
flushed the game from cover; birds of all sizes, from herons down-
wards, were the quarry.

Such were Henry's favourite recreations; but beside the primitive
energy which he devoted to them, he was also the possessor of an
acute mind that delighted in quick wit or in eloquence, as illustrated by an incident from the life of St Hugh of Lincoln. The bishop
had incurred his displeasure for excommunicating a royal servant.
When he came in answer to the king's summons, he found him
and his court resting in a forest clearing. No one moved or greeted
him, knowing how matters stood between him and the king; and
Henry ignored him, asking instead after a few minutes' silence for
needle and thread, with which he began to stitch up a leather
bandage on one of his fingers. The bishop realised that this was all
for his benefit, to intimidate him and make him withdraw his excommunication and plead for pardon; but, knowing Henry, he
merely bided his time, and at last said: 'How like your cousins of
Falaise you are.' Henry dissolved into helpless laughter, and finally
explained to his amazed courtiers that the jest referred to his great-
grandfather William, reputedly the son of a tanner's daughter
from Falaise. The bishop was at once restored to the royal favour.[11]
      Nor, in an age when the idea that kings should be literate
was a novel one, was Henry daunted by scholarship; he had received a particularly good education, and enjoyed arguing with the
learned men who frequented his court. He read a great deal when
affairs of state permitted, and it was said that he knew every

language from the coasts of France to the river Jordan. Perhaps this was an exaggeration, since very few of the most learned men of his day knew Greek or Hebrew: but that he continued the family tradition for wide culture, best represented by his great-uncle and cousin, Baldwin III and Amalric I of Jerusalem, is unquestionable.

The king was equally accessible to scholars and to the meanest of his subjects, and if he knew how to delay affairs that he did not wish to settle, he could not be accused of being difficult of approach. As soon as he left his residence, he might be assailed by a crowd of noisy suitors, shouting their pleas and complaints, and dragging the king along with them; yet he would hear each man out, and bear no anger for the almost physical violence offered to his person, although, if too hard pressed, he would withdraw again to more peaceful places.[12]

Apart from the work of government, Henry's major legacy to his successors was his great series of buildings, both for war and peace. To him many English castles owe their existence, most notably the great keep at Dover, guarding the gateway to England. The stone building that looks out over the Channel today has only once fallen into foreign hands, and the £6,000 that Henry spent on replacing the wooden structure left by the Conqueror has proved a good investment. At Orford, an experimental design was used for the keep of the castle that was to deter both the Flemish invader from landing there and the ambitions of Hugh Bigod; and although now ruined, the polygonal tower still stands by the peaceful Suffolk estuary. Other fortresses at Newcastle and Bowes were constructed on the more conventional square keep design. Elsewhere, the old wooden motte and bailey design, providing little more than a fortified enclosure, was replaced by stonework. With peaceful ends in mind, the castles at Winchester, Windsor and Nottingham were converted into residences in keeping with the royal dignity, combining for the first time some degree of comfort with the more austere demands of defence,[13] although lesser castles such as Marlborough and Arundel had their gardens and other amenities.[14] Less of Henry's military building remains abroad; Gisors, now ruined, Chinon, of which parts survive be-

neath later work, and Niort in Poitou were the chief products of
his activity, besides large-scale rebuilding at Arques, Neaufles and
Neufmarché in the eastern part of Normandy.[15]

As to Henry's secular residences, these fall into two classes:
the humbler houses and lodges associated with the royal forests,
and the great residences at which he held court.[16] Most of the first
type lay well within the boundaries of the royal hunting-grounds,
and were no more than adequate resting-places, with a hall,
kitchen, chamber and chapel and separate gatehouse inside a
moated palisade. The king was rarely likely to use these lodges for
long periods, and no large retinue had to be provided for. The
palaces—no other word describes their spacious proportions and
luxurious details—at Westminster, Woodstock and Clarendon
were a different matter.[17] Westminster was not only the chief
royal residence in Britain, but also the home of the exchequer and
the king's court. Although the main treasury remained at Winchester, Henry set up a subsidiary branch here and established the
palace by the Thames as the centre of his administration. With
two great halls, a great chamber and wardrobe for the king's use,
apartments for the queen, besides the usual domestic offices and a
quay on the river, it was so complex a cluster of buildings that a
resident engineer, Ailnoth, was needed to supervise repairs and
construction there throughout Henry's reign. The internal decora-
tions and finish were still primitive, however, in spite of the use
of glass windows in some parts of the building.[18] Panelling may
also have been used: but the rush-strewn floor and central open
fire, the smoke from which escaped through a vent in the roof, were
to be found in the meanest baron's hall and in the king's most
magnificent dwelling alike.

Clarendon and Woodstock were similar in that they both
developed from hunting-lodges of earlier days. By the end of
Henry's reign, Clarendon boasted a great hall with pillared arcades
and a dais at one end; a chapel with marble columns; and a variety
of chambers, kitchens and other domestic offices, including a vast
wine-cellar. Woodstock, though it could not rival Clarendon's
situation overlooking the valley where Salisbury now lies, was a
more interesting place. The house itself was on the same lines as
Clarendon, but had fascinating associations. Here it was that

Henry's amours with Rosamund were reputed to have taken place; and it seems that a small group of buildings not far from the palace itself formed a rural retreat which was the setting of this dalliance. The nearest parallel to this pavilion was to be found in Sicily, where the Norman kings took their ease in such ornamental summer-houses as this. Everswell, as these buildings were called, was grouped round three pools, the plan of which John Aubrey drew in the seventeenth century; and it is curious that the whole setting of a particular episode in the legend of Tristram and Iseult was re-created here. 'In this poem the lovers were accustomed to meet in an orchard near the royal castle in which Isolde lived. This orchard was surrounded by a strong palisade, and at one end of it there was a spring from which water first tilled a marble pool, and then continued in a narrow channel which ran through Isolde's apartments in such a way that Tristan was able to communicate with her by dropping twigs into the stream. Whether at Woodstock the channel actually passed through Rosamund's chamber is not clear, but the chamber and the running water were undoubtedly in close proximity. Everswell, in fact, provided the complete *mise en scène* of the poetic episode: the enclosed orchard; the spring with the stream flowing first into an artificial pool and then into a narrow channel; the chamber or "bower"; and finally the lovers, in the persons of Henry and Rosamund.'[19] Since the poem was certainly known to Henry, and one version may even have been written for him, it is far from impossible that, once he had decided on the building of such a pavilion—which, if we might hazard a not improbable conjecture, may well have been planned for Eleanor in the first place—he should model it on the poet's fancy.

Henry left no other monuments in England. There is no English parallel to the great hospitals at Angers (1173) and Le Mans (1180) which still survive, although put to different use; the great hall of the former is one of the remaining glories of the secular architecture of the period. A similar foundation at Caen (1159) no longer exists, and the park of Quévilly, originally made for Henry's own pleasure but later turned by him to charitable uses, has also vanished. More impressive than any of these monuments to the Angevin's activity in ordinary building is the great dyke that runs the length of the Loire and holds its floodwaters in check from Ponts-de-Cé thirty miles upstream to Bourgueil, making the road along the valley safe even when the river is in full spate.

If the military works of Henry outweigh those for peaceful purposes, the king regarded the former as an insurance for peace rather than in an aggressive light; although he was continually at war, and always involved in fighting, he had a deep horror of bloodshed, and held peace to be the greatest good that a king could bestow on his people. This was not hypocrisy, for in twelfth-century warfare very little loss of life occurred, especially since anyone of higher rank than a footsoldier would be held to ransom rather than killed. The chroniclers always have a long list of prisoners to record after a siege or skirmish, but deaths rarely appear in their pages. Pitched battles were avoided almost as studiously as nuclear conflict today; the attempts to break the enemy's nerve by drawing up an army in full battle order, and the hasty negotiations to prevent the unleashing of the holocaust, have a familiar ring. War on the fullest scale was not the standard instrument of foreign policy that it was to become two centuries later. Hence, although Henry spent much time in sieges and in the field, the picture of his grief, 'far greater than the love he bore the living',[20] over those who fell in war, nonetheless rings true. Nor did he prefer armed combat to diplomacy, using the latter until either his patience or his skill was exhausted.

But there was a darker side to this picture of high ideals and industry, this concern for his people's welfare energetically transmuted into realities, which was at its most evident in the outbursts of rage inherited from his Norman grandfather, the first Henry. On these occasions he would tear his hair and clothes, throwing off his shoes and any loose garments, hurling objects on the floor, perhaps the precious silk covers of the couches, and finally, sprawling on the ground, he would begin to chew the rushes spread on it. Today such behaviour would betoken madness; but in Henry's day, there were fewer restraints on the display of emotion. Although the king's temper became a byword for its violence, his actions were never regarded as an eccentricity. He usually recovered rapidly enough from these paroxysms of anger, and only once did a remark made in fury lead to disaster.[21]

In similar vein was his elemental response, at rare moments, to the divine portents beloved of the age. Neither devout nor as inclined to scepticism as his contemporary, Frederick Barbarossa, the Holy Roman Emperor, he would occasionally be struck by one of the strange warnings which the religious fanatics of the age directed at him, and which he normally brushed aside with a jest or an absent-minded silence. Once, when a knight from Lincoln-shire came to him with seven commandments which the king was to obey, and which had been dictated by a voice from heaven, Henry sat up all night dealing with cases of justice which he had delayed too long, but at daybreak thought better of it and dis-charged the remaining suitors.

Yet if Henry was not devout, he was certainly as free with the royal bounty as his predecessors.[22] The religious order which most benefited from his gifts was that of the Knights Templar, who received wide lands in England, chiefly in London, Essex, and the Midlands and a regular income from alms paid by every sheriff in England throughout his reign.[23] Two of his close com-panions were Templars, Richard of Hastings and Tostes de St Omer, and the Templars helped him in a political manoeuvre in 1161, which perhaps explains their predominance in his favour. Regular orders received little from him except charters of con-firmation and minor grants of rights. The three monasteries which he promised to found in redemption of a vow to go to Jerusalem in expiation of Becket's death, were an evasion of the spirit of the promise, for he refounded existing houses at Waltham and Ames-bury; though reform was in both cases badly needed and the work valuable. Only at Witham did he create a new house; its prior, Hugh, was later that bishop of Lincoln whose quick wit won him the king's grace. To this monastery he was more generous; but Hugh still had to brave the royal wrath on several occasions and ask outright for support in cash or land. Once he had to return one of Henry's gifts in secret to its rightful owners; for the king, hearing that the monks of Winchester had prepared a beautiful new illuminated Bible for use in their refectory at meal times, asked them to give it to him. They could hardly refuse; but when

Hugh received it and discovered how it had reached him, he lost no
time in sending it back.[24] In France, we have fewer records of his
gifts; such as survive are often confirmations with added concessions, and the Chartreuse (Carthusian monastery) at Liget in the
forest of Loches was his only foundation, again in expiation of
Becket's death, and dating from c. 1176. He gave extensively to lay
charities, supporting the leper houses he had built at Angers and
Caen with gifts of land and money; and in time of famine he
looked after the poor, keeping ten poor men in each diocese during
the spring of 1176 from April 1 until August 22 and making
similar arrangements in Anjou and Maine, on which he spent all
the produce from his lands there.[25]

Nor, in spite of wild popular rumours about his relations with
his wife, did Henry have more to atone for than his predecessors.
Eleanor had once been accused of infidelity to Louis; and if all
the stories of Henry's misdemeanours were true, she was amply
punished by her second husband's behaviour. But most of the
stories about the king, even those current in his lifetime, had
the same political motive behind them as those told about Eleanor.
During the conquest of Brittany, he took many hostages for the
good behaviour of the lords, and in the revolt of 1166 it was
alleged that he had seduced and made pregnant a girl thus committed to his care;[26] but this is too obvious a rallying-cry for rebellion to be believed, especially since no supporting evidence was
produced. More serious, on the face of it, was the affair of Alice,
sister to Philip of France and fiancée of Henry's son, Richard.
His refusal to allow Richard to marry the girl naturally gave rise
to every kind of story. It was said that he had called Cardinal
Huguezon to England in 1176 in order to procure a divorce from
Eleanor and marry the princess himself. After his death, Richard,
not wishing to fulfil the engagement, produced witnesses to show
that Henry had had a child by Alice, whose evidence Philip
accepted and released Richard from his obligation. But Henry's
action was more probably due to Richard's value to him as an un-
attached and eligible candidate for marriage alliances; nor were his
attempts to maintain the *status quo*, neither implementing nor re-
pudiating the agreement, well concealed. In 1191, the marriage was

no longer of advantage for either Philip or Richard, and a good political excuse was needed.[27]

With Eleanor's imprisonment in 1173, Henry almost certainly grew unfaithful. Before this, he is reputed to have been passionately in love with the sister of the earl of Clare and with Avice de Stafford;[28] but it is in this year that the most famous of his mistresses makes her appearance: the 'fair Rosamond' of so much literature and legend. One of six children of Walter de Clifford, a knight with lands in Shropshire, she was openly acknowledged as the king's paramour only a little while before her death as a nun at Godstow in 1176, where she was buried. So much is within the bounds of history; but the stories of the maze at Woodstock which Eleanor penetrated in Henry's absence to offer her rival the choice between poison and the dagger, and of the wondrous casket kept there, are so much embroidery on a slender groundwork of reality. Although she may have lived at Everswell, Henry's pavilion near Woodstock, the chamber at Winchester named after her eighty years later is unlikely to have existed in her day. By then 'camera Rosamunda' had become the euphemism for the royal mistress's quarters. Even the grim epitaph quoted as adorning her grave at Godstow was borrowed; it really belonged to a sixth century Lombard queen of the same name, in spite of its strange appropriateness:

Hic jacet in tumba Rosa mundi non rosa munda;
Non redolet sed olet quae redolere solet.

(Here lieth in tombe the rose of the world, nought a clene rose; It smelleth nought swete, but stinketh, that was wont to smelle ful swete.)[29]

Yet it was this of all Henry's exploits that caught the imagination of the ballad writers of a later age; Becket was almost forgotten, and a whole series of poems and plays from the sixteenth to the early nineteenth century were centred on this passion. Even when the perspective of history was corrected, and Tennyson wrote his play on the struggle between king and archbishop, Rosamund remained a central character; Rosamund figures as Becket's ward, and is saved by him from the avenging queen, to appear, disguised as a monk, at his murder. The play ends with Rosamund kneeling over the martyr's body.

Thus a later age cast Henry in the part of romantic lover, at as far a remove from reality as could be imagined. A very different theme recurs in the last years of his reign, reflected in the dispute over Alice: that of dissension between father and sons. Henry was undoubtedly fond of his children; but once they were of an age when they might expect a share in the government, in those days about seventeen or eighteen, he made a series of political and psychological blunders in his handling of them. On the one hand, he was reluctant to part with the least shadow of power or sum of money to his heir, and on the other hand was too soft-hearted to follow through this policy consistently. Rebellion was followed by tearful reunion—and fresh rebellion. Even if the problem was largely political, it was complicated by Henry's personal feelings, and the family habit of internecine quarrels. Henry I had imprisoned his elder brother Robert for many years, and Matilda had quarrelled with him over her dowry; the Plantagenet himself had had to suppress several revolts on the part of his brother Geoffrey, and no tradition of loyalty existed. Henry's love or friendship could be strong: 'whom he once loved he hardly ever hated':[30] yet that was no reason for his sons to reciprocate it. Of his children, the young Henry occupied a special position as heir to the greater part of his father's domains, Richard always remained close to his mother, Geoffrey earned no special love or hate, and John was always his father's favourite. Hence between the varying loyalties of their father and the sons' self-interest conflict was inevitable and frequent.

The same clash between the interests of state and the king's personal position arose in the matter of Thomas Becket. In the early days of Henry's reign, while Thomas was still chancellor, the two were firm friends. When Thomas, as archbishop, opposed Henry over religious matters, the bond was weakened; but the days of friendship show Henry at his best, gay and tolerant, yet never abandoning statecraft for luxury and dissipation. One day, as they rode together through the wintry London streets, the king suggested that it would be a worthy act of charity to give a poor by-

stander a warm cloak, and offered the chancellor this opportunity
to gain merit. When Thomas hesitated, Henry tugged at the
splendid cloak his friend was wearing, and a friendly tussle ensued in which the chancellor eventually had to give in, much to
the poor man's delight. Henry would often join Thomas at table,
riding into the hall, dismounting and vaulting over the trestle to
sit beside his friend, where he would complain in jest that the
chancellor had such a brilliant household that the court itself was
almost empty.[31] But when it came to the question of the crucial
appointment to the archbishopric, Henry grossly miscalculated,
although to all outward appearances he should have known Thomas'
character better than any man living. If he could not be expected
to notice Thomas' abstinence and self-discipline as a dominant
trait of character, or to anticipate his sudden asceticism, he
should have remarked the high ambition and determination of
his closest helper. On these his plans eventually foundered.

    If Henry lacked the skill to tame those who were born
leaders of men and whose aims conflicted with his own, it would
be mistaken to brand him as a poor judge of character, since he
chose his ministers and subordinates with almost unerring skill.
Men like Richard de Lucy, Richard du Hommet, Robert de
Neufbourg, Earl Robert of Leicester, Ranulf Glanville, William
the Marshal and many others were of high character and untiring
energy, who built under the king's direction a system of government unrivalled in its time; and charges of corruption were far from
common among great officials. From the moment that he refused
to cede Anjou to his brother when he gained the English throne,
Henry had made it clear that he would brook no equal in his
domains. Yet the disasters of his latter years were the direct con-
sequence of his failure to deal with the one man in his realms who
could claim to be exactly his equal: his heir, crowned king of
England in his father's lifetime. After the younger Henry's death,
Richard, although without the same advantage of coronation, rebelled chiefly against the repetition of the treatment accorded to
his elder brother.

With a king of such character at its centre, who added to his other

traits of energy and determination a wide learning and varied
interests, the Anglo-Norman court could hardly fail to be distinguished in many ways. The culture of the twelfth century
knew none of the boundaries imposed by the later concept of
nationalism. Through the universal medium of Latin, the intellectual activity of a scholar in Spain or Sicily reached his fellows
in England without any hindrance save that of distance; and if
travel was not as easy as it had been a thousand years earlier,
political affairs had little effect on it, for pilgrims, students and
clergy flocked along the great highways of Europe to St James'
shrine at Compostella in Spain, the universities at Paris, Bologna
and Salerno, and to the Eternal City itself. Diplomatic missions
contributed to these exchanges; to Henry's court came the emissaries of Norway, Germany, the Eastern Empire, Castile,
Navarre, Sicily and Jerusalem; and English embassies made their
way to the various countries in return.

Foreigners were welcomed not only as guests but as residents
at the English court. France was hardly a strange country, and
numerous Frenchmen, both from Henry's own domains, and
from those of Louis, made their careers in England. Thence came
Hugh de Puiset, bishop of Durham; Peter of Blois, archdeacon of
Bath and a great writer of letters to whom we owe much of our
knowledge of Henry; Hugh, bishop of Lincoln, whom Henry
summoned to England to become prior of Witham; from Italy,
the great civil lawyer, Vacarius, who arrived in 1149 and remained
to teach at Lincoln; from the Sicilian court, Master Thomas
Brown, the royal almoner—such are a few examples of immigra-
tion to England. In the opposite direction, we find John of Bel-
meis and Gervase of Tilbury, having made their mark at the
English court, going to Sicily;[32] and Henry's daughters, married
respectively to the kings of Sicily and Navarre and to the duke of
Saxony, took English retinues with them, just as Eleanor had
introduced troubadours from southern France to the unappreci-
ative Londoners. Not all the exiles were happy in their new homes;
Bernart de Ventadorn's complaint at being left in London when
Eleanor had gone south, finding the chill, dank English autumn
little to his liking, showed another side of the picture of international movement.[33]

Most of the important officials in church or state had received some degree of training abroad. Eight of fourteen English bishops in 1166 had been to foreign schools of canon law;[34] Thomas Becket had been to Paris and perhaps also to Bologna to complete his studies, like many of his contemporaries. Paris was the intellectual heart of western Europe at the time, and even a satirist's account of it underlines its importance. In his poem *Burnel the Ass*, Nigel Wireker relates the adventures of an ass who seeks a means of lengthening his tail at all the great schools of Europe, by magic, medicine or pure learning; here is the description of his arrival at Paris and what befell him there:

> While of such things still wayfaring they speak,
> They come to Paris and there a hostel seek.
> Weariness by repose is there made good,
> And diet scant by lavish cups and food.
> Tired bones, soiled skin, strained sinews, worn with toil
> Of the long journey, are by baths and oil
> Refreshed; and newly bled and with trimmed hair
> Burnel, all combed and washed and dressed with care.
> Goes forth into the town; he prays in church
> Then for which school will suit him best makes search.
> And there with careful thought considering
> The Englishmen, to them he fain would cling;
> In wit and counsel shrewd, in courtliness
> Pre-eminent, handsome, charming in address,
> They rain their money on the folk, and hate
> The skinflints; many a course in lordly state
> Adorns their tables, wine abundant flows;
> All this attracts, only three faults he knows;
> But for these three he would all else commend;
> They are 'Wassail', 'Drink health!' and 'Lady friend'.
> Nor yet are these so reprehensible
> That in due time and place they serve not well;
> For two are banishers of grief and care,
> And open wide the way to glad good cheer;
> While the third takes the harm from violent passion
> (Which, so we're told, in France is all the fashion).

So with the English would he comrade be,
And live like them in their own company;
Which he desires the more for having heard
In public talk of them a certain word;
Company alters manners, and if so
Could not their company make something grow?
Nature to them past nature has been kind,
Why not to him—in front or else behind?
So with all zeal he buckles down to work,
To learn correctly and with taste to talk.
Alas his wits are dull, his headpiece tough;
Tis all in vain, he cannot learn the stuff.
Year after year passed by, the seventh now
Was near complete, but nothing yet, although
To teach him friends and masters laboured sore,
He had contrived to say except hee-haw.[35]

England could offer no rival to the city on the Seine, and although
Englishmen were some of the brightest individual stars in the
intellectual firmament, it was not until the following century that
Oxford became a centre of learning of any repute, after the political bonds with the continent had been loosened. In Henry's day,
western Christendom was to all appearances a single unit with
local differences. The intellectual life was not the only universal
element; besides the Church, a common language was shared by
all men who could read, and common pursuits by the noble
warriors who contested the rich prizes of jousts and tourneys. Coming from distant parts of Europe to compete in Flanders, they
found the count an ardent enthusiast for such pastimes at a time
when other rulers frowned on them. As a result, he gathered a
brilliant group of knights about him, and for some five years after
1175, made his lands the home of chivalry.

Even the central institution of western civilisation was in
Henry's day more truly international than it had been or was to be
for many centuries. Furthermore, at the beginning of his reign,
the Church had as its head the only Englishman ever to wear the
Fisherman's Ring: Nicholas Breakspear, otherwise Pope Adrian
IV. His career is a good illustration of the absence of national

F

divisions within the Church at this time. Son of a minor land-owner in Hertfordshire, he went to Paris on being refused entry to St Albans monastery, where his father had become a monk. Having risen to the position of abbot in a house near Avignon, the canons complained of his harsh discipline and tried to get rid of him. The litigation involved took him to Rome, where Eugenius III realised his ability, appointed a new abbot, and kept Nicholas at the papal curia, as cardinal-bishop of Albano. He was sent on a mission to Norway to establish a metropolitan see in 1152, and scored a considerable diplomatic success. On Eugenius' death he was elected Supreme Pontiff on December 4, 1154—a mere fort-night before Henry was crowned king of England. His period of office was brief, but he proved a statesman of ability, improving the Church's temporal position. Nicholas' course had a host of lesser contemporary parallels; Becket's close friend, John of Salisbury, is another good example. After twelve years at the schools of Paris and of Chartres, he was at the papal court from 1148 until 1154, leaving a vivid memoir of events there. Between 1154 and 1160, he returned three times to Rome, before be-coming Becket's most valuable supporter during his controversy with Henry, and sharing his exile in France. After his friend's death, he became bishop of Chartres, and ended his days there.[36]

Fed by this free currency of men and ideas, learning and literature flourished at Henry's court. Some fifteen literary works have sur-vived with evidence of dedications to Henry himself. Apart from the works presented to him by his masters, Adelard of Bath and William of Conches, and minor poems celebrating his accession, four major chronicles bear his name: Henry of Huntingdon's *Historia Anglorum*, Jordan Fantosme's account of the Scottish war in 1173-4, John of Marmoutier's history of the Angevin counts, and Robert of Torigni's chronicle. In an age when historical writing became as exact a science as could be hoped for under the circum-stances and something more than a literary exercise, it was fitting that some of the resulting works should be connected with their central figure and inspiration. Men closely associated with the government of Henry's realms left records which are invaluable today: one, Roger Howden, writing as a historian, and two others

portraying the state of their particular branch of activity. The
treatises on the exchequer and on the legal system, attributed to
Richard Fitz-Neale and Ranulf Glanville respectively, are both
dedicated to Henry, who had devoted much energy to both fields.
But besides the expected works of statesmanship, several purely
literary efforts figure in the list. Peter of Blois was a close friend of
Henry, and it is hardly surprising to find his Collected Letters and
Commentary on the Book of Job dedicated to the king. Even
Gerald of Wales, usually hostile to the ruler, who, he believed, had
unjustly hindered his promotion, offered his Topographia Hibernica
to the king, perhaps in hopes of reconciliation; but his over-effusive
final eulogy of Henry was hardly likely to be to the latter's taste.
It is the French works connected with the king that show the extent
of his interest. The Roman de Rou, the long poem on Normandy inspired by Geoffrey of Monmouth's great inventions about the early
history of Britain, was given jointly to Henry and Eleanor by its
author, Wace. Eleanor, a noted patron of literature, had already
received the dedication of his earlier verse translation of Geoffrey
of Monmouth, the Roman de Brut, which was one of the first
French versions of the Arthurian legend; and Henry, who may
have heard the Welshman's tales in his uncle's household at
Bristol in his boyhood, commissioned the new work from Wace.
But the dedication was not an entirely happy one, for by the time
the poem was finished, Henry had withdrawn his support because
Wace was making such slow progress and had asked another
writer to complete it. Turning from the epic to the fresh blossom-
ing of lyric poetry, the poems of Marie de France may be connected with Henry, if the identification of the elusive figure of
their writer with the abbess of Shaftesbury, a relative of the king,
is correct;[37] and a version of 'the fair tale of love and death',
of Tristan and Isolde, was perhaps dedicated to him.[38]

Much more literature connected with Henry must have
vanished; nor have we the least idea of the size or contents of the
royal library, in contrast to that of Becket, although Henry was
certainly a voracious reader. The slender list above, which coin-
cides well with the known traits of his character, must serve to out-
line his tastes. Theology plays no great part; scholarship and epic
works of days gone by predominate, while the two greatest works

are treatises on the state. It is as well to remember that the prime purpose of the king's attendant company of knights and clerks was to direct the government of the country. Anything else was mere recreation for minds busied with the vital interests of their lord; and John of Salisbury levels every charge at the hangers-on of the court except that of indolence:

> Who, pray, are these in such gorgeous attire, who haughtily strut about surrounded by a retinue of footmen, accompanied by a band of companions and messmates, saluted first in the market place, sitting in the first places at feasts, their ears tickled by the sound of their first names and by such words as have power to reach the sensitive ears of nobles, raised on high and held there by the oarage of fortune's wings, setting the style and changing the fashions of every house? Flatterers to be sure, who are ready to live at the beck and call of others, provided that they may swindle them out of everything.[39]

Even entertainers were rare at the Plantagenet's court; other than wandering minstrels and harpers of whom no record remains, in all Henry's reign payments were only once made officially to a 'fabulator', one Maurice, in 1166; but a solitary royal harper drew a regular salary from 1176 to the king's death.[40] Henry also kept bears for some time, doubtless of the performing variety.[41] Other diversions may have been of a quieter kind; chess and draughts were certainly known to him. But the ladies of the court were usually the chief patrons and encouragers of these diversions, their only other occupations being domestic: embroidery, sewing and weaving, and occasionally falconry, using the smaller kinds of hawk. The *jongleur* would find in them a ready and appreciative audience. To their patronage much of the code of courtly love was due; but even though Eleanor was interested in this cult, and gave judgement in several cases put to so-called courts of love, the temperament of the king and his northern companions did not encourage its introduction to his court. Blended into the romances of Chrétien de Troyes and others, it may have come to the king's ears; but the cult never gained a following in England such as it enjoyed in Poitou.

The king's closest friends were drawn almost exclusively from administrative circles, and were concerned with the business of government which occupied Henry's days, whether as judges, diplomats or warriors. Thomas Becket was his chancellor; Richard du Hommet, Richard de Lucy and Robert of Leicester his great officers of justice; Simon of Apulia, after spending many years in the service of the Sicilian kings, became dean of York and finally bishop of Exeter in reward for his discharge of various offices; Master Thomas Brown, also trained in Sicily, was a financial expert; Walter of Coutances, his last chancellor, had worked his way up from humble beginnings, and was typical of the new men who had made their names through an administrative career; Richard of Ilchester acted as his chief envoy to Germany and Italy. The only men who enjoyed Henry's confidence outside this circle were the princes of the Church in his domains. Many of these held their posts as rewards for years spent in the royal service; but there were others who had had a purely clerical career and yet were cherished by Henry: Arnulf of Lisieux, Gilbert Foliot, and Rotrou of Rouen—all of whom played a large part in the royal council as advisers on ecclesiastical affairs.

It might seem from this that Henry made his appointments purely on a basis of favouritism. Yet the reverse is true. He chose his officials for their qualities, and, unless he actually disliked them, personal matters were irrelevant. It was only because these were the men among whom he spent the greater portion of his time that his closest friends came from their ranks. Visitors to the court were rare enough, and were usually foreign missions or persistent plaintiffs disappointed in their lawsuits, such as Richard Anesty, who has left us the accounts of his expensive pursuit of royal justice in the matter of an inheritance.[42] Although the king was readily accessible to all comers, his circle of friends was a closed one.

Hence the character of the court was chiefly determined by the structure of the governmental hierarchy. In England, the functions of the royal officials were far more easily distinguished than those of their Norman or Aquitanian counterparts. It is a reasonable generalisation to say that governmental authority and system declined as Henry's realms extended southwards, England being the best governed and Aquitaine the least inclined to obedience. But even Henry's English 'civil service' cannot be represented as a rationalised organisation divided into well-defined departments. A royal official was concerned, except in a few cases where special skills were involved, with everything that touched the crown's interest; finance, justice, military duty, administration of the royal lands. The most important single class of officials was that of the sheriffs, each of whom was responsible for one or two shires. This office went back to Anglo-Saxon times, and in the hands of the great lord of the shire could be seriously misused. Henry was aware of this, and took care, as soon as he was sure of his position, to replace such men by others of lesser influence. However, the sheriffs spent most of their time in the country as the chief royal agents in their various localities, and rarely earned promotion to the king's immediate circle; it is unusual to find them appearing at court except on special business, and their annual journey to report to the exchequer in London at Michaelmas more often than not found the king absent.

The real link between central and local government was formed not by the sheriffs but by the itinerant justices, whose office had been devised partly to make good the lacunae of the legal ability of the sheriffs and county courts, and partly as a check and supplement to the sheriff himself. Henry himself on his incessant wanderings was really attempting to do the tasks he delegated to them, but even with his enormous energy, efficiency could not be achieved by one man alone. Commissions were therefore issued for the holding of so-called 'pleas of the crown'— trials involving legal questions reserved for the royal judgement; but the itinerant justice was usually responsible for finances and military arrangements as well, his range of work being much wider than the name implied and almost as great as that of the sheriff. Nor were the justices a special class of men devoted to this one task, but men of importance at court. Almost every major figure closely associated with Henry performed this function at some time, including the financiers of the exchequer, who were the only true specialists among Henry's servants.

In view of this versatility, the lack of precise definition of function within the court is not surprising. Great offices did exist—chancellor, chamberlain, butler and marshal—but these had originally belonged to the household of the king in the strictest sense of the word, and extended their influence to other matters in varying degrees. The brilliance of Thomas Becket's chancellorship was exceptional, and even as guardian of the great seal the chancellor did not necessarily have political influence. The seneschals and constables enjoyed traditional perquisites and duties rather than fulfilling a vital role in government, and the only regular officer of purely administrative importance was that of grand justiciar. This was at first what it had been in Henry I's day: a kind of permanent regency. The two justiciars could represent the king whenever necessary, but no real initiative power went with the title until it was held by one man, Richard de Lucy, during the revolt of Henry Plantagenet's eldest son in 1173–4. Under him and his successor, Ranulf Glanville, it became a position almost equal to that of chief minister, with wide powers and competence.[43]

In addition to the English great officers, Henry was also accompanied by their continental counterparts. The composition of the court varied from day to day and depended largely on which part of his realms he was resident in. The most important function of the royal officials was to continue the process of government in the king's absence, and hence only a very few men are found in constant attendance on him—a group that varies from year to year. All the continental fiefs had their seneschal, Poitou and Anjou having constables as well, while Normandy had a similar arrangement of great officers to that in England. It is not always easy to identify the holders of these titles, since many lesser men held offices similarly named, but one man from each region can usually be found as its representative in the framework of the household. Their functions varied considerably. In Aquitaine, the real power lay in the king's hands alone. On two occasions, governors were used to control the unruly lords of the south, and little permanent organisation existed other than that of the provosts: personal agents common to all landowners from the least baron to the duke himself. The Angevin homelands enjoyed better government; under seneschal and constable, and later seneschal alone, the royal provosts worked effectively, and the king's demesne lands yielded rich revenue. In both regions, the chief officers were always great barons, powerful enough to enforce the king's will with their own resources: a system adequate enough except in times of general discontent.

Normandy presented a much closer parallel to England. The same division into local and central officers appeared, and the intermediaries between the two worked on a similar basis. Local government was less well arranged, however; here there was a multiplicity of agents whose titles varied more than their tasks: bailiffs, provosts, vicomtes and others. Part of Henry's work was to reorganise these often conflicting elements, as a result of which the bailiff emerged as the most important. Itinerant justices were also introduced on a basis akin to that across the Channel, the personnel being important figures at court. At the highest level, regional differences ceased to matter; once accepted as part of the central organisation, a man might be appointed to office on either side of the Channel; Ranulf Glanville, Robert of Leicester and Richard of Ilchester all played important parts in Norman affairs, the latter two exercising powers equivalent to those of the English justiciars. A small core of Normans formed the more permanent element of the administration, however; Richard du Hommet and his son William as constables, Robert de Neufbourg, Rotrou of Evreux and William Fitz-Ralph as seneschals, were exclusively Norman figures.[44]

If the picture given of Henry and his court must remain a sketch, without depth or colour, it is because Henry himself is the only person who can be clearly characterised. Few anecdotes are recorded of his companions, and these more often than not shed light on the king rather than his friends. Yet, even in the dry records of the exchequer or the law courts, something of the activity and enthusiasm of Henry and his helpers comes down to us, and in the chronicles and literary scrapbooks of the time, we can begin to make out a figure which is more than a royal effigy or a flatterer's colossus, whose vices and virtues, foibles and traits are those of a remarkable individual. But to appreciate the true quality of the man, we must turn from the static picture of the king in his court to the active side, and watch his character emerging in the challenges of his mature life.

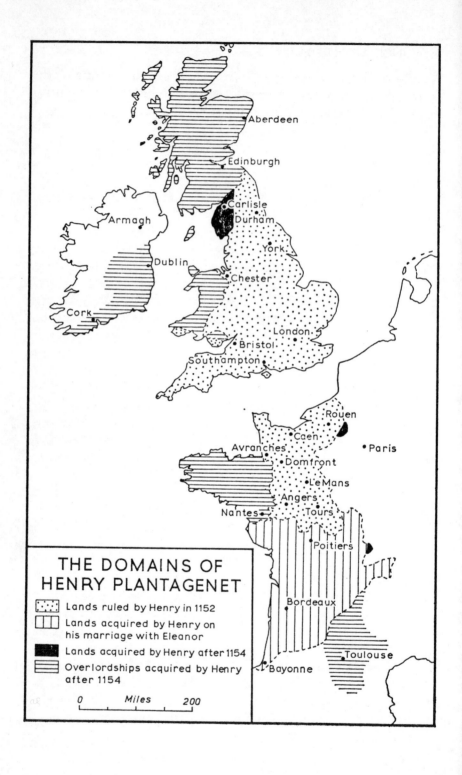

THE DOMAINS OF
HENRY PLANTAGENET

:::: Lands ruled by Henry in 1152

||| Lands acquired by Henry on
    his marriage with Eleanor

███ Lands acquired by Henry after 1154

≡≡≡ Overlordships acquired by Henry
    after 1154

0   Miles   200

4

The New Order

THE EXTENSIVE domains over which Henry now ruled contained a variety of language, law and tradition within their borders, in contrast to the more universal outlook of the educated men who ruled them. The southern boundary of his continental domains lay along the valley of the Dordogne and the foothills beyond the Gascon plain; in the south-east it reached into the heart of the Auvergne mountains, while the Atlantic coast from Bayonne almost to the mouth of the Loire was in his hands. In the north, Eu, on the Flemish border, marked the limit both of the French king's overlordship and of the Norman state, a fixed and ancient division: but the western boundary with Brittany was uncertain and fluctuating. Across the channel, England and south Wales acknowledged him as ruler, although Cumberland and Westmorland remained in Scottish hands. Four languages were spoken by the common people of these lands: English, Welsh, Provençal and northern French, besides the ubiquitous Latin of educated men. A variety of customary laws prevailed: in England, the Anglo-Saxon system had been infused with the feudal custom of Normandy, while overseas, Norman, Angevin and Poitevin each had their own traditions in spite of the common base of Charlemagne's codes. Their feudal law, which formed the bulk of civil as distinct from criminal law, was for the most part the same, since they all acknowledged the kings of France as overlords.

Henry's task was formidable enough without these added obstacles. Four years' work in Normandy and Anjou was only just beginning to produce tangible rewards. England, where the royal power had partially disintegrated in Stephen's reign, was at once

the richest and potentially best governed of his four major territories, followed by Normandy. Henry had relied on the strength
of his power in the latter to gain his new crown; now that he had
achieved his object, he found some of the machinery of government built up by his mother's father still in reasonable condition.
There was less need to reconstruct than to set in motion again the
processes of administration and to make them effective. This was
speedily done. Within a few months of Henry's accession, the
English exchequer was again in full operation, and once more
presented a model of financial organisation to the rest of Europe.
From the accounts of the third year of Henry's reign, we can
estimate the damage done to the royal finances in England by the
warring factions and turbulent barons, since the payment of taxes
was excused if the land was too ravaged to bear the burden, and
such sums were accounted for as waste. In the south-east, the
area formerly under Stephen's control, bounded by Hampshire,
Buckinghamshire and Cambridgeshire, had a waste percentage of
one quarter of the anticipated revenue, Cambridgeshire, Hunting-
donshire and Oxfordshire being the worst affected, while Kent and
Sussex were almost unscathed. Similar damage is recorded for the
counties most loyal to the Angevins: Somerset, Gloucestershire,
Worcestershire and Herefordshire. The Midlands, which, to all
outward appearances had enjoyed the normal feudal government
of their lords,* were in the worst condition, almost half their
quota being unpaid. Most of the serious military action had taken
place there, and the tyranny of their lords had often proved worse
than lack of defence. Yet for all this dismal record of devastation,
the revenues of England were still worth, on average, £12,000 per
annum.[1]

The first action of Henry as king of England was to issue a
coronation charter, as Stephen and Henry I had done before
him.[2] But whereas his grandfather's charter had been a list of
specific promises to the Church and to the barons, and that of
Stephen had defined the royal duties towards the Church, the new

* The chief of these were all related—Robert of Leicester, Waleran of Meulan,
the earl of Northampton and Roger of Warwick.

charter was much less explicit, and instead of offering concessions, set a strict legal basis for the beginning of the work of reorganisation. Henry did not include the expected clause confirming the grants of lands and liberties made by his predecessors. Instead he chose to promise a return to the *status quo* at his grandfather's death in 1135. This was calculated both to dismay the many barons who had profited from the late king's weak political position to extort concessions, and also to bring the Church to order, which had in the interval tacitly assumed many exemptions from royal surveillance, besides those formally recognised. All such gains were now subject to Henry's good will and the issue of a new charter; and he could revoke any grants of crown land made by Stephen. However, he proceeded circumspectly and treated the matter to a great extent as propaganda designed to show Stephen as a usurper, rather than as a means of regaining the lost lands and privileges. No murmur of organised revolt was heard for the moment, although the king had only just assumed his new dignity. Henry had too secure a hold on Normandy, where he had been able to revoke his father's grants three years earlier; most of the important English barons held lands there which they were loth to risk. His personal prestige, combined with the powerful backing of the Church under Archbishop Theobald's leadership, also played its part in preventing trouble.

The king spent Christmas and the New Year (1155) at Bermondsey, where he promulgated the first measures towards the execution of his plans. Before any action could be taken he required a reliable central group of officials. Stephen, from the few traces of his government that remain, seems to have lacked this nucleus, so essential to good organisation, and to have worked largely according to the needs of the moment, Hence there was no body of experienced men on whom Henry could rely, and with the youthful king, a largely youthful body of men took charge. The most important nomination at the beginning of 1155 was that of Thomas Becket as chancellor. As archdeacon of Canterbury, he had been of great service to his archbishop, and Theobald strongly recommended him to Henry for this post. He had taken Becket with him on an important mission to Rome in 1143, when he was attempting to solve the problem of the papal legation for

England. This appointment carried with it authority almost as great as that of the pope himself, and was usually held by the archbishops of Canterbury, if it was granted at all. Henry of Winchester, however, had succeeded in obtaining it in 1139, and was using it to undermine Theobald's position. Theobald and Becket failed to regain it for Canterbury, but in 1145 the new pope, Eugenius III, granted the request.[3] Becket had accompanied Theobald, in spite of Stephen's prohibition, to the council of Rheims in 1148, where questions of a political nature had been discussed. Finally, he may have been instrumental in persuading the pope to refuse Stephen's request for permission to have his son Eustace crowned in 1152,[4] in which he would have helped not only Theobald, but Henry as well. His training in the archbishop's household had fitted him admirably for the chancellorship and although fourteen years the king's senior, he could share Henry's enthusiasm for new ideas and radical solutions.

Two other men were closely connected with the king's plans. These were Robert, earl of Leicester, and Richard de Lucy, both of whom had been partisans of Stephen until Henry's campaign of 1153. Robert of Leicester was a man of great influence whether he held royal office or not; he had enjoyed the king's confidence since he first joined the Angevin party, for it was on his advice that the siege of Tutbury, which had led to earl Ferrers' surrender, was undertaken. With de Lucy, who had risen from being a knight of no great standing to become one of Stephen's great officers, he was responsible for royal justice from the earliest days of the reign. Richard de Lucy appeared for Henry in lawsuits at Abingdon and York, as well as in a protracted case over charters granted by William the Conqueror to Battle Abbey which involved most of Henry's principal officers.[5] Both were probably older than the king by several years.

Henry wasted no time in carrying out the implications of his coronation charter. In a week's hard work, before he went to Oxford on January 6, 1155, he issued orders establishing his own sovereign authority and completing the execution of the treaty of Winchester. Stephen had made little headway with the destruction of illegal castles, and Henry repeated instructions for this work and for the expulsion of mercenaries. He commanded the return to the crown of all castles, towns and lands which had been seized or granted away during his predecessor's reign. In addition he abolished all the earldoms given by Stephen to his partisans, and took back the portions of the royal demesne which had gone with them. Henry also profited from the death of the earl of Chester, whose lands lay in his wardship until the heir came of age, and from the detention of his murderer, William Peverel, whose lands fell to the crown.

This was a beginning to the restoration of the royal position. It helped the royal finances; and the king was beginning to over-awe the major barons by sheer territorial power once again. Much depended on how these enactments were interpreted by those carrying them out. There could be no doubt as to the question of the castles and mercenaries. Attempts to buy or beg exemption from the general demolition were rarely successful: Henry fully realised the dangers of too many fortresses in the barons' hands, and although the figure of 1,115 given for the castles destroyed is ridiculous,[6] a year or so later there were only 217 baronial castles as opposed to 52 with royal garrisons: one in every five castles thus belonged to the king.[7] The mercenaries, with the exception of their leader, William of Ypres, and a small number who went to join a settlement of Flemings on the Welsh border, had left the country within three months, and this major threat to civil peace removed.

The evidence as to the confiscation of former royal property is slender, and opinions drawn from it conflicting. The proclama-tion may have been intended only to ensure that irregular grants and seizures were easily detected when the exchequer officials came to draw up the list of royal lands. Alternatively, Henry may have wished to enlarge the royal revenue either by retaining it or by regranting it to its occupier for a fee. Judging by the reactions to the measure, it cannot have been a very radical or unexpected step, since no one raised any serious opposition to it, while the order regarding castles provoked only one open revolt. William of Aumale, a baron so wealthy as to be the uncrowned king of Yorkshire, had to be compelled to surrender his lands, but it was the loss of the castle at Scarborough which was the real cause of his reluctance. Furthermore, Henry certainly regranted a large amount of the disputed territories, and for this we have the evidence of charters. The earldoms were also granted again to their former holders, and hence Henry's intention must have been less to deprive the barons than to ensure that they owed their position, like the newly created earl of Norfolk, to his personal sovereignty. He even went so far as to ignore charters which he himself had issued during the anarchy, giving new titles instead of the confirmations that one would expect.[8] The black years of Stephen's usurpation were to disappear from administrative records, and his reign was to begin as prosperously as his grandfather's had ended.

Only among the Welsh marcher lords did resistance to the new order of firm government appear. They had always regarded themselves as semi-independent, and free from the strict letter of feudal law as applied elsewhere, because of their essential part they played in the defence of the realm. Roger of Hereford, who had been a loyal supporter of the prince in 1149 and 1153, refused to give up the castles at Gloucester and Hereford, but was persuaded by his cousin, Gilbert Foliot, bishop of Hereford, to surrender them peacefully. This he did on March 13, receiving wide lands in exchange. The bishop of Winchester also quarrelled with Henry over the surrender of his six fortresses, and chose voluntary exile rather than hand them over to him, whereupon the latter seized them and turned them to his own ends. Alone among the barons, Hugh of Mortimer preferred open revolt. Henry was forced to launch a campaign in May to deal with this problem, which involved three castles in the Midlands: Bridgnorth, Cleobury and Wigmore. Matters did not go so easily as the king might have hoped, and it was not until July 7 that Hugh was reconciled with Henry by formally making surrender of the castles at a council at Bridgnorth. During the siege, Henry had a narrow escape when an arrow aimed at him was intercepted by a knight of his bodyguard, Hubert de St Clair, who died of the wound. The king evidently did not feel his position to be strong enough to take drastic measures against Mortimer, who retained his lands.

The summer of 1155 was passed in the south of England in com-

parative peace. Henry could now appreciate the pleasures as well as
the cares brought to him by his new realms, and indulge his
passion for the chase in the huge forests created by his grandfather
and great-uncle. Not until Michaelmas did he return to major
affairs of state. About September 29, another great council was
held, at which the project of conquering Ireland was mooted. Such
an idea, new to English politics, was inspired partly by the internal
disturbances across the sea, and partly by the young king's in-
satiable ambition. He had already obtained permission from the
pope, to whom Ireland was held to belong under a spurious eighth-
century document, purporting to be a donation to the Church from
the Emperor Constantine, all islands formed part of the 'patrimony
of Peter'. Hence Henry, imitating William, his great-grandfather,
when the latter set out to conquer England, sought papal leave to
convert Ireland: a process which gave him some sort of title for
what was otherwise naked aggression. The exact form of the grant
does not survive, but John of Salisbury records how he used his
influence at the papal curia to obtain it, and how he brought the
document back to England together with a precious ring, both of
which were deposited in the treasury at Winchester.[9] Nothing in
the political situation appeared unfavourable, and Henry even proposed to give the intended conquest to his brother William; but
the queen-mother, Matilda, opposed the scheme nonetheless, and
her opposition carried sufficient weight with Henry for him to
postpone the idea indefinitely.

Matilda's caution was perhaps justified; for at Christmas, disturbing news came from France, where the situation had been potentially dangerous ever since Henry's accession in England. The promise
made in accordance with his father's will, that Geoffrey should
have Anjou and Maine, had not been carried out. Henry now had
additional reasons for avoiding the fulfilment of this, since as ruler
of Aquitaine, they were vital to communications between his
northern and southern domains. He left England from Dover on
January 10, 1156, having waited eight days for a fair wind, and
landed at Wissant, near Calais. On February 2, he was at Rouen,
where the count and countess of Flanders visited him, to arrange
details of Henry's wardship of Flanders when count Thierry went

G

on pilgrimage to Jerusalem in the following year. A treaty was also made between the two rulers by which Thierry was to receive certain lands in return for the services of 1,000 soldiers in England or Normandy, or 500 in Anjou, whenever Henry should require them. Whether Henry was thinking of the immediate situation or of long-term policy, the investment was a good insurance against future troubles.

A week later, he was better able to appreciate how matters stood. At a conference on the French border, at which Thierry, Louis of France and Geoffrey were present, Geoffrey rejected his brother's compensatory offers, although Henry had already taken the precaution of obtaining papal absolution from his oath on the grounds that it had been exacted under duress (a normal procedure in such circumstances). He further strengthened his hand by doing homage to Louis for all his continental domains, including those under dispute. Outmanoeuvred by his elder brother, Geoffrey left for Anjou, and Henry returned to Rouen. Civil war was plainly imminent.

The position of 1152 was now repeated, but Geoffrey lacked the support of Louis, and Henry could concentrate on the reduction of his brother's three fortresses. By July, Chinon and Mirebeau had fallen, and Geoffrey preferred to accept an offer of £1,000 in sterling and £2,000 Angevin to be paid annually. Later in the year, his position as potential rival to Henry was resolved when the citizens of Nantes ejected their duke, and offered Geoffrey the lordship. This thus provided him with a sufficient domain of his own, an arrangement which could hardly have been better from Henry's standpoint, since it also meant that the mouth of the Loire was now in friendly hands.

After this success in Anjou, Henry went briefly to Normandy and then south with Eleanor in October to Aquitaine—a part of his domains he had scarcely entered since he became its lord on his marriage. He had never received homage from its barons, and used this opportunity of so doing, making sure of his position by taking hostages as well. On November 11, at Limoges, he ordered the razing of the castle fortifications, and made peace between the town and the castle garrison. Christmas was passed at Bordeaux before his return north. One year had sufficed to settle his lands oversea, and the future seemed to offer peaceful prospects.

Henry sailed from Barfleur in early April 1157 and landed at Southampton. If the lords of France were quiet, or at least quiescent, there were still difficulties to be faced in England. One of these, the problem of the two northern counties of Westmorland and Cumberland—which he had given to David of Scotland in return for his support before his accession—had been simplified by the latter's death in 1153. But no action had yet been taken, and a council was summoned at Northampton on July 17, at which Malcolm, the new king, was required to surrender the lands. Simultaneously, William of Warenne and Hugh Bigod had to appear and give account of their actions. Threats proved enough. Malcolm received Huntingdon—a fief far less valuable to him—in return for the two northern counties; William of Warenne duly surrendered his lands and castles and was given back those held by his father in 1135, in direct contravention of the provisions made for him at Winchester. Hugh Bigod placed his castles in the king's hands. From these manoeuvres, Henry gained twelve castles, the most important being Norwich and Framlingham from Bigod, and Pevensey and Lancaster from William.

The same council also served to assemble forces for a campaign against the Welsh, for which knights were summoned from all parts of England. Henry had high hopes of success, and a formidable invasion was launched by land and sea. Events proved otherwise. Near Basingwerk, Owain of Gwyneth's levies under his son's command ambushed half Henry's force. The king himself was believed dead when the standard was dropped in a moment of confusion by the bearer, Henry of Essex. A disordered retreat ensued. The other part of the English forces, however, compelled Owain himself to retreat to his mountain fastnesses, and Henry— furious at the reverse—withdrew to Rhuddlan when he found pursuit impossible through the wilds of Snowdonia. Matters were made worse by the fleet's behaviour. The sailors had landed at Anglesey, but after pillaging two churches, were also forced to retire. The king, hampered by the oncoming harvest for which his troops, officially on forty days' service, would have to be released, deemed it prudent to withdraw. He made peace with Owain and managed to recover some of the lands which the latter had seized during Stephen's reign.

Political stability was now almost complete; but financial matters required attention. The revenues of 1156–7 were the lowest of the reign, and Henry took in hand minor reforms of the collecting system, besides ordering the levy of the first of a series of extra-ordinary taxes listed in the accounts as gifts. Furthermore, the coinage was reissued, in the form of new pennies of a higher purity, with almost ten per cent more silver in them. These 'short-cross' pennies were to be the standard coin of the realm for twenty years, and one of the best issues of coinage England had seen until then. This business, and a tour of northern and central England, occupied Henry until the Whitsun of 1158, when the court assembled at Worcester. Here the customary ceremony of crown-wearing was performed, as it had been at Bury St Edmunds the previous year and outside Lincoln the Christmas before. At the end of the ceremony, Henry and Eleanor laid their crowns on the altar of the cathedral and vowed never to wear them again. No reason is recorded for this decision, strange in an age when the out-ward pomp of majesty counted for much. Perhaps Henry's active temperament disdained such charades that served no apparent pur-pose and wasted valuable time. At the same time, Henry of Win-chester came to make his peace with the king, and to renounce the will-o'-the-wisp of political power which he had so single-mindedly pursued for two decades; once the greatest man in the realm, although unable to build himself a stable position, he now devoted himself to his see, occasionally appearing in public life as an elder statesman, beyond the heat of partisan views of the moment.[10]

    From Worcester, the progress round his kingdom continued for Henry, interrupted only by a Welsh attack on Gloucester while he was in the west country. In reprisal for this he invaded south Wales and obtained the submission of Rhys, the most im-portant of the Welsh princes. However, the following year brought renewed troubles, since Rhys was dissatisfied with the settlement made by Henry. Wales continued to be a problem which, although small compared with other tasks facing Henry, proved more intractable than any other.

When, in August 1158, Henry crossed the Channel once again his goal was again that consolidation of his lands which had occupied much of his time in England. Having received from Scotland the lost English counties, he now planned to recover the lost castles of the Norman Vexin from Louis. To this end he arranged that his son Henry—who had been heir apparent since his elder brother William's death in 1156—should marry Louis' eldest daughter, Margaret, and that the dowry should consist of the castles of Gisors, Neaufles and Neufchatel: exactly those which he had surrendered six years earlier. Such a triumph of diplomacy was not achieved without considerable effort. A preliminary mission led by the chancellor, Thomas Becket, departed for Paris before Henry himself had reached France. Its pomp and splendour, reflecting a certain theatrical streak in Becket's nature, made a deep impression on the French. An escort of more than two hundred rode with him, knights, squires and pages, with vast supplies of every kind of luxury to be distributed to the French court: silk, fur, cloaks and carpets, skins and ermine, 'such as are usually found adorning a bishop's chamber and bed'. Eight large waggons held these treasures, as well as Thomas' own wardrobe which included twenty-four changes of silk robes, his provisions, a portable chapel and kitchen, and equipment for his clerks. Two of the waggons carried nothing but ale, which was distributed to the populace, who found it vastly superior to their native wine. Twelve packhorses bore the rest of his equipment, treasure, plate and books. The passage of this procession was as impressive as the riches packed in its chests. First came two hundred and fifty footmen, hounds and greyhounds with their keepers, the great waggons with their hide covers, and the packhorses. Then the squires followed on foot, bearing their masters' shields and leading their horses, and then the falconers and the officials of the chancellor's household. Last of all, the knights rode two by two before the chancellor himself and his close friends. So vast was the company that it caused a shortage of food as it passed on its way, huge prices being paid for a single dish of eels. 'The king of England must be a marvellous man if his chancellor travels with such great display', murmured the French as the carefully staged pageant moved slowly into Paris.[11]

But the lavish outlay was well repaid, for Thomas seemed to have little difficulty in securing Louis' assent to Henry's plans. In addition to the marriage treaty, he obtained a free hand for his master in Brittany where the death of duke Geoffrey in July 1158 had caused new confusion. As seneschal of France, the hereditary post of the counts of Anjou, Henry was to judge between the rival claimants. This was really licence to create an Angevin puppet-state without any threat of interference from his overlord. Louis could do little else, for Brittany was surrounded for hundreds of miles by Henry's domains. When Henry himself appeared, he travelled in striking simplicity. This, after Becket's display, made an even deeper impression than a second lavish pageant would have done. His chancellor had indeed done his work well, for the final terms were quickly settled. At Neufmarché on August 31, he met Louis. The details, although simple, were the vital part of the marriage agreement, and although Henry might have hoped for more, they could have been far less favourable. Prince Henry was amply pro-vided for, being given the city of Lincoln, £1,000 revenue and a fief owing three hundred knights' service in England and a slightly smaller endowment in France, to ensure that the couple could live in appropriate style. The castles were to be put into the custody of the Knights Templar until the marriage took place. Arrangements were also made for Henry to visit Paris and take back with him his son's fiancée, which he did shortly afterwards. He was lodged with the canons of Notre-Dame and splendidly entertained by Louis. On his return to Normandy, the three-year-old Margaret was placed in the care of Robert of Neufbourg, the viceroy, to await either the day when she came of age or when Henry felt the acquisition of the dowry, and hence the marriage, to be imperative. That day was to come sooner than Louis had expected.

Meanwhile, preparations had begun for a campaign in Brittany. After Geoffrey's death on July 26, 1158, Conan IV, nephew of the duke whom the Plantagenet had replaced, had seized Nantes. Henry accordingly sent orders for his forces to assemble at Avranches to besiege the disputed town unless Conan previously surrendered it, and confiscated the English revenues enjoyed by the latter as earl of Richmond. This and the news of Henry's successful negotiations with Louis were enough to overawe the interloper. Formal surrender was made on September 29, 1158, the date on which the Angevin forces were to have foregathered. Relieved of the need for military action, Henry went instead on pilgrimage to Mont St Michel, where he heard mass at the high altar and dined in the monks' refectory with his barons. From there he proceeded to inspect his newly acquired city, valuable both for its high revenue and strategic position on the mouth of the Loire.

Throughout Henry's reign, his domains, taken by and large, were usually at peace. The moments were nonetheless rare when some minor disturbance was not taking place, especially among the unruly lords of the south, though not always on a scale to require the king's personal attention. Henry normally preferred to wage his own wars and to leave the less exciting administrative side of his duties to his deputies when the choice arose. His next expedition made a great impression on his contemporaries. We know little of the details except that it was aimed against the lord of the reputedly impregnable castle of Thouars on the borders of Poitou and Anjou. Henry seems to have used a force of mercenaries, for the Norman knights would not have served so far from home, and there is no evidence of a summons to the men of Anjou or Poitou. In any case, the dramatic speed with which the castle fell—its resistance lasted a mere three days—implied some new method or a higher than usual standard of military efficiency. The mercenaries were no new institution, for Stephen had used them, and others before him. Henry, however, succeeded in changing them from an ill-organised treacherous rabble to a highly effective force, loyal and well-disciplined, under recognised captains. With the fortress fell one of the key factors in twelfth-century strategy: the assumption that impregnable castles situated at vital positions were an adequate defence, and that no major field forces were needed for a successful campaign. If such fortresses could be taken in a mere three days, whole regions might fall within a few weeks now that siegework no longer involved long delays. Nor was this success a mere flash in the pan. His mercenaries and siegecraft were Henry's great asset for the next fifteen years, and not until the French began to play at his own game did they present a serious challenge to his military superiority.[12]

When Louis met Henry again soon afterwards, he was in no way to quarrel with his successful vassal. A warm display of friendship marked a joint pilgrimage to Mont St Michel, where they heard mass together. Returning by Avranches and Caen, they parted on the best of terms at Rouen. Louis had during this time reconciled Henry with his old enemy, Theobald of Blois, and a treaty fixing the eastern border of Anjou was made soon afterwards. Theobald gave up the Loire castles of Amboise and Fréteval, and an exchange was arranged with his brother-in-law, Rotrou of Mortain, by which Henry gave up Bellême on the Norman border for Moulins nearer the centre of Normandy: another step towards making his domains compact and well-organised.

Eleanor, who had been acting as regent, joined Henry for Christmas at Cherbourg. After the festival, he began to plan a new expansion of his effective domains, perhaps with her encouragement. Eleanor's forebears, the lords of Aquitaine, had at one time been lords of Toulouse; but the counts of Toulouse claimed that William VIII, Eleanor's grandfather, had given them full lordship in bond for a loan made to him when he went on crusade in the early years of the twelfth century. Since the money had not been repaid, they now regarded themselves as independent. Louis, when he was married to Eleanor, had planned an expedition to re-establish her rights, but this never materialised. He had chosen instead to make an alliance with the count of Toulouse by marrying his sister Constance to him. Henry decided to revive the claim, and began his plans accordingly. The campaign would be fought far from the lands of his trusted northern knights, and he placed little reliance on the men of Gascony and Poitou. Therefore, on Thomas Becket's advice, he turned to a form of taxation, first used in the early years of the century, which would enable him to raise the army of mercenaries he needed and would relieve his knights of irksome duty in the far south. By this system, each knight paid a specific sum—five shillings—for the service he owed. If a baron held lands for which the service of twenty knights was due, instead of raising the contingent himself, he paid the appropriate assessment of £5 to the king, who then organised the levy and wages of the army himself. Henry furthermore made an alliance with Count Raymond of Barcelona, by which his third son, Richard, now aged eighteen months, was (in due course) to marry the count's daughter.

Only one possible danger threatened: that of Louis' intervention on behalf of his brother-in-law. Henry hoped to avoid this. Yet the French king could hardly afford to allow his already overpowerful vassal to appropriate more lands. A meeting at Tours proved unsuccessful from the Angevin's point of view, since Louis refused to make any promises not to intervene. Plans were nonetheless continued, and a general summons for the army issued on March 22, 1159; the meeting place was to be Poitiers, on June 23, for those knights who chose to do their service in person. A fresh attempt to appease Louis was made at Heudicourt three weeks before the expedition was due to depart, but once again the French king refused to give Henry a *carte blanche* similar to that granted for Brittany in the previous year.

Henry had been active in other diplomatic fields. A mission was sent to win over the German emperor, Frederick Barbarossa, to his side; but his envoys arrived at the Imperial court at the same time as those of Louis and embassies from Greece and Hungary. Even the goodwill gained on a previous embassy in September 1157, when a huge tent of marvellous workmanship had been presented to Frederick, was insufficient to extract more than the 'prudent words and royal gifts' distributed to all alike.[13] Frederick, already involved in Italy and at home, had no desire to assist Henry in his ambitions, which, if nourished, might one day cross with his own; from Toulouse, it was not far to the discontented cities of northern Italy, which lay uneasily under the emperor's yoke, ready allies for ambitious interlopers.[14]

The army that left Poitiers on June 24, 1159, was of impressive size. Only a few knights came with the barons of England,

Normandy and Anjou; but Scottish and Welsh contingents, forces
raised by the count of Barcelona, and an innumerable host of
mercenaries gave Henry reason to hope for swift success. At first
all went well. Sweeping southwards, minor castles on the road to
the city of Toulouse fell rapidly before him. Malcolm of Scotland
was knighted by Henry at Périgueux on the last day of June,
perhaps in token of some special feat. A week later, the host lay
encamped before the walls of Toulouse itself. Most of the count's
lands, including the important stronghold of Cahors, lay in
Henry's hands by early August through Becket's exertions at the
head of a separate squadron. But the defence had been strengthened by Louis' presence within the city; he had moved south to
resist his vassal's ambitions, and now encouraged the defenders.
In addition, the besiegers were hampered by long supply lines,
their nearest base being forty miles distant. When an epidemic
attacked his troops, Henry deemed it wise to withdraw, giving as
his excuse his wish to avoid attacking his overlord in person.
To have Louis as his prisoner would certainly have placed Henry
in an awkward situation, but he had not hesitated to run this risk
on earlier occasions. Leaving garrisons in the castles that had been
taken, and giving Thomas the command of the rearguard, Henry
withdrew northwards via Uzerche and Limoges at the end of
September, cutting Louis' line of retreat. He reached Normandy
in October, where Louis' brothers had attempted to create a
diversion by ravaging the border; Henry retaliated by laying waste
the lands round Beauvais and burning many towns. The count of
Evreux surrendered three castles between Evreux and Paris to
Henry as the price of peace, with the result that Louis could no
longer travel in safety to Chartres from his capital, and the blow
was aggravated when the count did homage for all his lands to
Henry, not excluding those he should have held from Louis. A
truce was the only solution for the French king, and in December
1159 a truce was made until Whitsun following.

Henry spent this seven months' respite in reorganising the
internal affairs of Normandy. Two important changes had taken
place during 1159. William of Warenne, Stephen's heir, had died
on the Toulouse expedition, and Henry had retained his possessions, which included the county of Mortain on the western border

of Normandy. He had also lost a much-valued servant, Robert de Neufbourg, who had been seneschal and viceroy for several years; feeling that his days were drawing to a close, Robert became a monk at Bec in July, and died there at the end of August. Hence new arrangements were needed, and Henry took the opportunity to add certain reforms, promulgated at his Christmas court at Falaise. The tenor of these was that judgements, whether ecclesiastical or civil, should not be made without evidence from witnesses and persons who knew the defendant. These 'honest neighbours' were in effect the same system of sworn inquest instituted by Geoffrey Plantagenet, but the procedure had never been applied so extensively until now. As to replacing Robert, Henry did not act until he left for England four years later; while he himself was present, no viceroy was required.

The end of the truce was approaching by the time Henry had inspected his Norman domains, but both sides desired a permanent peace, which was arranged at Whitsun 1160. It involved a return to the position before the war began; the count of Evreux was to go back to Louis, and all other conquests, except certain castles in the south, were to be returned. Thus the Toulouse expedition—Henry's one attempt at extending his rule by force of arms—ultimately proved little better than a fiasco, and a costly one at that. Henry knew that he could not repeat the effort immediately, and hence had to make such terms as he could, although he had made a much better military showing than the French king. The terms of the treaty were confirmed in October, when Prince Henry did homage to Louis as heir to Normandy.

Frederick Barbarossa had stood aside from this quarrel in the west. This did not mean that his actions were to occupy a wholly separate sphere, and the attention of Louis and Henry was now occupied by repercussions of the emperor's schemes in Italy. Adrian IV, the English pope, had died the previous year, and a successor hostile to the emperor elected, under the name Alexander III. Frederick's influence was great enough to secure the election of an anti-pope, Victor IV. Both now claimed recognition as rightful pope, and synods of the clergy were accordingly held to deal with the problem. A council in London in June 1160 decided for Alexander, presumably with Henry's approval, for the Norman kings claimed the choice between pope and anti-pope as a matter for royal discretion. A similar decision was taken at the council of Norman prelates at Neufmarché in July, and a joint council with Louis at Beauvais ratified this. Louis left the actual announcement to be made at Henry's discretion, evidently failing to realise that this gave him an excellent means of extracting concessions from Alexander if he chose to delay it.*[15]

Another death, that of Louis' queen, Constance, in the summer of 1160 produced disproportionate political reactions. Louis, anxious for an heir, married again within a fortnight in almost indecent haste, choosing this time the sister of the count of Blois. This meant that Margaret, Prince Henry's fiancée, was less likely to inherit her father's domains or a portion of them; and if an heir were born, Louis would be reluctant to let her dowry be paid. Henry moved swiftly, for he could not reckon on one convenient factor for very long, namely the presence of papal legates in Normandy. Using the threat of a delay in the announcement of the recognition of Alexander, he obtained permission for the marriage of Henry and Margaret, in spite of their youth, and on November 2, 1160, the legates themselves performed the ceremony. The castles of Gisors, Neaufles, and Neufmarché were handed over by the Templars who had acted as custodians, and Henry rewarded their complicity with considerable gifts to themselves and to their order in England.

The expected consequences followed: Louis and his brother-in-law, Theobald of Blois, attacked Henry. But Henry reacted swiftly and seized Theobald's newly-fortified castle at Chaumont, strengthened Amboise and Fréteval on the border. He then retired to winter at Le Mans. From here, he ordered the garrisoning by royal officers of all Norman castles, and put Gisors in a state

---

* The decree of the council of Pavia, recognising Victor IV, in February 1160, had had Henry's name among the list of approving sovereigns; his acquiescence was said to have been signified 'by letter and by his legate'.[16] Perhaps this was also used by Henry in persuading Alexander's legates. That some diplomatic use of the situation was envisaged is implied by his anger with those bishops who recognised Alexander *after* Beauvais but *before* his announcement.

of defence. Anjou, too, was put on a war footing, and when hostilities broke out again in the spring of 1161, nothing more than skirmishes ensued. Peace was made about midsummer; Henry retained the dowry since he had both legal and military arguments on his side. This time there was to be no renewal of the conflict for six years, and the borderlands were able to recover from the annual devastations of the past. The profits of Henry's military campaigns since his accession were far overshadowed by his diplomatic gains. In France, he had an unofficial protectorate over Brittany, and had acquired the Vexin and Nantes, besides which the conquered castles in the south won by force of arms were unimportant. In England, the recovery of the northern provinces was of more value than the minor successes in Wales, and he had gained possession of almost all the baronial castles that he required.

The latter half of 1161 was occupied with lesser matters. Among these were a building programme for peaceful purposes in Normandy, including a park near Rouen and a leper-house at Caen. In August 1161, he reduced a strong fortress in Gascony at Castillon, to the amazement and terror of the local lords. Christmas was spent at Bayeux with Eleanor, and the New Year of 1162 saw a consolidation of Henry's position in Brittany. An old enemy of the Norman dukes, Geoffrey of Mayenne, surrendered three castles on the Breton border which his father had usurped from Henry I thirty years before. In the same area, the death of the lord of Dol in June gave Henry a chance to exercise his rights of wardship over the heiress, a normal perquisite of feudal lords, once he had retrieved the girl from her uncle, Ralph of Fougères. The latter had hoped to keep her—and the disposition of her marriage —in his own hands.

Henry had felt for some time that he should return to England, and at a council at Rouen, in February 1162, he began to put matters in order. He rebuked the viscomtes for their maladministration, and adjusted certain fiscal matters. It was not until the following December, however, that he was able to finish his arrangements, and he was then detained by contrary winds. After spending Christmas at Cherbourg, he landed at Southampton on January 25, 1163. He had been absent for four years and five months, and there was much to be done.

5

The Central Problem

HENRY'S FIRST decade as ruler of England had been in the nature of a prelude to greater things. Now that the time of preparations was over, sweeping changes, transforming the English political scene, were to ensue in the next six years. The first of these had already come about when Henry reached England. After a long and controversial primacy of twenty-two years, Theobald, archbishop of Canterbury, had died in April 1161. When he was elected to the see, Stephen's brother, Henry of Winchester, held the office of papal legate, and the archbishop of York was trying to assert his independence from Canterbury's jurisdiction. The archbishop's position could hardly have been more beset by difficulties; but, avoiding all the diplomatic pitfalls presented by the immediate situation and by the transfer to the Angevin dynasty later on, he had restored the see of Augustine to its ancient influence. His part in negotiating the settlement with Stephen had earned for Theobald Henry's highest confidence.

Henry did not hasten to fill the vacancy, although he seems to have had no doubt in his own mind as to whom Theobald's successor would be. His enemies accused him of prolonging the interregnum because during that period the rich revenues of the see fell to the treasury. Weightier matters brought about the delay. In the course of the various diplomatic missions Henry had exchanged with the Holy Roman Empire, it could hardly have escaped his notice that the emperor had resolved the problem of relations between Church and State by giving the office of chancellor to the archbishop of Mainz, his foremost prelate. Henry now had an opportunity of copying this pattern; and there were other good grounds for choosing Thomas Becket. He had been closely associated with Theobald, as member of his household and later as archdeacon of Canterbury. One of the archbishop's last acts had been to write to him demanding that he return to see him before his death. Furthermore, Henry felt that Becket, his closest friend, was completely loyal to him and could safely be entrusted with the great power attached to the office of archbishop; and that, knowing the royal will in such matters, would readily comply in carrying it out. With Church and State in the hands of himself and of Becket, whose ability to work in complete accordance with his plans was already proven by seven years of diplomatic, administrative and military success, Henry could make himself master of England to a degree beyond the most secret ambitions of his predecessors. The dangers of the Church as an opponent had been starkly demonstrated by Stephen's troubles: when he had tried to imprison cantankerous bishops, he almost lost his throne, and the pope's refusal to assent to his son's coronation during his lifetime had given fresh impetus to his rival. Henry, like every other monarch of the day, was only too conscious of the potential of the Church's weapons of excommunication and interdict, and he had no intention of finding himself threatened by them. On the other hand, he realised that he was liable to arouse the Church's enmity, in the course of his schemes for establishing strong government. To make Becket primate would not only dissolve this ever-present threat; it almost seemed to place those very weapons in the king's own hands.

The chancellor was leaving for England to deal with such matters of state as could not wait the king's return, when Henry broached the subject to him in private. Thomas' response was perhaps the only one possible in the circumstances. Knowing that Henry's will was as good as law, even if the law of the Church demanded a free election, he answered, smiling and indicating his rich and colourful clothing: 'How religious and saintly is the man you want to appoint to that holy see!' He went on to point out that he might not always see eye to eye with the king, and that he did not want to lose Henry's friendship.[1] It seems certain that Becket was already aware that, once he had accepted such high office in the Church, his sense of vocation and dedication to the task in hand would prevent him from taking a complaisant view of Henry's ecclesiastical policy as he had done until now: to serve God and Mammon would become impossible for him. Just as Henry failed to assess this trait in Becket's character correctly, so Becket failed to appreciate the degree to which Henry felt that he might legitimately interfere in Church affairs. Becket was trained in canon law, the code of the Church, which had only been properly worked out in the previous two decades.[2] The tenets which forbad excessive interference by the secular powers were commonplace to him but far less familiar to Henry. The king was either ignorant or contemptuous of these edicts and of the idea of Church independence. The chancellor had, it was true, applied scutage to Church lands nominally exempt from tax as well as to those of the lay magnates; but the Church owed feudal service on this type of property; scutage was paid in lieu of feudal service, and the point was certainly debatable. Otherwise, there had been few occasions on which Becket would have discussed ecclesiastical affairs with the king. Theobald had usually had his own way, and nothing more than minor details had found Henry and the previous archbishop at cross-purposes. That Becket should have taken up the archbishopric fully conscious of the dangers ahead and pursued a single-minded course of resistance is most unlikely in the light of subsequent events; his resolve hardened with the course of time, and for the moment the problem of relations with the king seemed to him 'a cloud no bigger than a man's hand', and before he left for England he accepted the king's choice.

Soon afterwards, Henry sent two bishops and Richard de Lucy to England to make the necessary arrangements for the election, taking with them writs directing the monks of Canterbury, on whom the duty of choosing the new archbishop fell, to put Thomas forward. Before de Lucy left, Henry, apparently doubting his zeal in the mission, called him aside in private and asked him: 'If I were lying dead on my bier, would you do everything in your power to put my son Henry on the throne?' De Lucy answered: 'All I could.' 'I want you to do as much to get the chancellor elected to the see of Canterbury', was Henry's injunction.[3] Yet before the royal wish was realised, there were many pitfalls to be avoided. The king enlisted the papal legate, Henry of

1. The image of a Plantagenet king: English illumination of Saul from the Winchester Bible, depicted in contemporary twelfth-century costume

2. Count Geoffrey of Anjou, depicted on an enamel memorial plaque hung over his tomb at Le Mans

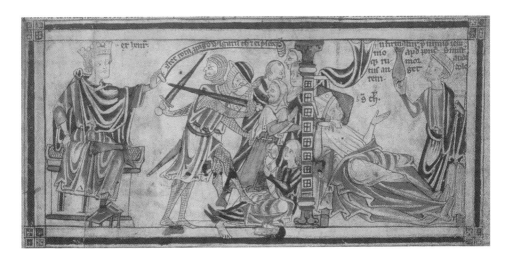

3. Left: Henry II (on left) banishes all Thomas Becket's relations; right: Becket lies sick at Pontigny Abbey

4. Thomas Becket takes leave of Pope Alexander III in the autumn of 1165

5. Left: Thomas Becket excommunicates all his enemies in 1166; right: Becket pleads his case before Henry II (above) and Louis VII (below)

6. Thomas Becket leaves Louis VII and Henry II in January 1169

7. Left: the coronation of Henry the Young King by the bishop of London; right: Henry II serves his son at the coronation feast, 1170

8. Becket returns to England in December 1170

9. Henry II at Becket's tomb. 13th century stained glass window from Canterbury Cathedral

10. Henry II, Eleanor of Aquitaine and their children present the great east window to the cathedral at Poitiers. Donor image from the foot of the east window, Poitiers Cathedral

11. Orford Castle, built by Henry as a fortress, but with architectural echoes of contemporary palaces

Pisa, and Bishop Henry of Winchester, to overcome any last doubts in Becket's mind. At the election itself, one influential prelate, the ascetic Gilbert Foliot of Hereford, opposed the choice of Thomas, whether from personal aspirations or from a genuine concern from the church's welfare. Certainly Thomas' ostentation in public and lack of apparent concern for ecclesiastical matters hardly made him seem the ideal candidate. In May 1162, the desired election was made. On June 2 Thomas the archdeacon became Thomas the priest; on June 3 he was consecrated archbishop in the old cathedral of Canterbury. Almost at once, he made his own independent will felt; and his first action as archbishop held in it the germ of much of the controversy that was to follow. Instead of executing Henry's designs, he sent the king his resignation from the secular offices he held. In so doing, he may have felt that he was justified; for when he was elected, Prince Henry, acting for his father, had released him from lay obligations at the request of Henry of Winchester.

Whatever dismay Henry may have felt on receiving the news, his next meeting with Becket was full of the old cordiality. All the same, in the six months' interval he must have learnt of the change that had come over the archbishop; of his rejection of the splendid show in which he had once delighted; of his zeal in pious works; and of his humble and ascetic way of life which in its way was almost as ostentatious, though more sincere.[4] When the king landed at Southampton in January 1163, the archbishop and Prince Henry, his pupil, awaited him; and Henry displayed as much joy in seeing Thomas as over his own son. After the tumult of the first meeting, they rode together to the royal lodgings. Soon afterwards, Thomas, seeing that the king was weary from the journey, discreetly withdrew until the following day, when they continued on their way together. Henry may have had doubts about his decision in the interval; but in the presence of his friend and reassured by the appearance of complete loyalty these quickly vanished.

A formal council and court were held at London on March 3, at which plans for the work of the next months were laid. A long

H

overdue ceremony of homage to Prince Henry was performed by
the English barons; he had been heir apparent since the death of
his brother William in 1156, but the formal recognition had
never been made. It is possible that Henry was thinking of crown-
ning his eldest son at this time, since a crown was prepared for
him;[5] but the necessary permission from the pope does not even seem
to have been requested. Measures were approved for an expedition
against the Welsh to attempt to settle the border troubles which had
continued intermittently since Henry's last incursion into Wales.

At the same time two great inquiries into the state of the
realm were set in motion. The first, concerned with the feudal
tenure of land throughout England, was designed to assert royal
rights which had lapsed during Stephen's reign, and to discover
how far the increase in military power commanded by the barons
had led to an increase in the number of knights' fiefs. Three
questions were put to the barons: How many knights' fees had
they under Henry I? How many knights did they owe in service
to the king? To how many additional knights had they given fees
since Henry I's death? The results of this inquiry were recorded at
the exchequer when the findings were completed three years later.
Whether the actual changes that arose from it were important or
not—there is very little evidence on this—it marks a departure
from Henry's political theme up to this point—that of reversion
to his grandfather's day—and a change to the beginning of a
programme of clarification and reorganisation. But first a word of
warning: we must not speak of Henry's 'reforms', for the established order was sacrosanct to both laymen and to the Church; the
king had sworn to uphold it at his coronation. Any changes had to
be justified as a revival of old customs, as was sometimes genuinely
the case, or as extensions of arrangements which were no longer
adequate in changing circumstances.[6] The idea of a fixed society,
governed by laws which reflected in their immutability God's unchanging order in which each individual had his appropriate place,
was to persist for many years to come.

A further inquiry by the archbishop of York and Reginald
de St Valéry overhauled the nation's finances. The regular annual
revenue, as showing by surviving records, declined by nearly
£4,000 in the year ending at Michaelmas 1163: a sum representing

almost one-third of the average total. This regular income was raised for the most part by the sheriffs, who paid a fixed sum into the exchequer for the various levies due to them. Hence, if increased prosperity meant an increase in the sheriff's revenue, the king drew no benefit; and eight years of peace had restored the economy of the kingdom. So the most important and simplest measure resulting from the inquiry was the raising of these fixed totals or 'farms' to a level closer to the new financial conditions. However, the king could not do this except when the occupant of the sheriff's office was changed, and by 1165 only four counties had been raised, the increase being about a quarter. Even more important, however, Henry seems to have managed to reduce the costs of government and to pay off some of the debts to moneylenders outstanding since the early days of his reign.[7]

Thomas had meanwhile crossed the Channel to represent the English Church at the council of Tours, where many decrees affecting the state of the Church as a whole were passed; and on his return he carried out a review of his new diocese, setting right some of the matters to which he should have attended as archdeacon. If he had changed his way of life from courtier to monk, he had lost none of the business acumen which had distinguished him as chancellor. Much of the property of Canterbury had been sequestered during Stephen's reign and among the more important items not returned were the castles of Rochester, Saltwood, Hythe and Tonbridge—the last being of vital strategic importance and in the hands of the powerful earl of Clare. To these the archbishop laid claim, reinforced by the canons of the council of Tours against those who held land usurped from the Church. In so doing, he aroused the king's anger. Nor was his action in excommunicating an important baron, William of Eynsford, over the right to appoint the vicar of Eynsford, calculated to please Henry. Since William I's day, it had been the custom that no man who held lands directly from the king, a tenant-in-chief, could be excommunicated without the king's permission, since the sentence might impede them in the execution of their royal duties; but this Thomas refused to acknowledge, saying that the Church alone was arbiter in such matters.

These were still minor matters such as might be expected to arise while the archbishop was settling in to his new office. A little goodwill could render them harmless. But the first opportunity for so doing—at a council assembled at Woodstock on July 17, 1163 —led only to further quarrels. In the course of the financial inquiry, a reform in the payment of certain taxes had been proposed, whereby the money traditionally paid direct to the sheriff to defray the costs of local government and defence of the shires should now be paid into the exchequer. This scheme would have given Henry further means of controlling his local officials, besides preventing extortion by them. The archbishop, however, took offence at the idea, declaring it to be an arbitrary innovation, and said that he would refuse to pay anything from the Canterbury estates. Why Becket chose to act thus is mysterious; there may have been aspects of the scheme which were genuinely harmful, but at moments the archbishop's conduct seemed to border on megalomania, in which he saw himself as the self-appointed champion of the liberties of England, often without much real cause or following. At best, his stand on a purely constitutional issue, which could hardly be regarded as an especial threat to the Church, was tactless in the extreme. Henry had to abandon the scheme under this pressure, which undoubtedly rankled in his mind. Some bishops were alienated by Becket's action; his old opponent Gilbert Foliot, newly translated from Hereford to London, refused to renew his oath of allegiance to the truculent archbishop.

Events during the spring and summer brought to the fore a much more important issue between king and Church. There were in England two separate systems of jurisdiction, covering the entire country: the royal courts, and the ecclesiastical courts. The latter were responsible for all men in holy orders and other matters ranging from Church property to marriage contracts, oaths and wills. If a man who was no more than a deacon or clerk committed an offence, it was to this court that he had to answer. Henry's complaint was not against the competence of the Church courts, but their lack of punitive powers. A layman committing murder would be heavily fined, mutilated or imprisoned; a cleric guilty of the same offence would be deprived of his orders and go scot-free, defrocking being the greatest punishment that the ecclesiastical court could impose. Henry, seeking to give his subjects a more equitable system of justice, was made all the more conscious of this loophole when one Philip de Brois was accused of homicide in the bishop of Lincoln's court, and secured a somewhat dubious acquittal. The sheriff of Bedfordshire had the case reopened, but failed to get any further, and was reviled by Philip in open court. This was brought to the king's notice since it constituted lèse-majesté; but even the king could only obtain a sentence in the ecclesiastical courts of a year's exile. When a further case of seduction and murder by a clerk at Worcester came up, Henry demanded a trial in the lay court, but found that he was directly opposed by Thomas, who managed to thwart the king's designs. The same happened in the case of a clerk who had stolen a silver chalice from a London church, although the archbishop decided that some conciliation was needed, and ordered that the man should be branded, a punishment forbidden by canon law. Yet another case occurred in the diocese of Salisbury, where a priest was accused of murder by the victim's relatives, and failed to clear himself by oath. On the archbishop's orders, the man was deprived of his benefice and condemned to perpetual penance in a monastery. Nor were such cases isolated incidents. According to the royal justices, more than a hundred had occurred since the beginning of the reign. The offences had included theft, rape and murder— all of which had gone unpunished by the lay courts.

Despite Thomas' placatory gesture, Henry had by now determined to treat the question as one of principle, relying on the practices of his forebears and the phrase in canon law regarding criminous clerks: 'Let them be handed over to the secular court.' He demanded that the bishop's court should degrade the offender, thus laying him open to royal judgement, and then hand him over to the lay courts for punishment. But both his arguments were doubtful. There is little evidence that the 'benefit of clergy' had not been applied in his grandfather's time, and it had been so widespread in Stephen's reign as to constitute a major scandal. The latest collection of canon law to be made—the great and authoritative work of Gratian of Bologna—preferred the principle 'God judges no man twice in the same matter'. On this Thomas based his counter-argument: degradation, according to him, was sufficient, and he could not permit any second punishment to be imposed. The weakness in Becket's argument lay in its disregard of Henry's careful proposal that no second trial should be held. The ecclesiastical courts could still acquit a man and have their sentence respected; but if they found the accused guilty, their powers would be strengthened by those of the lay courts. The decree that Becket quoted applied only to double trials and judgements. Yet Henry's canon-law case had a similar flaw; for the phrase on which it rested was intended only as a measure to ensure that the accused was properly identified as entitled to benefit of clergy. Once this was done, and the lay court satisfied, the accused was returned to the ecclesiastical court. So neither side had a clear-cut case, and the issue degenerated, as arguments from dubious premises always will, into a clash of personalities.[8]

The first public demand for the punishment of clerks guilty of felony in the secular courts was made by Henry at a council held at Westminster on October 1, 1163. Originally, this assembly had been summoned to deal with a very different, but equally embittered problem: that of the claim of Canterbury to authority as primate over the see of York. The king announced his new object as soon as the notables had gathered, and in a forceful speech which showed how near to his heart the issue stood, argued that the threat of losing holy orders was hardly likely to act as a deterrent to any cleric capable of committing such crimes; that clergy deserved a greater punishment since their guilt was the greater; and that canon law sanctioned his proposal. Thomas replied with a long oration pointing out the precedents for clerical immunity, and begged the king not to make this innovation which might threaten his kingdom's stability if he was forced to oppose it. His fellow-prelates, heartened by his example, supported him against the king.

Thomas should have known better than they that Henry's reaction to direct opposition was not to yield but to redouble his attack. The king now phrased his request differently, asking the prelates to swear to obey the royal customs. Refusal carried with it more than a taint of treason, while acceptance of the undefined 'royal customs' left them at the king's mercy. Thomas saw through the manoeuvre, and replied with a similar piece of verbal chicanery, promising that he and his brother bishops would observe the custom 'saving their order': a reservation which entirely defeated Henry's particular object. The king then attempted to break down this united front, but only succeeded in getting the bishop of Chichester to alter his reservation to 'in good faith' which did not placate him in the least. He roundly declared that they were using poisonous phrases and sophistry to evade his reasonable demands, and insisted on an unqualified oath. Thomas fell back on another line of defence, saying that their oath of fealty to him 'in life and limb and earthly honour saving their order' was already sufficient, since earthly honour included the customs, and that they could not make any new promises. At this Henry withdrew in one of his royal rages, without taking leave of the prelates, who vented their feelings on the unfortunate bishop of Chichester for his alteration of the formula. It was Henry's first serious reverse in the execution of his ambitions.

The following day, Henry had decided that he could make no further headway. After forcing the archbishop to hand over the various castles of which he had been given the custody when chancellor, he broke off the negotiations without any settlement. Without announcing his departure to the gathering, he rode off to the city of London. Before the end of the month, however, he summoned the archbishop to Northampton for a further interview, hoping that if he could persuade his erstwhile friend to comply, the remaining bishops would follow. The meeting took place outside the town, since there was not room for both the king's and the primate's retinues within. The king drew the archbishop aside, and reproached him with ingratitude; to which Thomas replied that the Church could not obey its secular rulers in defiance of divine laws, and offered to take the oath with the clause 'saving his order'. This once more proved unacceptable to the king. A new course was now adopted by Henry, who, knowing the foibles of his prelates, worked on Roger of York and Gilbert Foliot to arouse their old jealousy of Becket.[9] In this he was successful: at Gloucester, they promised to obey the customs, in return for the king's promise that he would make no demands on them which ran counter to the privileges of their order—verbally, a small difference, but one which left Henry ample room to manoeuvre. Soon afterwards the bishop of Chichester joined the royal party, and the Norman prelates began to take a hand: indeed, it was Arnulf of Lisieux who had advised Henry to adopt these new tactics.

By now, the rift between king and archbishop, although only a few months old, had attracted attention abroad. Pope Alexander III was prevented by his political situation from taking a firm stand on such matters, but sent letters by the abbot of l'Aumone urging Becket to comply with Henry's wishes.[10] Threatened by the existence of the anti-pope Victor IV, Alexander feared that any resistance by him might lead to the transference of the allegiance of the English king to his rival. In face of such persuasion, there was only one course open to Becket, whatever his conscience dictated. Soon after receiving the papal messengers at Harrow, he went to the king at Woodstock, seemingly of his own accord, and offered to submit unconditionally to the customs. Henry accepted this, with the proviso that the agreement should be ratified at a great council at Clarendon the following month, in the presence of the magnates of the realm. Since the archbishop's resistance had been public, his agreement should also be made in public.

On January 25, 1164, the magnates and prelates assembled at the royal hunting-lodge near Salisbury to witness Thomas' public profession of obedience. It seemed that the storms of the Westminster council had at last blown themselves to calm. But Thomas had had time to ponder his decision, and knowing the king's habits, to consider the ways in which Henry might take advantage of his promise. Hence he hesitated for a day or more after the council opened from making the agreement. Only by the persuasion of the bishops of Salisbury and Norwich, the earls of Cornwall and Leicester, and two distinguished Templars, was he induced to perform the ceremony. The promise was made; and all retired for the night, feeling that the six-month-old quarrel was now over.

The following morning was to prove otherwise. Thomas'

worst suspicions were confirmed. The king ordered—probably in accordance with a prearranged plan—that the ancient customs of the realm as practised by his forbears should be recorded by those of his barons old enough to remember his grandfather's days. The finished document was presented to Thomas on the following day in the form of a chirograph.*[11] The archbishop read the document. Apparently taken completely by surprise, he refused point-blank to seal the document, protesting that these were not practices that had ever obtained in England but 'pernicious innovations' and furthermore that his position forbad him to assent to such breaches of canon law. Nor could Henry's threats, his barons' efforts at persuasion, and the bishops' fears, move him to do more than assent to the document verbally, with much reluctance. The final record of the agreement, now known as the Constitutions of Clarendon, could only claim that the 'aforesaid customs and privileges of the Crown' were 'confirmed by the archbishops, bishops, earls, barons, nobles and elders of the realm at Clarendon'. Henry had won a Pyrrhic victory; for the struggle between him and the archbishop had begun in earnest. No quarter was to be shown by either side from now on. Behind the high phrases and solemn arguments of law and theology, the clash of proud wills could be discerned, now veiled by principles and doctrines, now degenerating into open stubbornness. Faced with a determined opponent, Henry resolved that the archbishop's downfall was the only solution. It was only a question of finding the right opportunity. Thomas fully realised that peace was even further off than at the end of December 1163, and resolved equally that he would not bow to the king, cost what it might.

The Constitutions of Clarendon have for so long been one of the great landmarks in English history that to consider them afresh would seem superfluous, if it were not for the lesson that they contain about Henry's personal attitude to law and order, and the means by which he was prepared to enforce it. Moreover, recent

* Two copies of the text written on one piece of parchment. When the agreement was made, the parchment was torn in half, and the irregular edges tallied to prove the authenticity of the copies.

work has clarified the legality of Henry's position in canon law, and shown that Becket was less justified than had been thought hitherto. Even at the time, the most impartial judge among contemporary historians and the most fervent of the archbishop's admirers alike admit that the Constitutions are part of a larger scheme of undoubted value to the kingdom and politically reasonable. Henry aimed at establishing a written and clearly recorded definition of the laws of England, which could not be disputed or suffer from the absence of central authority, as had happened to his grandfather's customs during the reign of Stephen. He had as a basis the treatise *Quadripartitus*, a summary of Old English Law, and a supplement to it, outlining—but neither in clear terms nor as an official document—those customs prevailing in Henry I's day. Many essential questions of jurisdiction were not recorded in it, or had arisen since the time of writing; and the king was determined to improve the standard of justice.

It was perhaps unfortunate that he chose to start by trying to define the position of the most powerful single interest in the feudal structure of England: the Church. Having once formed such a far-reaching scheme—and it is probable that it was in his mind before Theobald's death—Henry was bent on seizing any opportunity of making it reality. Hence the Constitutions of Clarendon should be considered not as an attempt by an angry ruler to break the opposition to his schemes, contrary to canon law, but as a reasonable interpretation of the part that the Church might play in a feudal state, and especially of the dual position of the bishops, at once ecclesiastics and feudal barons. The problem was no new one: the so-called 'Investiture Contest' over the respective rights of pope and emperor, as spiritual and feudal lords, had long been a major factor in European politics. Henry was once again unfortunate in that his efforts came at a time when the Church had begun to gain the upper hand elsewhere, strengthened by internal reforms. That his conception of the customs had a strong basis in feudal law becomes clear when the 'Constitutions' are analysed.[12]

Of the sixteen clauses, thirteen define the position of the Church in the feudal structure of England, as regards ownership, jurisdiction, services owed, and rights of other landowners. The most important group are those seven clauses which deal with jurisdiction, the issue which had originally aroused the controversy. Under William the Conqueror, ecclesiastical and royal courts had been carefully separated, and the bishops' application of canon law carefully separated from the administration of royal justice. Four clauses reinforce this arrangement and provide the church courts with effective means of implementing justice. Two clauses deal with minor matters, confiscation of goods and cases of debt. Other non-controversial clauses prevent the loss of feudal services due to the king when land was given to the Church; nor are villeins allowed to evade their masters by taking holy orders. The compromise reached on the matter of investiture which had elsewhere provoked such difficulties is recorded in another clause. Henry I and Anselm, then archbishop of Canterbury, had agreed that royal assent was required for the election, and the oath to be taken to the king was 'for life and limbs and earthly service, saving the order': a phrase all too familiar after the Westminster council.

There were, however, besides these stipulations which Becket accepted with more or less good grace, five articles which aroused his unconditional opposition. The first clause of the document declared that questions of the right to appoint vicars and curates, which often belonged to lay lords, should be treated in the royal court as though affecting lay property. Becket claimed that this was, on the contrary, a matter of the care of souls; and that in Stephen's reign the ecclesiastical courts had dealt with such matters. A similar provision declared that the question of whether disputed holdings of lands were free of military obligations (frankalmoign) or owed such duties (lay fee), should first be decided in the king's court by a jury which would give a sworn opinion; and any further question as to ownership would then be referred to the appropriate body, lay or ecclesiastical. This the church's lawyers held to be a breach of clerical privilege, and Becket protested against the encroachment. Two other clauses dealt with appeals and communication with Rome. Henry, wishing to safeguard his sovereign rights, attempted in these to prohibit all movements of native clergy outside England, and all appeals beyond the archbishop's court (i.e. to Rome) without his express permission; and there was undoubtedly some basis in custom for this. Although the arrangement favoured the archbisnop, Becket could not allow this, trained as he was in the continental tradition of the papal supremacy; especially as his authority over York was none too secure, needing reinforcement from Rome at intervals. Finally, the vexed question of the criminous clerks was raised once more in the following terms:

> Clerks cited and accused of any matter shall, when summoned by the king's justice, come before the king's court to answer there concerning matters which shall seem to the king's court to be answerable there, and before the ecclesiastical court for what shall seem to be answerable there, but in such a way that the justice of the king shall send to the court of holy Church to see how the case is there tried. And if the clerk shall be convicted or shall confess, the Church ought no longer to protect him.

The procedure envisaged was therefore this. The clerk accused of a serious crime should be brought before the lay court, where he could plead 'benefit of clergy'. Once his right to this was established, the case was to be transferred to the bishop's court, and only if he were found guilty and reduced to a layman's status was he to be returned to the secular authorities, as the last sentence implies, for mutilation or death. The presence of the royal officer was intended merely as a precaution to prevent the escape of the accused. This clause has provoked more argument than any other of the proposed customs. Henry appealed to canon law in justification of his demand. Certainly the procedure of identification in the lay court was reasonable, and there was never any suggestion that the trial should take place in the lay courts. It was the last sentence that caused the real difficulty. The closest parallel is to be found in Roman law, which had been introduced into England in the previous decades. Canon law was more specific: the authority of the secular court was only to be invoked in the case of a cleric who defied the bishop or the bishop's court, but this nonetheless constituted a precedent for a double sentence. The distinguished contemporary canonists, Rufinus and Stephen of Tournai, supported Henry's reading of 'Let him be handed over to the secular

court' against Becket's reliance on a clause forbidding any appearance whatsoever by a cleric in a lay court, and it was recognised
practice in northern Europe. Becket's quotation, 'God does not
judge twice for the same offence', came not from canon law, but
from St Jerome, and hence lacked the same force. In the absence of
any clear authority, Henry was making a reasonable and equitable
claim, which Thomas resisted as a matter of conscience rather than
because an established tradition was being brushed aside.

The archbishop's immediate reaction to events at Clarendon was to
abstain from celebrating mass until a letter requesting the pope to
absolve him from the oath to obey the Constitutions had been
answered. However, Alexander directed him to resume his priest's
office without giving the absolution, evidently realising the consequences of the latter. After a vain effort to see the king at Woodstock, which only led to the park gates being shut in his face, the
archbishop tried to escape abroad, where three rulers, Louis of
France, the count of Soissons and the count of Blois had already
offered him refuge. The first attempt was repelled by a contrary
wind; and on the second the sailors recognised him and put back
for fear of the king. Even flight seemed to be impossible; so
Thomas resolved to seek another interview with the king, who had
meanwhile remained impassive, waiting for the archbishop's nerve
to break. Although Henry feared the archbishop's escape, which
might entail a papal interdict and immense political advantage for
Louis of France, more than his presence at the interview, he
received Thomas coldly. Only once did he refer to the quarrel
asking, half in jest, whether he wanted to leave the country because
it was not big enough for both of them.

Henry's only action in the interval had been to seek another
diplomatic advantage. Sending messengers to the pope, he requested a legation or delegation of papal powers to be conferred on
Becket's implacable enemy, the archbishop of York. The pope was
willing to grant a legation, but not disposed to grant him powers
against Becket. Although this might have been of some use, it was
not what the king wanted; the letters conferring the office were
politely returned.

The initiative now lay with the archbishop's enemies, all too numerous at court. Jealous of his rise to power, and irritated by his resistance to the king, they gained Henry's ear without difficulty. The position of Becket was made worse by the death of the king's youngest brother, William of Anjou, on January 30, 1164. Rumour had it that he was heartbroken because Becket had forbidden him to marry the widowed countess of Warenne on the grounds that they were related within the prohibited degrees. The king had no lack of arguments presented to him for dealing summarily with the archbishop. His attempts at flight, contrary to the Constitutions, rendered his lands forfeit, some claimed; while a certain John the Marshal, having a suit in process at the archbishop's court, made use of one of Henry's new rules of procedure to make difficulties for Thomas. Under this provision, any vassal failing to obtain justice at his lord's court could swear with two witnesses to that effect and have the case transferred to the royal court. John took this course, perhaps with Henry's encouragement, and Thomas was duly cited to answer the complaint on September 14, 1164. He was too ill to appear, but sent two knights to make excuse for him and to deliver a protest in which he accused John of having sworn a false oath on a hymnbook instead of a bible. Henry was in no mood for excuses; here was the moment for which he had been waiting. He treated Thomas' absence as contempt, and ordered that a general council of the realm be summoned at Northampton on Tuesday, October 6, at which the archbishop should be arraigned. This was quite without precedent. Archbishops might threaten kings with spiritual penalties, but never before in England had a king invoked the full force of secular law against a prelate of Canterbury. Exile had been the fate of Anselm, one of Thomas' predecessors, but it was obvious that the king, besides the penalty, intended public humiliation as well.[13]

Men could not remember such a magnificent concourse of the great men of the kingdom since Henry's coronation. Only one of the bishops was absent from the proceedings, and almost all the lay magnates were assembled. But this was no festive occasion. All the notables save one had been summoned by personal writ, as was the custom; and all knew who the exception was. The gratuitous insult of summoning Becket through the sheriff of Kent as though he were a private person of no importance was perhaps a blunder on Henry's part, insistent as he was on the proper observance of the letter of the law. The king again showed his mood by arriving late at night on the appointed day. He had passed the time by pursuing his favourite sport of hawking along every stream and river on the way.

It was not until after mass on Wednesday morning that Thomas was able to see him. First, one of the minor disputes which always seemed to recur at crucial moments to exacerbate the quarrel, over one of the lodgings allotted to the archbishop which a baron had occupied, was settled. Then the king listened to the archbishop's case, a résumé of events so far, in which Thomas reiterated the charge of falsehood against John, and complained of the lack of personal summons. Henry, when John's absence was remarked, explained casually that his duties as marshal had kept him at the exchequer, but that he would appear the next day, and that he, the king, would hear the matter personally. Meanwhile, the archbishop was to return to his lodgings.

The following day, in the presence of the full assembly, Henry calmly and deliberately set about the work of humbling the stubborn spirit of Becket. He acted now as if performing an unpleasant but necessary task, without anger but with a far more threatening cold determination to undo the mistake of having appointed Thomas at all. The archbishop was formally accused of contempt of court in the case of John, having neither appeared nor sent a valid excuse. Thomas' defence—that the matter lay within his jurisdiction and that John's oath was void—was rejected out of hand. In view of the oath taken by Thomas to the king at his consecration, 'in life and limb and earthly honour', the court held that he should forfeit all his goods and movables at the king's mercy. After some dispute as to who should pronounce sentence, the aged bishop of Winchester was finally compelled to do so. Thomas' reaction was forceful: 'Even if I were to remain silent at such a sentence, future ages will not.' He denied the competence of the court to judge him, their spiritual father. Only at the bishops' insistence did he let his fury subside and make submission;

with the notable exception of Gilbert Foliot, they all stood bail for him.

So far the anger had been on Thomas' part; Henry had remained calm. The king had not finished with his victim yet. Later that day, Becket was sued for £300 that he had received for work on the castles of Eye and Berkhampstead when he was chancellor. Thomas pleaded that it had been spent on the castles in question and on the Tower of London. But Henry remained inexorable, saying that it was done without his authority, and Thomas, for the sake of peace, agreed to find the sum, for which several laymen stood surety: a sign that Henry was beginning to alienate the opinion of some influential barons.

Friday brought new demands, conveyed to the archbishop by royal messengers. All concerned details of his work as chancellor: accounts for 500 marks spent on the Toulouse campaign; 500 marks raised on royal security on another occasion; the proceeds of the archbishopric and other bishoprics and abbacies he had held in ward as chancellor—in all perhaps £20,000, a sum he could never hope to raise. He returned the answer that these charges were not the reason for the summons to Northampton, and that he would make satisfaction if due time and place were named for the hearing. Henry replied by demanding sureties for his appearance. No one was in the least doubt by now as to the king's intentions; and barons and knights were careful to avoid visiting the archbishop, lest the association might lose them the king's favour.

The weekend of October 10–11 was occupied by consultations among the clergy and the archbishop, while Henry waited patiently for Becket's will to break. The bishop of Winchester suggested that the king might be pacified by an indemnity of 2,000 marks; but this was a sad misreading of Henry's objective. Other clerks of Becket's household urged him to rely on the formal quittance he had obtained when consecrated, which released him from all secular obligations. His opponents among the bishops, notably Hilary of Chichester, hinted that he should resign, or at least throw himself on the king's mercy, to avoid rash action by Henry. They argued that he knew the royal mind much better than they did, and must see the dangers. Nothing could have pleased the king better than resignation or an appeal for mercy, and the suggestion may have been made at Henry's instigation in the hope that the archbishop might choose the easiest way out of his difficulties. What Thomas answered to this is not recorded: perhaps he was already ill, for on the Monday he sent his messengers to the court to say that he was suffering from a fever and could not attend. Henry, who was himself rarely ill, regarded this as an evasion, and replied with a demand to know whether Thomas would offer security for the money demanded. The latter promised to appear in court on the next day, October 13.

As the fateful Tuesday dawned, some of the king's followers accompanied the archbishop to mass, which he celebrated at an altar dedicated to St Stephen. Instead of the customary service, Thomas used the Mass for St Stephen's day, with its Introit, 'Princes sate and spake against me'. This liturgical irregularity was at once reported to the king; the bishop of London later accused Becket of sorcery for so doing. Henry was thus forewarned that defiance might be expected. When the archbishop dismounted at the castle where the court was to be held, he took his cross from the bearer and, to the horror of the assembled bishops, strode into the council chamber with it held before him; nor could he be persuaded to relinquish it. Roger of York, evidently warned of Becket's move, had his cross borne before him when he entered a few moments later, although he was not strictly entitled to do so outside his own diocese. By the time the bishops were summoned before the king, the talk among Becket's entourage was of what should be done in face of violence. Herbert of Bosham was all for immediate excommunication; but William Fitzstephen counselled moderation. Meanwhile, the bishops told the king how Thomas had reproached them with excessive severity in their sentence, reminding them that the customary fine for forfeiture of movables in Kent was only forty shillings, and that a single absence was in any case inadequate cause for such a sentence. Further, he had appealed to the pope and forbidden the bishops to judge him on any secular charge concerning his chancellorship.

For the first time during the proceedings, Henry lost his temper. He sent the earls and barons to find out if this prohibition had been made, in defiance of the provision at Clarendon that

I

bishops should sit in the royal court except when sentences of blood were being heard; and if the archbishop would give pledges for rendering account of his chancellorship. Thomas made an eloquent answer, admitting the appeal and refusing to give pledges; he questioned the court's competence in anything apart from the case of John the Marshal, and recalled the quittance from secular obligations. Henry was not the only one to find himself in check now. The bishops turned to him, pointing out the difficulty of their position, since Thomas might invoke ecclesiastical censures were they to pass sentence, and obtained permission to dissociate themselves from the judgement. While Henry deliberated with his barons, realising that it was now plainly a case of State judging Church, the bishops rejoined the archbishop in the outer chamber, where they complained of his attitude, but he reaffirmed his belief that the Clarendon acts were null and void. They withdrew once more to hear the lay lords passing judgement. A bold stroke might yet win victory for Henry.

At last the dreaded moment came; the door of the inner chamber opened once again, and Robert of Leicester, Richard of Cornwall and other barons appeared to pronounce sentence. But the earls hesitated and tried to delegate the task; at which Hilary of Chichester declared that there was no doubt as to the archbishop's treason. Becket took advantage of the confusion to speak: 'What is this which you would do? Have you come to judge me? You have no right to do so. Judgement is a sentence given after trial, and today I have said nothing in a formal lawsuit. I have only been summoned here for the case of John, who has not appeared to prove his charges. With respect to this, you cannot pass sentence. Such as I am, I am your father, and you are magnates of the household, lay powers, secular persons. I refuse to hear your judgement.'

The sentence unspoken, his would-be judges retired abashed. Before the king could make a further move, Becket rose and departed as he had come, carrying his cross, amidst the taunts of the bystanders. Not one tried to bar his way; and what the sentence of the court would have been remains unknown to this day.

Henry realised that he had been outwitted. Becket's one weapon was his refusal to acknowledge the court's powers; and he had used it skilfully. When the king heard of Becket's withdrawal, and of the insults offered to him by the onlookers, he issued a proclamation forbidding such behaviour towards the archbishop, knowing that reports of it would make a bad impression abroad. He was also anxious that Becket should not be driven to flight. After supper, three of the bishops arrived, asking for permission for the archbishop to depart. Henry appeared cheerful, having evidently found some new plan for dealing with the crisis, and deferred his answer until the next day. This seemed ominous to Becket, who, leaving the town under cover of darkness, made his way secretly to the Channel coast. On November 2, 1164, he landed in Flanders. The exile had begun.

Henry's immediate reaction to the news of Becket's escape was not the Angevin fury that might have been expected, but a calm appraisal of the situation. He saw that, in spite of the diplomatic advantages which his continental enemies might gain, exile was now perhaps a simpler solution than any that he might impose. Hence, officially in view of the appeal by both sides to the authority of Rome, the archbishop's lands were left in peace, and a mission sent to the pope to plead the king's case.[14] The hearings opened on November 26, at Sens where Alexander himself was in exile, since emperor and anti-pope held Rome. Alexander supported Thomas, refusing his proffered resignation, but took no active measures against Henry. Thomas withdrew to the Cistercian abbey at Pontigny, where he remained until May 1166. He was soon joined by his kinsfolk. Henry, having failed to gain his object with the pope, had expelled them at Christmas, besides taking in hand the revenues of Canterbury. This was an unnecessary provocation, and only served to arouse sympathy with Thomas; Henry's patience, already strained by the archbishop's successful defiance, was near exhaustion.

Yet now that the archbishop was outside his power, Henry had to quell his irritation and play a waiting game until some new opportunity arose. Diplomatic exchanges followed for the next two years. Alexander annulled the Northampton sentence in June 1165, and sent a series of warnings to Henry. But, even though the papal exile ended and he returned to Rome in November that year, he did not feel secure enough to support Becket with any more radical action. Indeed, the emperor had succeeded in winning the support of two English envoys at a great assembly at Würzburg in May 1165, when Alexander was publicly abjured and the new anti-pope, Paschal, formally recognised. However, Henry did not ratify their action, although no official denial was issued. The incident was arranged to provide a precedent or excuse if and when a change of loyalties seemed necessary. Besides, opinion in England seemed hostile; the earl of Leicester, the chief justiciar, had even refused the kiss of peace to the schismatic archbishop of Cologne when he came to England in April to arrange for the marriage of the Duke of Saxony and Henry's daughter Matilda.

The archbishop himself was engaged in working out the theoretical grounds from which he could continue his argument, and in winning support at the French court. An attempt to win over Matilda, the queen-mother, produced little result. In England, the 'royalist' group of bishops grew stronger under the leadership of Gilbert Foliot of London, who had become Henry's chief spokesman and adviser in the quarrel.

The fire of controversy had died down by the Christmas of 1164, and Henry was free to turn to other matters. In Lent 1165, he crossed to Normandy for a conference at Gisors with Louis on April 11. This was to have included the pope, but Henry refused to allow him to bring Thomas, and the discussions were mainly on feudal questions. At the beginning of May, Henry was joined by Eleanor and three of the children; but barely a fortnight later, he had to return in haste to deal with troubles in Wales.

It was not until the beginning of the following year that the work of legal reform could be continued. An inquiry into the feudal service due to the king had been in process since 1163; but the events of Clarendon and Northampton had hindered the execution of any further plans the king may have had. The next great project was likewise promulgated at the hunting-lodge near Salisbury, in the first months of 1166. Attended by no dramatic scenes, it is known to historians of governmental institutions rather than to the general chronicler, yet its implications were in many ways wider in effect than those of the Constitutions. The assembly was a sitting of the royal court, and the resulting document was called the Assize of Clarendon.[15] In it, Henry laid down his provisions for the maintenance of public order in a fashion hitherto unknown in England. His problem was to prevent criminals from escaping justice by taking advantage of the dual nature of the English system. At the local level it was often in baronial hands, while the national courts were under the royal aegis. Furthermore, justice and its administration brought with it certain profits, which the local lords would have been loath to lose; on the other hand, the efficiency of their courts was questionable. A careful course had to be steered between the conflicting interests.

Henry's objective was not a single unified system of royal justice, as has sometimes been implied, but the repression of lawlessness. In doing this, he was more interested in repairing the failures of the existing system than in building afresh; the architecture of his legal structure was that bequeathed by tradition, and Henry's work on it was aimed at renewing its defective parts. He was less the builder of the medieval English legal system than the preserver of an older tradition. To do this, he had to extend the powers of the itinerant justices by declaring them his representatives, so that the court held by them was equivalent to his personal sessions; and he had to give the sheriffs adequate means of enforcing his intentions. But the result was the filling of a vacuum rather than any diminishing of baronial rights. Had Henry attempted the latter, we might know more about the proceedings of the council, which seems to have passed off without controversy.

Immediately after the end of the council, Henry left for Southampton, and on March 23, 1166, crossed to Falaise. In spite of the difficulties with Becket the preceding five years had been a time of prosperity and peace. He left the kingdom in good order, and with every hope that the future was secure. Free from doubts about the state of England, he could turn again to the diplomatic problems presented by the archbishop's exile.

6

This Low-born Clerk

THE INTERVAL of three years since Henry had last spent any length of time abroad had seen a gradual extension of his power and prestige everywhere. His work on the Norman and Angevin administration had stood the crucial test of a long absence well, and even Poitou, where his authority was much less secure, had remained quiet. On the diplomatic front, the German emperor had sent an embassy seeking the hand of his daughter Matilda for Henry the Lion of Saxony, and the subsequent betrothal strengthened the king's hand against Louis of France and the pope simultaneously. Only one event had gone against his hopes: the birth of a son, Philip Augustus, 'Dieu-donné', to Louis. Margaret, Henry's daughter-in-law, was no longer heiress to France, and one of his deeper schemes had gone astray. However, the possibility of a heir to France had perforce entered into his plans when Louis remarried in 1160.

Brittany was the only place where problems had arisen in connection with the Plantagenet's ambitions, and it was to these that he turned first. The intransigent lords who had resisted him in 1162[1] had now risen in open revolt. Although the fortress of Combourg had fallen to the seneschal of Normandy, Richard du Hommet, in August 1164, the revolt had only become serious in the following year, when the conduct of operations was entrusted to Eleanor with instructions to use negotiations as well as force. The nobles of Maine and Brittany proceeded to form a sworn confederation against anyone who might attack them. In answer to this dangerous threat, which seemed liable to extend the revolt into the heart of his domains, Henry took over the command as soon as he arrived. With his habitual swiftness, he summoned men from as many of his continental lands as possible, and struck at the heart of the rebellion. The retreat of most of the rebels on the arrival of his army, and the absence of help from France, enabled him to seize Fougères, whose lord had been the leading spirit of the resistance, and to raze the castle to the ground. This exemplary punishment, combined with a diplomatic marriage between his fourth son Geoffrey and the daughter of Conan, claimant to the ducal title, brought about the submission of almost all the Breton barons. Homage was done to Henry at Thouars, and he set out on a progress through his new dominions: at Rennes, he took formal possession of the duchy, and proceeded to Combourg, Dol, and Mont St Michel. Here he offered his prayers in the abbey church, and received William the Lion, who had just succeeded Malcolm on the Scottish throne, and had come to perform the required homage for his English lands to Henry.[2]

If success crowned Henry's military efforts, he had fared worse during the summer in the negotiations with Becket. There had been an attempt to arrange a meeting between Henry, Louis and Pope Alexander on April 19, 1166, at Pontoise. Henry still refused to negotiate in the archbishop's presence, and he met Louis alone on April 24 at Nogent-le-Rotrou. The conference was amicable, but almost fruitless; the only tangible result was an agreement to send financial help to Palestine, where the Saracens had made fresh inroads.

Becket had restricted himself to intrigue during the first eighteen months of his exile, but without much result. He had attempted to enlist the Empress Matilda to support him; but she had complained that Henry no longer consulted her on such matters, and had been unable to make any headway with her son. Alexander had annulled the sentence of Northampton, and generally furthered Thomas' cause with such authority as he could afford to exert. On the other hand, the negotiations at Würzburg had weakened his position, Henry having shown that he was quite aware of the possibilities of a change of allegiance. Alexander urged moderation on Becket, forbidding him to take active measures for a while.

Henry's first move in the summer was to profess himself willing to allow appeals to Rome subject to royal permission and to hold a council on the matter if the pope felt that it infringed his rights. This adoption of a conciliatory attitude may have been merely to gain a temporary respite, since Becket had returned to the attack. In three letters sent to Henry between January and May 1166, he reproves the king for his attitude.[3] The first is brief, requesting that the heavy hand of oppression be lifted from the Church, and that the king meet him soon for a conference. In the next, Thomas' severity grows; he sets out his concept of priestly and royal power, a matter which he had pondered at his retreat at Pontigny, and ends with an exhortation to the king to repent. The third would seem to have been written after the archbishop's unsuccessful efforts to meet the king in April, for he begins: 'I have long desired to see your face and to speak to you; much for my own sake, but even more for yours . . . for three reasons: because you are my lord, my king and my spiritual son.' The tone of the letter is set by the lack of formal salutation. With passionate eloquence, Thomas urges the superiority of the priest-hood to the secular power, and repeats his previous commands to set the Church free, listing those parts of the Constitutions of Clarendon to which he objected. Finally, he sets out his demands. The king must not communicate with the schismatics to the dis-advantage of Rome; he must restore the rights and property of the see of Canterbury; and 'if it be your pleasure' he himself is to return, to serve the king 'faithfully and devotedly . . . with all our strength, in whatever ways we can, saving God's honour and that of the Roman Church, and saving our order also'. The archbishop concludes menacingly: 'Otherwise you know for certain that you will incur the vengeance of Almighty God.'

Henry now feared that the archbishop would use his dreaded spiritual weapons. The last letter implied that such action was not far off. Becket had been encouraged to adopt a stern tone by Alexander's authorisation of censures against those who had in-vaded the property of Canterbury. These were issued in April, and a papal warning to Roger of York that only the archbishop of Canterbury could perform the English coronation rites had fol-lowed, since it was suspected that Henry was considering the crowning of his eldest son. On April 24, 1166, Alexander appointed Thomas legate for England, and a week later reiterated the need for censures on the Church's despoilers. In May, however, he warned Thomas to deal gently with the bishop of Salisbury, in spite of the latter's obduracy in refusing to carry out Thomas' commands.

Although Henry had not deigned to answer Thomas' letters, he was fully aware of the danger of his position. He held a conference at Chinon, at which he displayed violent agitation, calling Thomas' supporters traitors, and asking for suggestions as to how he should deal with the rebellious power of the Church. Arnulf of Lisieux suggested that the interdict and excommunication which everyone felt to be impending might be forestalled by an appeal, and this was set in motion. Henry wrote to Alexander complaining of his machinations against him, and to the Cistercian abbots blaming them for having sheltered Thomas in one of their houses, threatening that he would take action against their English branch. Arnulf of Lisieux, the archbishop of Rouen, and the bishop of Séez, were sent to try to appease Becket, but failed to find him at Pontigny and had to return empty-handed.

Disaster seemed imminent and, had it not been for the king's illness, Thomas might well have used the most powerful spiritual weapon at his disposal: that of excommunication. Instead, while Henry lay sick at Chinon, the archbishop waited until Pentecost. Then, on June 12 at Vézelay, he fulminated against John of Oxford, who 'had fallen into a damnable heresy in taking a sacrilegious oath to the emperor' and against the other envoy to the Würzburg council, Richard of Ilchester. As despoilers of the Church, he excommunicated Richard de Lucy, the justiciar of England, Jocelyn de Balliol, Ranulf de Broc, Hugh de St Clair, and Thomas FitzBernard. Finally, he called upon the king, under pain of anathema, to make amends for his actions against the Church, condemning the Constitutions of Clarendon once again.

The thunder had been loosed, and the situation was far less desperate than it might have been for Henry. Alexander confirmed the sentences; but the king was able to enlist the support of the English bishops and clergy against Thomas, who, they felt, had taken too extreme a course. The matter now degenerated into a battle of propaganda. On June 24, the clergy of England appealed to Alexander against the archbishop's high-handed behaviour, protesting that Henry was eager for reforms, an upholder of peace and order, a just and energetic ruler; his apparent infringement of clerical immunities stemmed only from a desire to preserve peace. A remonstrance in similar terms was sent to Thomas himself. Although some of Thomas' more fanatical supporters were hoping for a sentence against the king on July 24, the war continued to be one of letters. Becket's partisans produced lengthy answers to the appeal; the archbishop himself did no more than send a stern letter to Foliot reprimanding him for opposing his primate's will. The bishop of London replied with a lengthy defence of his actions and of his disinterested status. He denied that he had ever sought the archbishopric for himself, and recommend gentle dealings, for the king could not let it seem that any concessions had been extorted from him by use of force.[4]

Tempers were rising on both sides. Thomas, attempting to establish his control over the English clergy, summoned various of them to appear, and used their failure to do so as a pretext for threatening them with sentences. He denounced Henry before the pope once again, and called Foliot a 'tumour'. It was murmured that the marquis of Montferrat had sent an embassy requesting the hand of one of Henry's daughters as a bride for his son, in return for which he would use his influence among the cardinals to procure Thomas' deposition, and that the mission had been well received. Nothing came of the supposed plan, and it may have been an invention of Henry's enemies. On the other hand, an English mission was sent to Rome at this period, consisting of a group of important officials—among them the excommunicated John of Oxford—to put the king's case to the pope once again.

Diplomatic intrigues continued to be Henry's chief weapon. In the autumn he conferred with the count of Flanders, and received a papal envoy at Rouen. He protested his goodwill towards the pope so volubly that the messenger was unable to deliver the reproaches he had been commanded to deliver over the treatment of another envoy who had been imprisoned. About this time, Arnulf of Lisieux, who was suspected by Henry of playing a double game in the dispute, attempted to leave the king on the ground of poverty; but Henry forestalled this by paying off his debts. The bishops of Worcester and Hereford, who inclined to the archbishop's views, were given permission to join Thomas provided that they did not return.

In December 1166, Henry's envoys at Rome were successful in obtaining the appointment of commissioners to arbitrate between the king and the archbishop: the first positive move of the year. William of Pavia and Otho, the cardinals chosen, were more acceptable to Henry than Becket: William had a bad reputation of corruption, although Otho was said to be fair-minded, 'but a Roman and a cardinal'—in other words, open to secular persuasion. The Empress Matilda and Archbishop Rotrou of Rouen were also asked to mediate. John of Oxford was absolved and—most important of all—Becket's powers as metropolitan of the English bishops were suspended. He was now unable to take action without the pope's permission. The news was greeted with rejoicing by Gilbert Foliot and his party, Thomas' inveterate enemies; but even a cooling in French hospitality failed to discourage Becket. He had had to leave Pontigny for a new refuge at Sens on November 11 because Henry had threatened the Cistercians who sheltered him at Pontigny with action against their English brethren and property.[5]

The papal legates did not reach France until October of 1167, and until then little change in the positions of either side occurred. Henry gained another advantage over his adversary through his emissaries at Rome, when he secured a papal mandate for Roger of York[6] to crown his son, Prince Henry: a step which he wished to take as soon as possible in order to secure the succession to the English throne.

The political situation nonetheless kept the king fully occupied. Henry's authority south of Poitou had never been very secure, and in March 1167 a revolt broke out under the leadership of William Taillefer, Eleanor's uncle. Fortunately, Henry's officers were able to suppress this rapidly, and to strengthen their position. At a conference at Grammont during Lent, he was able to follow this up by securing the overlordship of Toulouse, which the count now offered him, thus achieving the object of his war eight years before. This aroused Louis' enmity, and when the count of Auvergne started to create difficulties the latter was able to repudiate his homage to Henry, and make an alliance with Louis. Henry retaliated by invading his lands after Easter, realising that the good relations which he had enjoyed with Paris for the last six years were now at an end. A dispute over the collection of the subsidy for Palestine from the bishopric of Tours, which lay within Henry's domains but belonged to the hierarchy of the French Church, aggravated the differences. A conference was arranged for June 4 at the traditional meeting-place at Gisors. Both sides arrived with armies, and no results were possible. The familiar pattern of Norman-French warfare was set in motion: castles were provisioned, and the French made an attack near Mantes, while Henry replied with an attack on Chaumont-en-Vexin, where the French supplies were stored. The defenders made a sally, but the Welsh troops swam the river and set fire to the town. Count Theobald of Champagne was captured, Louis' brother Henry was besieged in the citadel, most of the French army's supplies were either burnt or seized by the Normans. Louis could only devastate the unimportant towns of Gasny and les Andelys before beating a retreat. To add insult to injury, he lost many of his men in the exceptional summer heat as they withdrew, large numbers dying of thirst. A threatened invasion of England by Matthew of Boulogne came to nothing, although Richard de Lucy had to make hasty preparations for the defence of the coast. The French, exhausted, had to agree to a truce from August 1167 until the following Easter.

Henry had reason to seek an interval of peace, for fresh troubles had arisen in Brittany, and he had no desire for action on both fronts simultaneously. Eudo of Porhoet and his father-in-law, Guiomarc'h, had raised the standard of rebellion, and Henry launched a campaign against them in September. Once again, he was able to reduce his enemy by a few bold strokes, penetrating for the first time in his Breton campaigns to the distant county of Lyonesse, and damping the rebels' ardour by destroying many of their castles. Yet, though the campaigning season ended with the Angevin arms everywhere triumphant, the disadvantage of the

breach with France and the prospect of renewed conflict in the
following year remained.

A personal sorrow was the only misfortune to befall Henry
during these months: the death of his mother, the Empress
Matilda, at Rouen on September 10, 1167.[7] Her latter years had
been devoted to good works, for her health, impaired by an illness
contracted after the birth of her youngest son, had prevented her
from leading the more active life to which she had been accustomed. She had been Henry's mentor in much of his political
training, in compensation for the lack of attention during his early
years, when she was fighting in England and he was with his father
in France. She it was who taught him to keep all men dependent on
himself, protracting their business, making no gifts on other men's
recommendation, and to retain everything that fell into his wardship for as long as possible. Walter Map, recorder of many details
of Henry's court, says that she illustrated such advice with a
parable: 'An untamed hawk, when raw meat is frequently offered
to it, and then snatched away or hidden, becomes more greedy
and obedient, and will hold fast to its master'; and Map con-
fidently imputes all Henry's unattractive qualities to her teach-
ing.[8] This is perhaps unfair; but the harsh school in which the
empress had learnt the ways of power—the civil strife in England
—justified her cynical opinions of royal followers. Henry was in
Brittany at the time of her death, and does not seem to have
attended her burial at the abbey of Bec; on his return, he piously
distributed large sums to churches, monasteries, leper-houses and
the poor, in memory of her.

Towards the end of October 1167 the legates, whose arrival had
been so long expected, reached Normandy after a brief conference
with Becket at Sens. Henry met them, but had no wish to come
to an immediate settlement, since the archbishop's demands remained unchanged. He realised that the legates were unlikely to
hasten back with nothing accomplished, and therefore used their
presence to shield himself from any censures Becket might wish
to launch, since he knew that the latter's powers would not be
restored until the results of the mission were known.

Having discovered what was in the king's mind, the cardinals summoned Becket to meet them near Gisors on November 11. Becket, albeit protesting at the unnecessary distance and his lack of sufficient horses, went to meet them. Henry's terms were not specified; but the legates recommended that he should make peace with the king without mentioning the customs, because if the king accepted this, the archbishop could then regard them as null and void, and it would save Henry the embarrassment of retracting something enacted in his full council. Becket, supported by the French king, saw the matter differently. He felt that he had no alternative but to press for this retraction, and the conference proved fruitless.

The two cardinals returned at once to Argentan to confer again with Henry. Although the king knew them to be favourable to his cause, he was in stormy mood when they arrived on Sunday, November 26. After two hours of consultations on the Monday, the king was reported to have said as the legates departed, 'I hope to God I never set eyes on a cardinal again', threatening to turn Mohammedan to avoid them.[9] He dismissed them before their horses had been brought, so that they had to borrow what mounts they could find to get back to their lodgings, while Henry continued the discussions with his own clergy. The following day, the clergy acted as intermediaries; and on Wednesday, the king went hunting, leaving them to confer and to announce their decision to the legates: a lengthy attack on Becket, a protestation of complete obedience to the cardinals, and a repetition of Henry's willingness to waive the clause about appeals. This was of little effect, and the negotiations ended on December 5. The king entreated the legates as they left to persuade the pope to rid him of Becket altogether, and wept publicly. William of Pavia was seen to do likewise, but Otho, less favourably inclined to Henry, and perhaps remembering the king's words on the first day of the meeting, could scarcely restrain his laughter. But the year ended unfavourably for Becket: he was restrained from laying an interdict on England, and the bishops of Norwich and Chester were given power to absolve those excommunicated at Vézelay.[10] Furthermore, plans were being made to secure Thomas' translation to another post. Only a new legation or a change in Alexander's political position could lead to a turn for the better; and since the pope was again hard pressed by Frederick, the outlook seemed bleak for the archbishop.

Henry's stalling tactics had proved very successful, and in view of the increasing poverty of the archbishop, every month that passed without action favoured the king. But a tacit truce with Becket was also needed to keep him free to deal with the increasing hostility of France. At Christmas, he held a great court at Argentan with Eleanor in the newly-built hall. In January 1168, Henry had to leave in haste for the south, where the counts of Marche and Angouleme, and the Lusignan family had renewed the troubles of the previous spring. The castle of Lusignan fell rapidly, and Henry destroyed many of their towns and fortresses, leaving garrisons under the queen's charge, and giving her Patrick, earl of Salisbury, to assist her as governor. He then returned north to prepare for the expiry of the truce with the French at Easter. Hardly had he gone when Patrick and a few attendants were ambushed by the Lusignans; the unarmed earl was felled by a blow from behind, and one of the squires, William the Marshal, taken by the Poitevin rebels. Eleanor ransomed the latter,[11] and continued to manage affairs alone. The Poitevin malcontents exchanged hostages with Louis, and succeeded in preventing a permanent agreement at the meeting between Henry and the French at Pacy on April 7, 1168. Only the nobles were present to meet Henry, and in Louis' absence all that was arranged was an extension of the truce to July 1, for war was renewed however, not in France but in Brittany; and Henry welcomed the three months' respite. He was able to secure successes over the Bretons which rendered them incapable of causing him embarrassment during his dealings with France.

The new negotiations were no more successful. Louis had promised not to make peace unless the Bretons and Poitevins were included. The leader of the former, Eudo, complained not only of military injuries, but also that Henry had seduced his daughter, who had been given as a hostage, while the Poitevins demanded restitution of their lands. Long discussions followed, which ended with Henry offering to settle the latter claim, except in the case of the abbey of Clairvaux, which was not French, as the abbot

claimed, but his and the pope's. This was not good enough for
Louis, who demanded restitution of Clairvaux on principle, and
summoned Henry to appear within two days at a named rendez-
vous. Henry remained six miles away, and only approached at
nightfall of the second day, with his entire army. Both sides
retired, and war began afresh. The results were even more futile
than the previous year's skirmishes. Neither side wished to risk a
decisive pitched battle, a fear that shaped the pattern of all Henry's
campaigns. In the course of the manoeuvres that followed, Henry
scored a diplomatic victory by gaining Matthew of Boulogne to his
side by paying him a large sum for his claim to the county of
Mortain in Normandy. Otherwise, Louis burnt Chenbrun in
Normandy, and Henry ravaged the counties of Perche and Le
Vimieu, the latter because its lord had tried to prevent Matthew
of Boulogne from coming to help him. The campaign petered out
about the beginning of December, and Henry retired to Argentan
to hold his Christmas court.

Immediately after Christmas, two new legates began work. These
were Simon, prior of Mont Dieu, and a monk of Grammont,
Bernard de la Coudre, appointed by Alexander on May 25. A conference between them, the two kings and Becket, was held at
Montmirail in Maine on January 6, 1169.[12] It was the first occasion on which king and archbishop had met since Northampton
and the beginning of Becket's exile. For once we know nothing of
their personal reactions, which seem to have been concealed under
a diplomatic show of sang-froid. The business of the conference
opened with negotiations for peace between Louis and Henry,
which was rapidly attained. Prince Henry did homage for Anjou
and Brittany, and Richard for Aquitaine, while the king himself
did homage for all his dominions overseas. Richard's marriage to
Alice, Louis' daughter, was also arranged,[13] although the English
prince was already engaged to the daughter of Raymond of
Barcelona; either Henry had abandoned this alliance, or the count
had taken advantage of the troubles in the south to join Henry's
enemies. Full restitution was to be made to the Breton and
Poitevin barons.

A few days later, Henry received papal letters from the

legates, commanding him to do his utmost to make peace with Thomas. The most difficult part of the discussions now began. There had never been any question of the desire for an end to the archbishop's exile on both sides; on the other hand, the price demanded by each meant that concessions would have to be made. There was a general feeling that Becket had perhaps been a little too obstinate in his stand, and almost everyone present urged him to submit unconditionally to the king's mercy. This course had much to recommend it. Henry could scarcely exact dire punishment; but on the other hand, Thomas would probably have to comply with the Constitutions of Clarendon, excepting only the clause about appeals which the king had already offered to withdraw. To avoid the extremes of obstinacy and compliance, Thomas took refuge in the old expedient of making the offer of surrender 'saving God's honour'; but the mediators were quite aware of Henry's probable reaction to this, and at length virtually succeeded in persuading him to abandon the clause. However, as the archbishop was on his way to face the two kings, one of his more extreme followers, Herbert of Bosham, warned him that he would only repeat the difficulties he had encountered when at Clarendon he omitted the phrase 'saving his order'. Thomas took heed, and went on his way. Coming into the kings' presence, he threw himself at their feet. Henry, touched by this gesture, raised him gently. Becket then put forward a very moderate view of the events of the quarrel, and declared himself ready to submit and throw himself on the king's mercy and judgement. Just as the bystanders felt that peace had come at last, he added 'saving the honour due to God'. Henry, who had evidently believed with the rest that victory was in sight, was seized with anger, and abused Becket roundly. The latter was unperturbed, and even Louis' support of Henry failed to trouble him. 'My lord, do you seek to be more than a saint?' asked Louis sarcastically. It was evident that the negotiations had failed, and though the argument ranged long and heated, the archbishop was unmoved.[14] Dismayed, the prelates and princes went their various ways: Louis to Paris, Henry to Normandy.

Peace with France was now secured.* But Becket was moving to

* This had been finalised at a conference between the two kings at St Germain-

K

more active measures again, in spite of Alexander's appointment
of a new legatine commission at the end of February, consisting
of the cardinals Vivian and Gratian.[15] On Palm Sunday, April 13,
1169, the archbishop issued from his residence at Sens the most
drastic series of excommunications yet. At the head of the list
stood Gilbert Foliot, bishop of London; and the nine other victims
of Thomas' wrath included Jocelin bishop of Salisbury, Hugh
Bigod, earl of Norfolk, and Richard of Hastings, head of the
English Templars and an intimate friend of the king. Besides this,
Geoffrey, archdeacon of Canterbury, Richard of Chester, Richard
de Lucy and two others were threatened with like penalties on
Ascension Day unless they mended their ways.[16] The blow was not
unexpected, for both Gilbert and Jocelin of Salisbury had appealed
in advance against the censure. It nonetheless presented a new and
almost insuperable obstacle to reconciliation. Henry could hardly
swallow this fresh insult; equally, Becket was unlikely to retract
the sentences.

Henry was occupied during the following months in quell-
ing a revolt in Gascony; but he kept in touch with developments,
writing to Alexander in protest against Thomas' action, which,
he said, touched him as closely as if it had affected his own
person.[17] In correspondence with Gilbert Foliot, he was more
vehement: he advised the bishop of London to disregard the excommunication—'the outrage which that traitor and enemy of
mine, Thomas, has inflicted upon you and other subjects of my
realm'—and encouraged him to appeal to Rome. As a further
measure to obtain support, Henry began to intrigue with the
Italian cities, who might assist him against the pope, and paid
large sums to Milan, Cremona, Pavia, Parma and the nobles of
Rome in return for their influence with the pope to obtain
Thomas' deposition or translation.

---

en-Laye at the beginning of March 1169, and was concerned with the fulfilment
of the political agreement of Montmirail. Prince Henry had been to Paris on
February 2, where he formally did the duties of the count of Anjou as seneschal
at the king of France's table, and did homage to Louis' son Philip, now four
years old, for Anjou and Brittany. In March, Geoffrey, Henry's third son, did
homage to the young Henry, in obedience to his father and with Louis' approval.
Finally, Louis and Henry swore an alliance against their enemies, the only condition being that no dowry should be given to Richard with the princess Alice.

Alexander was still not prepared to support Becket to the full, as is shown by a letter of his in June, regretting the censures. However, the cardinals Vivian and Gratian, when they arrived in July, gave Becket to believe that the pope was favourable to his cause, and the third series of negotiations began with both sides still firmly entrenched in their respective positions. Thomas' close friend, the philosopher John of Salisbury, met the legates at Vézelay on July 22. A month later, they saw the king at Domfront.[18] The meeting opened inauspiciously, since the cardinals had to withdraw to avoid two of the excommunicates, Geoffrey of Canterbury and Nigel de Sackville, who arrived at the same time. The king arrived towards evening with Prince Henry; the latter gave Vivian and Gratian the spoils of his days' hunting, and his father entertained them. A long and unsuccessful discussion until late at night ensued on the next day. The king retired from it angrily, swearing: 'By God's eyes, I would act differently if I were you.' Gratian answered: 'Do not threaten us, my lord, for we fear no threats, coming from a court used to ruling emperors and kings.'

A further meeting at Bur-le-Roi on September 1, at which Henry conferred alone with the legates, enabled him to extract the absolution of the excommunicates, and late in the evening, Henry offered the archbishop peace, tenure of his office and return of his possessions if he would go back. But a further demand, that one of the legates should go to England to perform the absolutions, led to a violent scene. Vivian and Gratian refused, whereupon Henry —saying: 'Do what you like; I could not care less for you or your excommunications'—strode out and mounted his horse as if to ride off. Fortunately he was persuaded to return by the bishops present, and to write to the pope offering terms for Becket. Impatient of the delay in making out the document, he withdrew again, and when told that the legates were authorised to take action against him, answered: 'I know, I know; they will put an interdict on my lands. But if I can capture the strongest of castles in a day, can't I take one cleric who puts an interdict on me?' At last the king was pacified, and agreed to the document drawn up.

The next day, however, he again raised the question of the excommunicates, which was a real problem to him in that it

hindered several of his officers from doing their work, since an excommunicate was technically cut off from the society of all fellow-
believers, and anyone wishing to evade one of these men could
take advantage of the fact. New negotiations began; and, tired after
two exhausting days, Henry insisted on the inclusion of the phrase
'saving the dignity of his kingdom' in the peace offer, which
Gratian refused, knowing it to be unacceptable to Thomas. Although continued debates led eventually to a settlement over the
excommunicates, the king's insistence on the new clause continued at renewals of the discussions in Caen and Rouen, and no
agreement was reached. Expecting the storm to burst about him,
he took what precautions he could, ordering that after October 9
anyone found carrying letters from the pope or from Thomas into
England was to be treated as a traitor. Any clergy obeying an
interdict issued by Becket were to forfeit all their property; and
any of them outside England were to return by January 14, 1170.
All appeals to Thomas or the pope were forbidden. All laymen and
clerks coming from abroad were to be searched, and clerks who
had no royal permission to enter were to be sent back. Finally,
everyone was to swear to obey the articles, and all men over the
age of twelve were to abjure Thomas and the pope on oath.[19] This
was an open declaration to all involved in the quarrel between king
and archbishop that Henry was going to do all he could to defy
the pope and his powers.

Thomas now felt himself justified in taking the action that
Henry feared. He sent letters to England threatening an interdict on February 2 of the next year, 1170, unless the king repented.
One of the legates, Gratian, returned to Rome to report on the
situation, feeling that deadlock had been reached. But soon after
his departure, Vivian held a conference at Montmartre, on
November 18, which opened in very hopeful circumstances.[20]
Henry, having got wind of the archbishop's proposed censure,
offered full restitution to the archbishop, withdrawal of those
customs to which Becket objected, and the submission of the outstanding differences to Louis, the French clergy, or the scholars of
Paris. Becket, on his side, withdrew the clause 'saving God's
honour', and agreed to go back to England at once. Peace seemed
certain. But Henry, because he had once sworn never to give

Becket the kiss of peace, refused this vital condition of pacification, for the kiss ratified any agreement and indicated the good faith of both parties. It was a guarantee of royal protection, without which Becket could ill afford to face his many enemies in England. Once again, talks dragged on late into the night, and no solution was reached. Henry, who had to ride twenty miles to his quarters at Mantes, retired furious. The third legation had failed; but Vivian and Gratian had left a good basis for future negotiations, and had brought the two sides closer than at any time since 1164.

Even if Becket was his predominant political problem, Henry could not abandon his other work. He kept Christmas at Nantes in Brittany with his son Geoffrey, and afterwards made a solemn circuit of the Breton castles, taking oaths of fealty from the Breton barons. He finally settled his score with Eudo of Porhoet by confiscating his estates, and returned to Normandy, having assured his son's position and given a definite shape to his re-organisation of Brittany. On March 2, 1170, he crossed to England in a violent storm, during which one ship sank with the loss of some four hundred men, and the rest were dispersed, making their way to various ports along the south coast. The French were firmly convinced that Henry had been drowned; but he reached Portsmouth safely the following day, and at once set about the variety of business which awaited him. He had received letters from the pope informing him of yet another commission to negotiate between him and Becket, consisting this time of Rotrou archbishop of Rouen, and Bernard bishop of Nevers; and he knew that he had only a short while in which to carry out much work. Soon after Easter, which he kept at Winchester with King William of Scotland and the latter's brother David of Huntingdon, a council was summoned at London. For once, Henry had been seriously let down by his servants: the sheriffs had profited by his absence to indulge in a variety of malpractices—a risk always inherent in the essentially personal nature of Angevin government. A detailed edict ordered an inquiry into the behaviour of both them and other royal officers: a complete résumé of almost all business transacted by them since 1166 was demanded, to be presented on June 14 at London. It was 'a wonderful inquisition',[21] and the time allowed for its execution very short.

At the same time, plans were made for a political move, which, although actuated by other motives, was bound to vitiate relations with Becket: the coronation of Prince Henry. Plans had been made for this perhaps as early as 1161-2, as a means of ensuring a peaceful succession; these were revived in 1167, but laid aside. The prerogative of crowning the kings of England belonged traditionally to the archbishops of Canterbury, but Henry was relying on the letters authorising the archbishop of York to perform the ceremony, issued by Alexander when the idea was last mooted.

Becket could not allow this affront to his authority to go unchallenged, especially since the long-standing dispute about the primacy of Canterbury over York remained unsettled. He therefore wrote to the bishops of England forbidding them to take part in the ceremony, and to Roger of York—an old rival from their days together in Theobald's household—prohibiting his performance of the rite. These messages reached their destination in spite of Henry's orders that anyone bearing such instructions should be arrested. But the king was close at hand and impatient to proceed, and Becket's threats seemed less real a menace than the royal wrath. Accordingly, the prince was crowned at Westminster Abbey on June 14, 1170, with all due pomp. Henry himself was in defiant mood, for a notable absentee was Margaret, the prince's wife. He must have foreseen that this insult to his daughter would provoke Louis; for by right she should have been crowned with her husband. After the rite, so the story runs, the king served the prince, henceforward called the 'young king', at table; and when the archbishop of York remarked that no prince in the world enjoyed such distinguished service, the young king retorted: 'Why are you astonished? Should not my father do this? He is lower in rank than I, the son of a queen and a duke, while I come from royal blood on both sides.'[22]

There was not much time for feasting, however, for matters in France were rapidly coming to a head. Henry had only prevented the archbishop of Rouen from crossing the Channel by promising peace, and the new commissioners, reinforced by William, archbishop of Sens, were active in France. On landing, Henry was met by the bishop of Worcester, who although ordered by the king to attend the coronation, had been restrained from crossing by the queen and the constable of Normandy, Richard du Hommet, since they had learned that the bishop would do all he could to prevent the ceremony. Henry refused to believe this story, and called him a traitor, only later being persuaded of the truth of the explanation. His temper was not improved by the bishop's reproaches, and knights of the king's entourage remarked that it was lucky he was a priest; yet when one of them reviled the bishop openly, Henry's anger turned against the knight instead, and later he and the bishop talked amicably about a reconciliation. Henry might be quick of temper: he was rarely in the long run unjust or untrue to his purpose as a result.

The tide had now turned against Henry. Alexander authorised the legates to use an interdict against Henry's continental domains if no results were reached, and no such measures as those in force in England could protect Henry against this. Becket could pose as the injured party, a prelate suffering under a tyrant's rule, now that these royal prohibitions were generally known and the coronation had taken place. The legates were disturbed by the challenge to their authority, and Louis was offended by the insult to his family. Henry must have considered either that his opponents were weaker than they actually were, or alternatively that reconciliation was impossible. At the beginning of July, he began to realise his miscalculation. On July 16, Becket agreed to attend a conference with Louis and Henry on July 20 at Fréteval. The meeting opened with a parley between the kings, perhaps following up Henry's talks with Theobald of Blois on July 6, at which he had promised to mediate between Louis and the count.[23] The real business began on July 22. The same terms as at Montmartre were offered and accepted by Thomas: peace and security publicly granted and withdrawal of the offending customs. Thomas made no mention of the kiss of peace, and at long last agreement was reached. It was nearly six years since the archbishop had set foot in England and as long since he had talked alone with the king, his erstwhile friend and companion. At the end of the parley, Henry and Thomas turned their horses aside and rode alone across the meadow. Thomas asked the king for permission to act against the bishops who had taken part in the coronation, and received consent. Gratefully, Thomas dismounted and knelt before the king; but Henry held his stirrup for him to remount, saying with tears in his eyes: 'My lord archbishop, let us return to our old friendship, and each show the other what good he can; and let us forget our hatred completely.' Reactions among the courtiers to the new situation were varied: some were overjoyed, while others who had used the quarrel to their own advantage were less pleased. A few felt that the peace could not last and was not really sincere.[24]

The work of restitution began at once; its progress was slow, but this was due to the complexity of the task rather than lack of good will. The financial side of Canterbury's affairs proved particularly intractable. Henry passed the next month in Normandy, and about August 10 fell seriously ill at Mote de Ger, near Domfront. The French believed him dead, and he himself was moved to provide for the division of his lands.[25] The young king was to have England, Normandy, Anjou and Maine, out of which he was to provide for his youngest brother, John. Richard was to hold Aquitaine directly from the French king, while Geoffrey's marriage to Duke Conan's daughter was to be celebrated and he was to hold Brittany on similar terms. This was the first attempt to solve one of the crucial problems of Henry's later years. He had recognised that some form of division was essential in his agreement with Louis at Montmirail in January 1169, but the precise terms were not worked out. It is remarkable that Richard and Geoffrey were to be independent of their elder brother; perhaps Henry's own experiences with his brothers as vassals led him to this solution. Finally, the king stipulated that he was to be buried in the chapterhouse at Grammont, at the feet of the master of the house. His fears were unfounded: towards the end of the month he recovered, and about Michaelmas made a pilgrimage to the shrine of Rocamadour in the south of Poitou, accompanied by a large protective escort, before resuming the negotiations with Thomas.

The delays had led William of Sens to obtain letters threatening the king with excommunication unless the settlement was rapidly made final, and the pope had demonstrated his support of Thomas by suspending the bishops who had crowned the young king. Henry avoided further troubles at a meeting at Amboise on October 12, 1170. He arrived with a large following, and was met by Thomas, William of Sens and Theobald of Blois. A full reconciliation took place next day. The archbishop 'was received into the king's grace and friendship; and he and all who had been exiled with him were pardoned'.[26] When Thomas came to mass, however, in hope of gaining the kiss of peace, Henry once again evaded the ceremony by ordering that a requiem mass should be said (in which the kiss is not exchanged), and he remained obdurate in face of an open demand by Thomas. A day or two later, Becket took leave of the king at Chaumont, and to Henry's expression of good wishes, replied: 'My lord, something tells me that I take leave of you now never to see you again in this life.' Henry bridled at this: 'Do you think me a traitor?' and the archbishop's swift denial hardly pacified him.[27]

Henry had promised to escort Becket to England; but he wrote to say that affairs in the south prevented him from coming to Rouen as planned. So king and archbishop went their separate ways: Thomas to England, where, due to Henry's poor preparations and tactless choice of the once excommunicate John of Oxford as escort, he landed with foreboding in his heart; Henry to prepare for a campaign in Berry. This area had long been disputed between the men of Aquitaine and France, and Henry now laid claim to the presentment of the archbishopric of Bourges in opposition to Louis. By November 23 he was at Montlucon with his army, and tried to reach Bourges itself, but Louis appeared with rival forces. In view of the oncoming winter, a truce was reached.

At Christmas, Henry was at Argentan in Normandy, gloomy and disturbed; reports arriving from England showed that Thomas was in no mood for compromise. His last act on French soil had been to send ahead letters excommunicating the bishops who had taken

part in the young king's coronation. Even if he had authority from
Henry to proceed against them, it was probably on the understanding that the sentence should be mild. This action by the archbishop questioned the validity of the ceremony itself, one thing
that Henry certainly did not intend to happen. The bishops had
arrived shortly afterwards at his court in Normandy and protested
strongly against the archbishop, calling his action treasonable.
Wild rumours of armed mobs at large in England led by Thomas
followed this complaint. At the Christmas court, the king asked
the bishops what he should do, and they referred him to his barons.
The council was assembled, and the argument was indecisive until
one of them burst out: 'My lord, while Thomas lives, you will
have no peace, nor quiet, nor prosperity.' The king's anger was
apparent to everyone; and he finally exclaimed: 'What idle and
miserable men I have encouraged and promoted in my kingdom,
faithless to their lord, who let me be mocked by a low-born
clerk!'[28] At this, four knights slipped quietly out of the company,
mounted horse, and rode to the coast. Their absence was only
noticed some time afterwards. Henry at once guessed their purpose. He gave orders that they should be stopped at all costs, and
that Becket should be arrested. This done, he could only wait
anxiously for news.

On January 1, 1171, the messenger, who remains as
anonymous as his counterpart in Greek tragedy, reached Argentan.[29] He did not go straight to the king. His tidings would fall
ill on the royal ears; and the courtiers endeavoured to postpone
the evil hour. But at length Henry was told: was told how the
knights had eluded their pursuers and, taking ship for England,
had hastened to Canterbury; how they had demanded that Becket
should absolve the excommunicated bishops and stand judgement
in the king's court; of Becket's refusal; of the last desperate scenes
in the cathedral: how the archbishop had stood firm and, realising
the truth of his last words to the king, had found death at sacrilegious hands in his own church. Hardly was the grim tale ended
than the king gave way to a paroxysm of grief, more violent than
his anger had ever been. For three days he remained shut up in his
chamber, neither eating nor speaking to anyone, pondering not
only the blame that was bound to be attached to him and the

desperate nature of his position, but also the days of friendship long ago, when he and Thomas had ridden and hunted and planned together for a new order in England: the new order of Church and State now for ever made impossible by the man who had once been his friend. Thomas the archbishop had lost and won.

7

The Western Edge of the World

HENRY REMAINED at Argentan for a month, doing what he could to forestall any immediate action on the part of the Church. William of Sens was now the chief agent in the negotiations; supported by Louis and Theobald of Blois, he was implacably hostile. His messengers returned from Rome with papal instructions—issued before Becket's death was known—to use an interdict on Henry's French domains if peace was not made; and in view of the circumstances, William felt justified in launching this sentence, in spite of the entreaties of Archbishop Rotrou of Rouen. Henry's only comfort was the firm support of this prelate, who with Arnulf of Lisieux, Giles of Evreux and other bishops and clergy appealed to Rome, and soon afterwards set out for the Eternal City. These men had been with Henry at the fatal council and when the messenger from Canterbury arrived; and none of them doubted the king's innocence of complicity in the murder. Rotrou, because of his great age, had to turn back, and the others, when they arrived in Rome, were at first refused all audience by the pope. Eventually two of them gained admittance and succeeded in obtaining a promise that papal legates would be sent to Normandy: cardinals Gratian and Vivian. More important, they averted the excommunication of the king, which had been planned for Maundy Thursday, the traditional time for announcing such sentences.

Meanwhile the king, accompanied by a large force, had gone into Brittany, and at Pontorson received the homage of Guiomarc'h of Lyonesse, who had just caused further trouble by murdering the local bishop. Duke Conan, who still held Guingamp and the honour of Richmond in Yorkshire, had died, and the lands had passed via his daughter to his son-in-law, Geoffrey. Henry could now unite the Breton peninsula under his son's lordship, and this was done without much difficulty, only Eudo of Porhoet resisting. With the latter's exile to Wales and the burning of his castle, the Breton settlement was at last complete.[1]

Returning to Normandy, Henry received an embassy from the south of France, coming from Humbert of Maurienne. This count's lands lay on the Alpine borders of Dauphiné and Lombardy, and compensated in strategic importance for their small size, since with them went control of the passes from France to Italy. Humbert was an old enemy of the count of Toulouse, and having recently antagonised his other neighbour, the German emperor, he was in search of a powerful ally. He therefore offered his daughter's hand and the inheritance of his lands to Henry for his son, John. Henry's ambitions in this area, from the borders of Toulouse into northern Italy, remain mysterious; it is possible that, with the defeat of Frederick Barbarossa in 1166, he had begun to think of expansion in that direction, and the payments of 1169 to the Italian cities of the Lombard League who were hostile to the emperor would support this idea. But the Angevin king was essentially practical, and must have realised the huge dangers and difficulties involved in such an extension of his empire. It is more likely that he preferred to make as many allies as he could, as befitted so great a prince; and the Italians might have been useful in his negotiations with the pope. Besides, it was Humbert who approached Henry, rather than the other way round: an indication that the two events were only tenuously connected. More important, this and the visit of the ambassadors of the Greek emperor, Manuel Comnenus, on a similar errand of match-making in the same year, show that Henry's prestige in western Christendom was hardly affected by the murder of Becket. The Greek terms, if our information is correct, were most flattering: John's hand was sought for the princess Maria, and on the emperor's death, he was to become ruler of Byzantium, for Manuel had no son. Henry received the ambassadors at Angers, and promised to reply within fifteen days; but evidently he felt the proposals of the count of

Maurienne to be more practical and likely to succeed, since no more was done about the Greek offer.[2]

Henry's lands on the continent had now reached their greatest extent, and the year 1171 marks a turning-point in his work abroad. There was very little room for further expansion; to the south-east lay Frederick Barbarossa's domains, to the east those of Louis, to the north-east those of the count of Flanders. The problem that faced him was that of maintaining the existing equilibrium, and avoiding the possibility of the formation of any powerful alliance against him. By themselves, none of his neighbours was likely to cause Henry trouble, and his object was to secure such alliances as might be useful to him. The increase in diplomatic business at the Angevin court after 1170 is no accident, and the machinations which henceforward occupy Henry reflect the new position in which he found himself, which made equally exacting if less exciting demands on his skill in government. From the great schemes of his earlier years and the grim confrontation of powers in the struggle with the Church, he turned now to the problem of maintaining a vast established empire—a problem which few European rulers before him had faced at all, and even fewer successfully, since the Roman sway had ended. The minutiae of these manoeuvres must bulk large in the history of Henry's later life; but no portrait of him can be complete without them.

The constant headache of raising enough revenue led, in the summer, to an order for an inquest into the revenues of Normandy. This was aimed at discovering the extent of his grandfather's estates, and what lands had been alienated since then. Anything that could be recovered went to swell the treasury's income. Henry's next great scheme, however, concerned his island realm, and was his last attempt to expand his realm. At a council at Argentan, he outlined the project: the conquest of Ireland. The king had two good reasons for departing for the western edge of the known world: he wished to avoid the legates, who had arrived about this time, and had tried to enforce an interdict; and he felt that events in Ireland meant that the moment was ripe at last to carry out a long-standing project. The attitude of the pope also played a part in his considerations. Alexander seems to have wavered between yielding to pressure from French and Roman circles to take drastic action, and temporising until the furore had died down. By putting himself out of reach in Ireland, Henry could hope to influence his choice in the latter direction. On August 1, the king left Normandy.

After a mere four weeks of hectic activity in England, Henry went to south Wales to wait for a fair wind. He had allowed himself time only to gather an army. He does not seem to have been eager to remain in England, where Becket was already worshipped as a martyr, and rumours of miracles connected with the dead archbishop flew thick and fast. Even so, he had one unpleasant moment. Almost as soon as he landed, he went to see the dying bishop of Winchester, Henry of Blois, the same who, sixteen years before, had done much to gain him the throne. The old man bitterly reproached him for Becket's death, and this sincere conviction that the king was to blame from one who knew the facts of the dispute intimately must have disturbed Henry. Others even better informed might exonerate him: the words of a man near death could not have failed to make a deep impression.[3]

The king had to spend a month in south Wales before he could cross to Ireland, and used the enforced delay to improve his relations with the Welsh princes. Wales and Ireland were the only two lands which he subdued by main force and held; the closest parallel abroad was Brittany, another Celtic territory, where he had a legitimate title which took him many years to secure.[4] The Welsh expeditions of 1156 and 1157 had not settled the question by any means; there had been trouble from Rhys ap Griffith in 1158, when Henry was elsewhere. If the prince eluded him, he had on one of these expeditions greatly discomfited the Welsh prophets, whose sayings enjoyed wide popularity. In pursuit of Rhys, he came to the ford of Red Pencarn, of which it was said that if a conqueror came and crossed it, the men of Wales would have become effeminate. The Welsh waited at a safe distance to see whether he would cross there or at another, newer ford nearby; when he chose the latter, they blew their trumpets in celebration, to their undoing. For this frightened the king's horse; it turned and bolted towards the old crossing-place, where Henry then went across.[5]

But success was none the nearer for such episodes. Five years later, he had to invade again, in April 1163, but made no more than a show of arms, although he received hostages from Rhys at Pencader. The next year more serious trouble broke out; Rhys invaded Cardigan and ravaged Roger de Clare's lands, while David, son of Owain Gwyneth, carried out devastations in the north as part of a concerted campaign against the English. Henry appeared in July 1163 and first went to forestall an attack on Rhuddlan castle which failed to occur; then, collecting reinforcements, he moved to Oswestry, where a united Welsh force opposed him. Neither side dared attack; but the king, knowing from bitter experience what the Welsh tactics were likely to be, had the surrounding forests cut down, and proceeded, undeterred by skirmishes, into the interior. His precautions proved vain, for he was defeated by weather: his provisions failed when the paths were made impassable by torrential rain. Enraged at the resistance of the Welsh, he gave orders for the hostages taken the previous year to be blinded. This was one of his rare acts of cruelty; but under the laws of the time, he would have been justified in ordering their execution when the rebellion started. He then encamped at Caerleon, where Irish ships came to meet him. The numbers of the fleet were inadequate, and with the abandonment of this scheme, the campaign petered out. The ensuing years had seen constant warfare along the marches, with castle burning and ravaging of lands. A major defeat for Henry had been the destruction of the fortresses at Rhuddlan and Prestatyn in the north after a three months' siege in 1166. Owain Gwyneth's death, however, removed one of the leading agitators.

When, in 1171, Henry reappeared in Wales, Rhys came to him and offered him 300 horses, 4,000 oxen and 24 hostages in token of friendship. In return for this, he was given wide lands in south Wales, including Cardigan. The next day, Sunday September 23, Rhys sent eighty-six of the horses to the king. Henry had gone on pilgrimage to St David's, where he offered two velvet choristers' caps and a handful of silver. The bishop invited Henry to dinner, but the king refused an elaborate meal, wishing to spare the bishop the expense, and he dined standing as did his escort of three hundred men. Soon after dinner, Henry mounted and rode

sixteen miles over the mountains through heavy rain to Pembroke
in the darkness, much to the discomfort of his attendants. On
finding the horses sent by Rhys, he returned all but thirty-six out
of friendship for him. Henry frequently had to endure such periods
of waiting, usually when trying to cross the English channel; he
beguiled the time with occupations which he did not normally
indulge in, such as going on pilgrimage, as well as his more usual
pastimes of hunting and hawking.[6]

During these early autumn days, Henry had plenty of time to think
over his plans for the conquest of Ireland. These went back to
September 1155, the first year of his reign, when messengers sent
to Rome had obtained the grant of Ireland for him;[7] only his
mother's opposition had prevented him from going then. The
island seemed to present an easy prey, for organisation of any kind
was almost totally lacking. The political structure—a loose feder-
ation of tribes and their rulers under the High King, or *ard-ri*—
was continually torn by civil war over minor disputes. The Norse-
men in the ninth and tenth centuries had had no difficulty in
securing bases in the island, which they continued to use; Dublin
was the most important of these. The last concerted action of the
Irish had been a century and a half earlier, when the expansion of
the Norse had been halted at the battle of Clontarf in 1014; since
then, the cycle of assassinations, abductions, cattle-raids and
resultant hostilities had been unhindered by any such outside
threat. Within the Irish Church, matters were only a little better.
In 1139, reforms had been carried out, under which the bishoprics
had been defined and the primacy of the archbishop of Armagh
recognised. The monasteries continued to be Ireland's chief glory,
and sheltered her culture; but the secular clergy and the laity were
scarcely distinguishable from pagans, so bad was their behaviour
and so strong the traditions of the older gods. The pope had little
authority in Ireland; it was indeed one of his major problems as
far as proper discipline was concerned, for the rules by which the
clergy were governed throughout the rest of western Europe were
scarcely known in the island. Hence Adrian IV had good cause to
encourage Henry to impose political order, so that order within the
Church might follow.

L

It was an episode in one of the civil wars between petty princes that first revived Henry's interest in possible conquest. Dermot MacMurrough, prince of Leinster, had begun to expand his kingdom in the early 1150s through a judicious alliance with two other strong princes, but had found himself at war with Tiernan O'Rourke. In the course of hostilities, Dermot abducted Dervorgil, Tiernan's wife, an action which is said to have earned him Tiernan's implacable hatred, and which led to a coalition of Dermot's most powerful neighbours expelling him. This was in 1166. Instead of intriguing with his own countrymen, he decided to apply to Henry for aid, having perhaps heard of the king's interest. He found him in France, and was given licence to seek assistance from any of the king's barons with royal approval. However, it was not until he approached Richard, earl of Clare, nicknamed 'Strongbow', one of the great lords of the Welsh marches, that he found the support he needed.

About May 1, 1169, the first company of Normans, under Robert FitzStephen, numbering 30 knights, 60 mailed horsemen and 300 archers, landed at Bannow Bay near Wexford. Richard himself had preferred to wait for Henry's permission before coming himself. With the aid of the Normans, Dermot easily won back Wexford, and went on to harry his neighbours, who were impotent against the minute force of cavalry. Further reinforcements came over during the following year, and Strongbow himself arrived in August 1170. By this time Dermot had set his heart on wresting the High Kingship from its holder, Rory O'Connor. In return for additional aid, he offered Strongbow the kingdom of Leinster and his daughter's hand. The high adventure of the early days of conquest culminated in the capture of Dublin in September 1170; although the official capital was at Ferns, Dublin was both Ireland's political centre and its richest town.

Henry was disturbed at these successes by men who were bound to him as their liege lord. The marcher lords were renowned for their independence and he feared that this spirit might move Strongbow to set up as a prince in his own right. He therefore determined to put a stop to their enterprise by recalling them under pain of forfeiting their English estates. Naturally enough, the invaders were loath to lose their advantages, especially since they were now threatened by an alliance between the Irish and the Norse who had formerly held Dublin. One of their number was therefore sent to Henry, while the rest defended the city against a strong onslaught. A daring sortie turned the tide in their favour, and in the ensuing carnage the Irish army was shattered. By the summer of 1171, Strongbow was master of the eastern seaboard, including Dublin, Wexford and Waterford. A further messenger sent to Henry reached Argentan while the council making plans for his expedition to Ireland was in session. An offer of the surrender of the three towns was accepted; in return, Strongbow was to keep his other conquests and his lands in Henry's domains. This settlement was made final in September, when the earl crossed to meet Henry at Newnham in Gloucestershire. In spite of slanderous reports as to his conduct, Henry received Strongbow well. Although the king took the most valuable part of his conquests, the earl of Clare was assured of royal support in his tenure of the rest of his Irish lands.

While Henry waited at Pembroke, twelve Irishmen, landing below the castle, came and offered to hand over Robert Fitz-Stephen, a knight who had fallen into their hands, as a token of good will, since he had betrayed Henry. This accusation was untrue; but, feigning anger against FitzStephen, Henry accepted the offer on the condition that he should decide on his sentence. The king wished to appear friendly towards the native Irish, and to arrive as upholder of their liberties against the over-powerful barons.[8]

Soon afterwards, the westerly wind at last died down, and on October 16 Henry left Pembroke to set sail from Milford Haven. He disembarked two days later, at Croch near Waterford, accompanied by 400 knights and a total force of perhaps 4,000 men. Strongbow surrendered the town, and the first of the Irish kings to bow to his new lord also appeared, Dermot MacCarthy of Desmond, who agreed to give hostages and pay tribute. Henry moved northwards to Lismore where he met the papal legate for Ireland, Christian O'Conarchy, and arranged for a great council of the Irish Church to be held. At Cashel, Donnell O'Brien, king of Thomond, submitted, and Henry sent officials to the chief towns of the two provinces now in his hands, Cork and Limerick.[9] The king went back to Waterford—where FitzStephen was released on confiscation of his lands—and then along the coast to Dublin, which he reached on November 11, having left Robert Fitz-Bernard and a garrison at Waterford. By now all the southern kings except the *ard-ri*, Rory O'Connor, had submitted to Henry in the course of what had been a triumphal progress rather than a campaign. Rory may have acknowledged Henry as overlord, but did not do homage. The latter does not seem to have intended to take military action and emphasised that the Irish had accepted him voluntarily. The northern kings, which he left undisturbed, were in any case too occupied with tribal affairs to interfere in the politics of the south, and Henry was not prepared to risk needless dangers in a strange land, especially as there had been some deaths among his troops because of the poor diet. He therefore spent the next three months at Dublin, in a palace built of clay and wattles in the native style. Here he kept his Christmas court with due splendour, much to the amazement of the Irish princes who were present.

The winter of 1171–2 proved stormy; wide stretches of the Welsh forests across the sea were blown down. Henry was forced to find occupation in organising the government of his newly acquired land and in dealing with the council of Cashel, and to lay aside all thought of contact with England. At the Cashel assembly which began on February 2, 1172, he gathered all the bishops of Ireland, save only the primate of Ireland, an aged and saintly man who lived entirely on milk, and could not come on account of his years. The remainder of the clergy favoured the reforms proposed by Nicholas, the king's chaplain, and Ralph, archdeacon of Llandaff. The resulting Constitutions brought the practices of the Irish Church into line with those of the rest of western Christendom on such matters as tithes, baptisms and marriage. By granting the clergy certain immunities and privileges, and showing them the papal letters issued seventeen years earlier, Henry secured their assent to his overlordship of Ireland, and the prelates swore an oath of fealty to him. The final clause of the Constitution drawn up at Cashel provided that all other matters should, when in doubt, be conducted according to the usage of the English Church: a

further opening for English influence.[10] As the one stable influential element in Irish politics, the priesthood's allegiance was
more valuable than that of the warring kings. By persuading the
Irish clergy to accept reforms, Henry also gained badly-needed
credit with the papacy. The council of Cashel was the most
important achievement of Henry's stay in Ireland. The other
major task—the transfer of baronial power to royal hands—might
have proved difficult in his absence, but his most persuasive
weapon was the confiscation of the barons' estates in his other
dominions, which could be done from the other side of the Irish
Sea without difficulty.

The barons were nonetheless the mainstay of Anglo-Norman
power in Ireland, and Henry could not afford to alienate them.
Hence his solution was to accept their lands in formal surrender
and regrant them to be held from him on conditions similar
to those on the Welsh marches, where the perpetual warfare
with the Welsh meant that the local lords had to be given a
certain degree of independence and freedom from feudal duties.
The only danger inherent in the system was that when the common
threat receded, civil war usually replaced it. Therefore Henry did
not rely entirely on the adventurers who had begun the settlement.
Dublin was placed in the care of Hugh de Lacy and a garrison of
twenty knights. Wexford and Waterford, more important
strategically as the ports for crossing to England, were garrisoned
by thirty and forty knights respectively. Their governors, William
FitzAudelin and Robert FitzBernard, were also members of
Henry's entourage. On the other hand, several members of Strongbow's circle were attached to the royal household and withdrawn
from Ireland.

The spring brought no change in the weather; the easterly winds
continued, and while messengers could easily come from England,
Henry was held powerless in Ireland. Nor was the news that
was brought such as to encourage him to stay longer than he had to.
Rumours of a conspiracy among his sons reached him, and there
was increasing pressure from the papal legates that he should return and answer the charges against him in connection with
Becket's murder. He had moved to Wexford about the beginning

of March 1172, but it was six weeks before his sailors were prepared to attempt the crossing. On Easter Monday, April 17, he
embarked at sunrise, the main body of his companions having left
the previous day. He landed the same day at Porth'stimian, about
a mile from St David's and made a pilgrimage to the cathedral. On
his way, he had to cross the river Alun; and there was a prophecy
attributed to Merlin that 'the king of England, conqueror of
Ireland, wounded by a man with a red hand in Ireland, would die
on Lechlavar'. As Henry was about to cross by the smooth stone so
named, a Welshwoman threw herself at his feet, crying: 'Revenge
us today, Lechlavar, revenge our race.' Henry, with his usual
contempt for such pure superstition, looked calmly down at the
stone as he crossed; and when he reached the other side, remarked:
'Who will believe that liar Merlin now?' But national prophets
are not to be discredited so easily: a bystander at once said that
Henry could not be the conqueror of Ireland.[11]

       Perhaps this was in a sense true; and it would have been rash
to predict that Henry's peaceful solution of the problems presented there was to outlast many of his most bitterly contested
achievements. Without striking a blow, he had established his
overlordship in three-quarters of Ireland, and the men of Ulster
whom he had left alone were unlikely to prove a serious threat. He
had prevented the establishment of an independent Irish kingdom under Strongbow. The Irish clergy had recognised him, and
incidentally provided him with a good opportunity of showing his
devotion to Rome. Between the three elements of Irish native
chieftains, Norman invaders and royal authority, he had created a
sound balance of power, and even in the darkest moments of
rebellion and disloyalty, Ireland always remained steadfast. Since
Henry was never again to visit the island, the history of subsequent
events form a suitable epilogue to the settlement of 1172.

The rebellion of 1173 in his other territories might have had repercussions there if Henry had not made Strongbow governor of
Ireland when he recalled the garrisons of the coastal towns. By
ensuring that the royal authority was in the hands of a man with
adequate resources of his own, he had guaranteed the security of
the country, the one risk being that Strongbow might attempt to

secede. But he proved loyal, and Henry left him in charge until his death there three years later. Meanwhile, Rory O'Connor, whose fealty to Henry in 1171 seems very doubtful, if made at all, had revised his judgement of the English king in face of his continued success, and sent his envoys to come to terms with Henry. The result was a treaty signed at Windsor on October 6, 1175. In return for formal allegiance and one hide for every ten cattle in Ireland as yearly tribute, Rory was given power over all the lands not already granted to Norman lords, and was empowered to ask the royal constables for help. This settlement, modelled on the position of Prince Rhys in south Wales, seemed a reasonable and indeed mutually advantageous solution.

Events were to prove that it was unworkable. Strongbow's death led to troubles among the Norman settlers, chiefly because they preferred Strongbow's lieutenant, Raymond le Gros, to the governor whom Henry wished to impose on them, William FitzAudelin. Henry distrusted Raymond and had attempted to recall him on his lord's death. But the following year, it was Fitz-Audelin who was recalled; Henry's plans had changed, and the restrictive policy of his governor, who attempted to hinder all further expansion by the barons, was no longer favoured. At a great council at Oxford in May 1177, the king set out his new arrangements for Wales and Ireland.[12] Whereas the Welsh princes had shown that they had effective control of their subjects, it had become apparent that the Norman barons were too powerful for O'Connor, whose régime would have to be supported if it was to survive. Hence, while David and Rhys of Wales were given new fiefs, the lands previously under the Irish prince's government were divided among the settlers. Meath went to Hugh de Lacy, Limerick to Herbert FitzHerbert and others, Cork to Robert FitzStephen and Milo de Cogan; although none of these lands were yet conquered, exact details of tenure were given. Most important of all, Prince John was made 'Lord of Ireland', holding it from his father, and the earl of Chester was sent across to prepare for the complete conquest of the land. Henceforward Wales and Ireland were no longer to be treated on the same principles; the former was to remain partially independent, but the latter was to become one of the major fiefs of the English crown, destined eventually to provide for Henry's youngest and favourite son.

The final conquest did not go as smoothly as the king might have hoped, for Irish resistance proved more stubborn than had been expected. But it was John himself who finally brought an end to Henry's plans. In the summer of 1184, Hugh de Lacy—who had shown signs of too much independence—was finally replaced as governor of Dublin by Philip of Worcester, with instructions to prepare for the arrival of John. The nineteen-year-old prince landed on April 25, 1185, lavishly equipped, with a considerable retinue and a large treasure at his disposal.[13] But John lacked the precocious skill of his brothers in handling men and affairs. Embarking on an indiscriminate aggression which scarcely distinguished between friend and foe, he deprived friendly Irishmen of their lands and insulted local chieftains who were not in the least hostile, even pulling their beards and openly mocking their uncouth manners. His only military operation—a raid into north Munster—was disastrous, and he lost many of his mercenaries. Fortunately, news of his conduct reached Henry, and a messenger was sent to recall him in September. John left just before Christmas 1185. In eight short months he had destroyed Henry's best diplomatic weapon: the idea that royal authority would replace the oppressive rule of the barons by a just impartiality. He had estranged the otherwise friendly Norman settlers and he had wasted the resources entrusted to him for the conquest.

The troubles of the last years of Henry's reign left him no time to reshape his plans after the disappointment of John's misbehaviour. John de Courcy was left as chief governor after the latter's departure, and the expansion of power became slower as the Irish adopted Norman tactics to withstand the barons. Hugh de Lacy was killed in 1186, and Prince John was sent to Ireland to seize his great estates, only to be prevented from crossing by news of his brother Geoffrey's death. Henry was still bent on giving the land to him, and even made arrangements with the pope, Urban III—who claimed the superior lordship of Ireland—to have him crowned. Messengers arrived later in the year, bearing the mandate and a crown of peacock's feathers, and legates were sent in 1187 to perform the ceremony. Matters came to a head in France in the meanwhile, and prevented Henry from persisting with one of his graver misjudgements. John's virtues may have been underestimated by later generations but they certainly did not include those required for a successful conquest and settlement of Ireland.

In 1172 all this still lay in the future. Fresh from his success, Henry spent no time in making his way to France; he met Rhys briefly at Talacharn on April 24, and then left for Winchester. About May 12, having decided that English affairs were in reasonable order, he embarked at Portsmouth for Barfleur. Four days later he was at Gorron in Maine, where he met the legates. Once again the rapidity of his movements astonished his contemporaries: to cover two sea-crossings and eight hundred miles in a month seemed little short of miraculous—or diabolic. The king of England seemed to fly rather than ride. Henry himself cannot have found it comfortable or easy, but such considerations weighed little against the advantages of taking his enemies unawares. Even when his opponents were cardinals, to be fought with weapons of the mind, there was much to be gained from speed.

8

The Great Rebellion

THE THREAT of excommunication or interdict on his
English lands had hung over Henry like a sword of Damocles
throughout his visit to Ireland. During his absence, his position
regarding the Church had hardly changed. The papal confirmation
of the interdict on his continental domains pronounced by William
of Sens and the arrival of the legates had both occurred before he
left for Ireland. In the interval, the archbishop of York and the
other bishops concerned in the coronation of the young king had
succeeded in obtaining absolution and restoration to their sees.[1]
The problem was now Henry's personal situation; and this was too
delicate a matter to be entrusted to intermediaries, although there
must have been some discussions before the first meeting between
king and legates at Gorron. Here the kiss of peace was exchanged,
and next day, Wednesday May 17, 1172, the negotiations began
in earnest at Savigny in the presence of the archbishop of Rouen
and many dignitaries of Church and State. However, although
both sides were evidently prepared for a reconciliation, the king
refused to give the legates an absolute mandate, mistrustful as ever
of the dangers of another power beside his in his own domains. He
left the assembly, angrily protesting that his long absence had
been quite justified, and that the legates could go anywhere in
his domains that they pleased in order to carry out their mission.
   The cardinals were undismayed. Henry's tactics were by
now well-known to them, and they succeeded in arranging a
further meeting for Friday, at Avranches in Brittany. One day
apparently sufficed to reach the terms of reconciliation; but much
had obviously been done at Savigny before the gathering there dis-

persed.[2] The absence of the young king was now the only obstacle to the completion of the concordat. When he arrived, two days later the ceremony of public exculpation and penance was performed.

Thus it was that on Sunday May 21, before the north doorway of the cathedral of Avranches, Henry came to face the legates. With one hand on the Gospels, he swore that he had neither ordered nor desired the murder of the archbishop of Canterbury, and that the news of it had caused him more grief than joy, adding —besides the prepared oath—that he had mourned neither the death of his father nor his mother so much. He would carry out whatever penance or satisfaction the cardinals ordered, for he realised that he had unintentionally by his display of irritation and anger caused the archbishop's death.[3] The legates then pronounced their terms: Henry was to send 200 knights at his own expense to the Holy Land with full equipment as approved by the Templars. All evil customs introduced in his reign, especially the Constitutions of Clarendon, were to be withdrawn and earlier abuses moderated; those clauses of the Constitutions to which the pope had objected were particularly specified. The possessions of the see of Canterbury were to be restored and due amends made for any losses. Finally, if the pope thought it necessary, Henry was to go to Spain to fight the Saracens. These conditions were announced in public; secret clauses enjoined various fasts and alms on the king, and an oath of fidelity from himself and his son to Alexander and his successors.[4] For political reasons, Henry did not wish to include these conditions in the general terms. He had once again averted a major conflict by alternating hard words and soft answers. The concordat of Avranches was a compromise between equal powers, rather than terms imposed on a defeated opponent of the Church. The king had every reason to be pleased with the conditions and cheerfully told the legates: 'My lords legate, my body is in your hands; I am prepared to go wherever you command, to Jerusalem, Rome or Compostella if you wish.' At the king's own desire, he was then led to the doorway of the cathedral, where he knelt to receive the absolution (though without the usual ceremony of stripping and flogging, because he had never been formally excommunicated). He then entered the cathedral to hear mass. On

May 30, at Caen, he repeated before a council of clergy and magnates the promises made at Avranches.

Louis had not been idle while Henry had been hard pressed
by the Church, and Henry had to meet him soon afterwards to
appease his claims. Now that the Plantagenet was once more in
harmony with Rome, Louis saw no real advantage in pressing
home his quarrel, and was prepared to make his peace. His chief
grievance was that his daughter Margaret had not been crowned at
the same time as her husband, even though he regarded the 1170
coronation as illicit. The diplomatic insult still rankled. Henry
mended matters by ordering a new ceremony on August 27, 1172,
at Winchester, this time with the legates' blessing and performed
by Rotrou of Rouen. Although Henry himself seems to have contemplated returning to England in June,[5] the legates required yet
another expiatory ceremony, again at Avranches, on September 28,
and the interval was spent in Brittany. Meanwhile, the papal bull
setting out the terms of the reconciliation had been issued on
September 2. With the final formality before a synod of the
Norman clergy at Michaelmas, the political settlement of the conflict between Henry's attempt to impose a universal standard of
justice and the Church's claim to immunity was complete.

To draw up an accurate balance-sheet of the gains and losses on
each side is very difficult. One thing becomes clear: that the compromise finally reached was nearer to Henry's aims than to those
of the pope. This was a major achievement on the king's part, if
hardly a triumph. The wave of hostility that had swept through
Europe on the first news of the murder had seemed to unite forces
against the Plantagenet that were bent on his total humiliation.
That Henry could make his side of the case heard in face of this
shows the great prestige which he enjoyed. He was helped by the
general loyalty of his subjects, who might make Becket a saint,
but did not turn his death into a political issue. The crucial point
—Maundy Thursday of 1171—once safely past, the passage of
time favoured the king. The reconciliation of the bishops and the
gradual return of the exiles meant that much of the rancour on
both sides had ebbed by the time that the negotiations with the

legates began. By May 1172, the legates had been in Normandy for nearly a year, and had accomplished nothing; they were all the more ready for a speedy solution when Henry at last appeared.

Henry had yet another weapon at his disposal once the treaty was made. The exact interpretation of the conditions left him a great deal of room to manoeuvre. He was helped by the probability that the pope would not go to extremes to enforce them. He succeeded in changing the first provision very soon afterwards, and instead of providing the 200 knights, he was to found three religious houses. His enemies accused him of keeping to the letter but not to the spirit of this: he had, they said, driven the nuns of Amesbury out because of their laxness and replaced them by a colony from Fontévrault, while at Witham he had replaced secular canons by regulars, and had done nothing about the third house.[6] Such evidence as there is shows that Henry kept his word more closely: Newstead in the forest of Sherwood and Vaubourg in Normandy were both founded about this time, the latter being a commandery of Knights Templar. Either Witham or the other Carthusian house founded by Henry, Le Liget (1175), may have been the third. The importance of Witham compensates in some degree for its being a refoundation: its first prior, Hugh, was later to become one of Henry's closer friends, bishop of Lincoln, and a saint.

The possible evasion of the cardinals' intentions over the first clause was a slight matter compared with Henry's treatment of the rescinding of the new customs. The king wrote to Bartholomew of Exeter within a week of the agreement, telling him of the terms, including the stipulation 'that I shall abolish all new customs introduced in my reign against the churches of my land (which I consider to be few or none)'.[7] He had reverted to the old argument that the Constitutions were no more than a record of existing usage; and there was no Becket to oppose him. Even if the clause was interpreted in the papacy's favour, he retained his jurisdiction over questions of patronage and presentment, and over all Church lands held as ordinary feudal tenements.

The practice concerning the disputed rights after 1173 is not always easy to determine. In the question of episcopal elections, greater freedom did prevail for a while. Although the election of

Richard of Dover to Canterbury was unhampered by royal suggestions,[8] there was on the other hand the Winchester election to
which Henry sent peremptory letters requiring the choice of one
candidate, Richard of Poitiers. In 1214, the archbishop of Canterbury felt that a renewed promise of freedom of election was worth
a struggle to attain, but it proved a hollow victory.

On the other hand, the most hotly contested issue, that of
the immunity of the clergy, was definitely a victory for the papacy.
Henry's action in codifying the law had in fact helped to crystallise
Roman thinking on this. Alexander, before becoming pope, had
written a commentary on the great law-book of the Church, Gratian's Decretum, in which he appeared to justify the double trial; but
after Becket's death, he issued a decretal on this point explicitly
precluding the secular inquiry. The legate Hugh Pierleone, sent in
1175, allowed one exception to this rule—arising from the great inquest into forest offences carried out at that time by the king—
in that clerics were summoned to answer before the forest courts
like any other offenders, and this formed a precedent for later
years. The practice of citing clerks to the secular courts continued
in parts of France until the following century, so that Becket's
victory in England on this point was a real one.[9]

More vital to the papacy was the question of appeals. Here
Henry had to yield and allow the free passage of all those who
wished to carry their pleas to the supreme authority; but it is
noteworthy that the ban was never, even in the most bitter days of
controversy, put into complete effect, since the king himself found
that appeals against his recalcitrant archbishop were one of his best
weapons. There had never been any questions of a complete ces-
sation of appeals, but only of royal assent. Since anything which
Henry refused to allow to go abroad remained in the hands of the
primate, the king found himself no better off. Perhaps a more important objective behind the clause was to restrict the growing influence of canon law, from which so many of the difficulties had
arisen. Frequently, the reply to an appeal would involve the cita-
tion of canon law, which might be in conflict with the existing
usage approved by the king; and if canon law gave no guidance, a
decretal from the pope would settle the matter, without the king's
being able to exert influence over his decision.[10]

During the remaining seventeen years of Henry's reign, a more moderate and conciliatory attitude prevailed between Church and State. The two major issues which came into dispute were both concerned with jurisdiction over property. Because the Church courts had the right to decide on legitimacy, and the results of such an inquiry were accepted by the royal courts, a direct conflict arose on a point of procedure. Canon law required that anyone whose land had been taken away by force should have it restored before the case began; but the reverse was true in the royal courts. The solution was reached when Henry obtained papal confirmation in 1178 that the ecclesiastical courts could only deal with legitimacy and not with actual possession.[11]

The more involved problem of right of presentation was also decided as Henry hoped, but without open recognition from the Church. Here the difficulty was that the right to nominate a parish priest was regarded as a property rather than a right, since it often proved a useful way of providing for younger sons or other dependents. The Church, naturally enough, felt that it should be allowed to settle disputes involving its own personnel. Furthermore, it was not always easy to distinguish between two clerks arguing over the possession of a benefice and two patrons claiming the rights to present: the former came under ecclesiastical jurisdiction, while the latter were answerable to the king's court. The decretal issued by Alexander III in 1179 did not take adequate account of the realities of the situation, while the Clarendon clause of 1166 also suffered from imprecise definition. What in practice happened seems to have been that the king's claims prevailed: the church council at Westminster in 1175 prevented one difficulty from occurring by forbidding that such rights should be given as dowries.[12]

Henry had retreated from his original aim of uniform justice in face of strong opposition; but it had scarcely been a dishonourable failure. Becket was not only a determined and sincere man, but he was also supported by a papacy long used to over-ruling the ideas of princes and armed with the new weapon of canon law. The English king, in trying to write down and clarify the laws of his land, was unknowingly taking part in a wider movement of which his opponents were the chief representatives: the change from traditional, local, remembered laws to a centrally administered body of recorded if not created law. In the later years of his reign, increasing quantities of papal decretals were directed to England; of 424 such mandates issued by Alexander III, just over half were specifically addressed to Henry's domains.[13] It was now impossible to resist this growing centralisation, even if Henry had had the desire or the time so to do.

The Plantagenet empire, to anyone present at the splendid gathering at Caen during the Christmas of 1172, seemed more firmly grounded and impressive than ever. The king enjoyed complete power, carrying out his plans through loyal officials whose degree of initiative and independence was entirely in his control. Even his own sons were thus employed. His lands were rich, prosperous and peaceful; no external enemies threatened their security.

Yet the first signs of the upheavals of years to come were already there for skilful minds to read. There had been rumours of conspiracy while Henry was in Ireland, and the young king, his eldest son Henry, had been growing increasingly dissatisfied with the emptiness of his title since his second coronation. With the glory of kingship, his father had given him no corresponding power. He and his wife had returned to Normandy on their father's instructions at the beginning of November, but under the pretext that Louis wished to see his daughter, they had gone almost at once to France.[14] Louis had advised his son-in-law, in a meeting at Gisors, to demand either the whole of England or the whole of Normandy to govern as soon as he returned to his father. If he was refused this, he was to come back to Paris. Henry had suspected that such plots might be laid, and at once recalled his son. The two kings kept their courts separately, the elder at Caen, the younger at Bonneville, although no public quarrel had occurred.

Early in January 1173, Henry summoned his son once more and they went together southwards into Auvergne to meet Humbert, count of Maurienne, at Montferrand-le-Fort on February 2. The counts of Vienne and Toulouse and the king of Aragon were also present. Two questions were to be settled: that of the marriage of Prince John to Humbert's daughter, first planned in 1171; and the quarrel between Raymond of Toulouse and the king

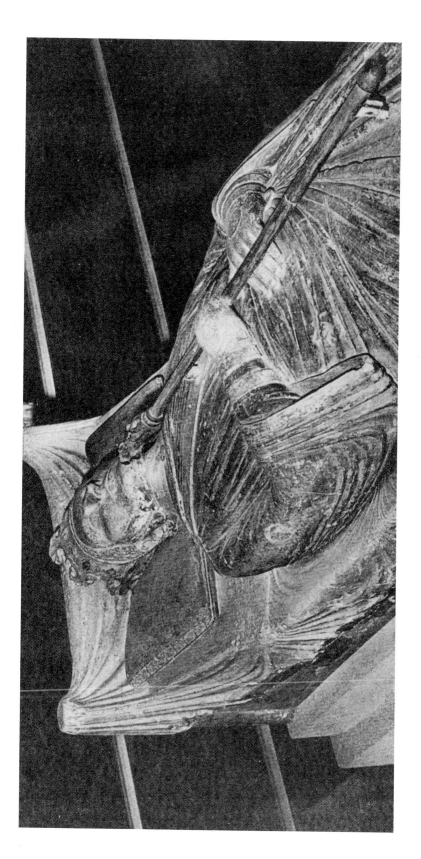

Funeral effigy of Henry II at Fontévrault

Great Seal of Henry II

The Murder of Becket

Chapelle du Liget in the forest of Loches

Effigies of Eleanor and
Richard at Fontévrault

Effigy of John in Worcester Cathedral

Interior of the Eglise de l'Abbaye, Fontévrault

of Aragon. The discussions started at Montferrand and were brought to a successful conclusion at Limoges. The settlement of the Aragon-Toulouse dispute—the first of several such achievements by Henry in diplomatic spheres where he held no direct interest—added considerably to his prestige and ensured friendly relations with neighbouring rulers. This time he secured a tangible gain in the shape of the homage of Raymond of Toulouse, on the usual terms of forty days service at the king's summons. He also agreed to come at the behest of Richard as count of Poitou, but any service beyond forty days was to be paid for. Henry was to receive from him 100 marks of silver or ten good warhorses annually.

The proposed alliance between the Plantagenet line and that of Maurienne seemed at first destined to similar success. Humbert offered either the succession to his lands or, should a son be born to him, twelve towns and castles, the city of Turin and many fiefs. In the event of his eldest daughter's death, the terms would hold good for his second daughter. For his part, Henry was to pay the count 5,000 marks. But one more point was raised by the count: John had no share in his father's domains. When would he receive this share, and what would it be? Henry suggested the three castles on the Loire: Chinon, Mirebeau and Loudun—the same that his own brother had held many years earlier. He cannot have been completely surprised by the reaction of his eldest son, who flatly refused to ratify the agreement as Henry's heir, and repeated his demand that he should govern England, Normandy or Anjou. He was encouraged in this by the barons on both sides of the Channel, who had begun to yearn for their old freedom and were finding Henry's hand too heavy for their liking.

Humbert accepted Henry's guarantee that John would receive the castles, and the young king's obstinacy made no difference to the settlement reached at Limoges. Henry realised all the same that action would have to be taken to prevent his son from becoming the focus of all potential discontent. At first he considered putting him in safe custody,[15] but finally decided that the dismissal of several of his intimates who seemed to be exerting a bad influence on him would be adequate; and Hasculf de St Hilary and other young knights were ordered to leave his company. At the end of the talks at Limoges, the two kings had returned to Nor-

M

mandy, and it was here that the father's decision was enforced. The reaction was immediate: the young Henry slipped quietly past the castle guards at Chinon the same night, having made them drunk beforehand, and rode post-haste to Alencon, a hundred miles away. His father discovered his absence the following morning, and set out in pursuit with equal speed. However, the fugitive had six hours' advantage, and when the old king reached Alençon, his son was at Argentan, forty miles north. It seems that his original objective had been to cross the Channel and to raise the standard of rebellion in England; but he now turned and headed eastwards for the lands of the count of Dreux, brother of Louis, crossing the border near Mortagne on March 8. Had the young king originally planned to make for Paris, he could have gone by a more direct route, up the Loire valley, or at least have crossed from Alencon into French territory.

There was no doubt now that the younger Henry would ally himself with Louis in an attack on his father's domains in order to extract the powers he demanded from him. The old king at once went to Gisors to supervise the strengthening of the Norman border defences. News soon began to reach him of further defections to France: Robert of Melun, who left his castles abandoned at Henry's mercy; Hugh of Chester, returning from Compostella; William Patrick, earl of Salisbury, and his sons. Worse was to follow, for Richard and Geoffrey joined their brother shortly afterwards, apparently at the instigation of the queen and her uncle, Ralph de Faye.[16] Eleanor herself attempted to reach French territory and, disguised as a man, made her way towards Paris. Henry's guards proved too alert for her; she was discovered and brought back. If her life with Henry had allowed her too little freedom, this rash action cost her what liberty she enjoyed, for the king no longer trusted her and feared her influence with his sons. Here lay the one great weakness in his statesmanship: in subordinating all matters of state to his own control, he had deprived his family, who in other circumstances would have shared the power as well as the glory, of their part. Eleanor had been allowed an occasional and rather nominal role, as head of the English or Norman government in Henry's absence; Richard and Geoffrey, although by title entrusted with Aquitaine[17] and Brittany respectively, were influenced by her and by their own proud ambitions to seek absolute power in those areas by joining their brother; while the young king himself had discovered that his new-found glory did not entail any practical outlet for his ambition.

The men who followed the king's sons on their rebellious path had similar reasons for finding Henry's rule displeasing. The movement towards centralisation of government and repression of baronial independence where the latter formed a threat to the state or to just rule was far from complete; yet enough had been done to provoke a reaction among those who had exploited the absence of a strong hand as Ralph de Diceto tells us:

> These men who for just and provable causes the king had condemned to forfeiture, joined the party of his son, not because they regarded his as the juster cause, but because the father, with a view to increasing the royal dignity, was trampling on the necks of the proud and haughty, overthrowing the suspected castles of the country, or bringing them under his own power; because he ordered and even compelled the persons who were occupying the properties belonging to his own house and to the exchequer to be content with their own patrimony; because he condemned traitors to exile, punished robbers with death, terrified thieves with the gallows and mulcted the oppressors of the poor with the loss of their own money.[18]

This revolt seemed the opportunity to reverse the trend; the future undoubtedly lay with the young king, and if he owed his position to the great lords, so much the better. Knowing the elder Henry's temper, the barons never envisaged complete reconciliation, and were prepared to exploit the situation for their own ends as best they could.

Henry was nonetheless reluctant to face the reality of the revolt at once, even though he had taken the necessary precautions, and still hoped for a way of escape. When the young king's household servants returned to him, bringing his seal and personal equipment, Henry received them kindly and then sent them back to his son. The latter, however, remained firm in his intentions, and

made them swear an oath to himself to the exclusion of his father.
Those who refused were sent back; and Henry could now do no
more than wait for his opponents' first move.[19]

Meanwhile, Louis had strengthened his protégé's position
by persuading him to make extensive grants of land to his allies
at a formal court at Paris. First of all, the French magnates took
an oath to support the young Henry in his warfare; and then with
due pomp and ceremony, using a new seal specially made for the
occasion, the young king distributed great fiefs in England and
Normandy. Philip of Flanders was to have lands yielding £1,000 a
year in England, the whole of Kent, and Dover and Rochester
castles; Matthew of Boulogne was allotted Mortain, once the
property of his father-in-law, Stephen; Theobald of Blois received
the disputed castle of Amboise; William of Scotland all the lands
north of the Tyne; his brother David was allotted Cambridgeshire,
and Hugh Bigod additions to his lands in Norfolk. In return, all
the recipients swore fealty to the young king, and offered him
assistance. If it might seem dearly bought to an outside observer,
the predominant influence of Louis must be remembered. He did
not wish the new ruler merely to replace the old: he was chiefly
interested in weakening the towering edifice of authority built by
Henry which now overshadowed his own small territories. Parti-
tion was suggested, Henry to have Normandy and the young king
England. Louis would have most liked to see a weak ruler, unable
to hold his barons in check, ruling all the Angevin territories.

A week after Easter, 1173, with this impressive list of supporters
and at least sixty-five lesser barons, chiefly from the ranks of the
ever-turbulent lords of Aquitaine, the young king went to war.
His father had spent the festival at Alençon, and was fully expecting the attack. For two months little happened, beyond further
defections to the rebels and the capture of Aumale castle on the
Flemish border. Normandy remained the stronghold of the old
king, while Aquitaine and Anjou were for the most part in revolt,
as was Brittany. Events in England were more serious; there the
earl of Leicester and the earl of Chester had joined the English
rebels, who now constituted a formidable party, and there was a
distinct possibility of a Scottish invasion. The young king had also

prevented the election of a new archbishop of Canterbury to succeed Becket. He wrote to the pope lodging an appeal, claiming
that this election was invalid without his approval. In another
letter, he promised to allow the English Church full liberty and to
repeal the Consitutions of Clarendon.

Henry seemed to take very little action to counter this
variety of threats. In contrast to his usual energetic movement in
summertime, he remained at Rouen until the beginning of July,
with the exception of a brief visit to England, of which nothing is
known save for a journey to Northampton by way of Southampton and Winchester. He publicly showed his lack of concern
by frequent hunting expeditions; but he was undoubtedly well informed as to the state of affairs. Louis had been before the walls of
Verneuil for a month when Henry was moved to retaliate at last.
Almost at once, the first piece of good news for many a long day
reached the elder Plantagenet. Having taken Driencourt, the young
king, with Philip of Flanders and Matthew of Boulogne, proceeded to Arques, where, on July 25, Matthew was mortally
wounded. It was five years to the day since Matthew had sworn
fealty to the elder Henry, the oath which he had just broken by
his rebellion. Stricken with grief at his brother's death, perhaps
also seeking an excuse to abandon a none too prosperous campaign,
Philip took this omen seriously and withdrew to his native Flanders. This was a grave blow to the young king's prospects; it would
be almost impossible, without Philip's help, to reduce the basis of
his father's power in Normandy and bring him to the point of
surrender.

Henry arrived at Conches, thirty miles south of Rouen, on
August 7, 1173, bringing a large army of mercenaries. Although he
knew that the inhabitants of Verneuil had agreed to surrender on
August 9 unless relief came, he waited for part of his army, and only
proceeded to within seven miles of Verneuil on August 8. Here, at
Breteuil, he drew up his forces in battle order, prepared but not
actively seeking to engage in a pitched battle. Louis was not enthusiastic about such an event, his troops being tired from the long
siege and probably inferior both in quality and numbers. He therefore sent three emissaries—the archbishop of Sens, his own brother
Robert and Theobald of Blois—to propose a truce until the next

day and a conference to establish peace. It seemed as though the great rebellion might peter out as a minor border raid, such as Louis had made at intervals on much slighter pretexts. Henry retired to Conches to await his enemy's arrival. However, the French king had other plans. In Henry's absence, he demanded the surrender of Verneuil, since relief had not arrived. This was granted, and the town opened its gates. Louis' treachery went further: against all his promises, he sacked the town and took its inhabitants into captivity in France. Henry had by then seen the flames and realised the deceit of which he was victim. Setting out in hot pursuit of Louis, he was in time to harass the retreating French army and take many prisoners, as well as the equipment left in the abandoned camp. Having repaired the walls of Verneuil, he forebore to raid the French king's lands by way of reprisal, but turned north, reducing the rebellious garrison of Damville on his way back to Rouen.

A second army had been fighting for Henry in Brittany while the king dealt with the besiegers of Verneuil; composed of mercenaries, its object was the suppression of the revolt raised there by earl Hugh of Chester and Henry's perennial opponent, Ralph de Fougères. This force had suffered a heavy defeat at the latter's hands when surprised during foraging. Henry is said to have come secretly to Brittany during the summer to attack Ralph, but finding his opponent too strong, to have retreated again.[20] Within ten days of returning to the Norman capital, Henry had fresh encouragement from this quarter. In an engagement at Dol, which Ralph had obtained by bribing the castellans, the Brabantine mercenaries revenged their earlier reverse, driving Ralph and the earl into the castle, and capturing several other leaders of the revolt, including Hasculf de St Hilary and William Patrick, earl of Salisbury. The news reached Rouen on Tuesday, August 21, Henry left that evening; travelling at incredible speed, he arrived at Dol on the Thursday, August 23, having covered some two hundred miles in two days. Three days later the castle surrendered in face of the siege-engines which had been rapidly erected on the king's arrival. This was a major victory, for besides Hugh of Chester and Ralph, sixty-seven other notables fell into Henry's hands, and there was no question of any further serious revolt in Brittany. Henry had showed the best side of his military genius in the episode: the employment of mercenaries under their own commanders—a system he had brought to the point where they could be entrusted with an important mission independently; his gift for immediate and unexpected action; and his skill in reducing strongholds in the shortest possible space of time.

It was now evident that the revolt would not bring easy success to its leaders. Henry had no desire to prolong the war, and a conference was soon arranged at Gisors, on September 25, 1173. Henry spent some of the intervening time at Le Mans, and met Louis and his own sons on the French border at the arranged date. In view of his son's conduct, the Angevin's offers were generous to the point of foolishness; but as his heirs, it was essential to satisfy them in order to ensure the peace of the realm. The young king was to have half the royal revenues in either England or Normandy, with either four English castles or three in Normandy and the revenues of Anjou. Richard was to have half the royal revenues in Aquitaine and four castles there; Geoffrey was to marry the heiress of the duke of Brittany and to have the lands which formed her inheritance. Any doubtful points were to be settled by the archbishop of Tarento and papal legates.

But Henry's generosity was more apparent than real, for in no circumstances would he part with the powers of government. Thanks to his financial reforms he had money to spare, although his offers would have laid a heavy burden on the exchequers. This was not what his sons wanted, and they regarded it as an attempt to buy off their political ambitions. Henry had never been conspicuously mean with his allowances to them, and this had not been one of their complaints. They were far more concerned with their father's apparent intention of retaining as much political control as possible until his dying day. Henry was only forty: the situation of the young king and his brothers threatened to remain static for another twenty years or more; and what was money without power? Such considerations as these, persuasively supported by Louis, prevailed in the young Plantagenets' minds, and the conference broke up with nothing accomplished. Further talks the next day ended in a skirmish between English and French

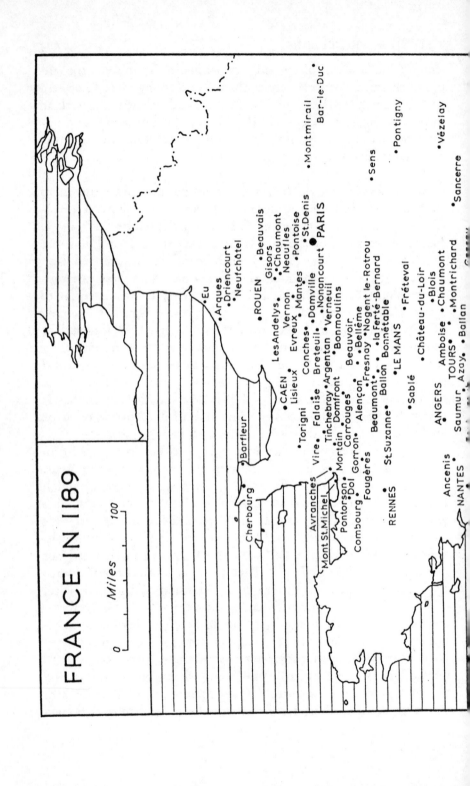

FRANCE IN 1189

Miles

0   100

Bar-le-Duc

Montmirail

Pontigny

Vézelay

Sens

Sancerre

St.Denis **PARIS**

Beauvais

Gisors Chaumont
Neaufles
Pontoise

Arques Driencourt Neufchâtel

Eu

•ROUEN

LesAndelys Vernon Mantes
Conches Damville Nonancourt
Breteuil• Verneuil
Evreux•

Frêteval

Château-du-Loir

Blois
Chaumont
Amboise Montrichard
TOURS •Ballan
Saumur• Azay•

•CAEN
Lisieux• Argentan Bonmoulins
Torigni Falaise• Tinchebray• •Beauvoir Bellême
Domfront Alençon Fresnay Nogent le-Rotrou
Vire• Mortain •la Ferté-Bernard
Carrouges Beaumont •LE MANS
Gorron• Ballon Bonnétable
Fougères St.Suzanne• •Sablé

•Barfleur

Cherbourg

Avranches
Mont St.Michel
Pontorson•
Combourg•Dol

RENNES

ANGERS

Ancenis
NANTES

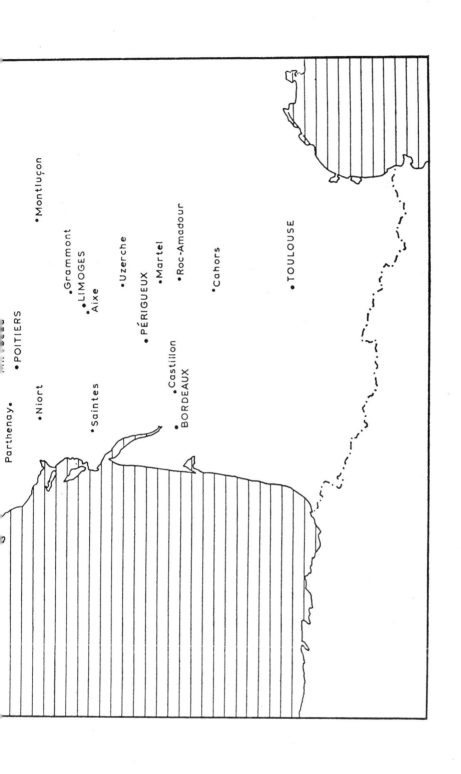

Parthenay.
•POITIERS
•Niort
Saintes
Castillon
BORDEAUX
•Montluçon
•Grammont
•LIMOGES
Aixe
•Uzerche
•PÉRIGUEUX
•Martel
•Roc-Amadour
•Cahors
•TOULOUSE

troops, in which a French knight was captured, and both sides withdrew.

The scene of the fighting now moved to England. The young king and his supporters had had little encouragement from the results of their continental efforts, and therefore sent the earl of Leicester with a body of Flemish troops to invade England. So far the only serious episode in England itself had been the siege of Leicester, on July 3. The town had been taken by Richard de Lucy and Reginald of Cornwall, after much of it had been accidentally burnt; but the castle held out. There had been trouble in the north: William of Scotland, while refusing the young king's offer of the lands north of Tyne for his help, had entered the war on his own account. He claimed Northumberland as his, on the grounds that it had been given to his grandfather by Matilda, and had been un- justly seized by Henry. With a large army, including many spear- men from Galway, he crossed the border from Caldenlea and besieged Wark castle. Meeting a spirited resistance from the castellan, Roger d'Estuteville, he made a forty-day truce and moved on to Alnwick, which likewise resisted. His first success was at Warkworth castle; but Newcastle held out, because William had no siege-engines—perhaps the reason for his first two failures. He next turned west and settled down to reduce Carlisle by star- vation; yet even here fortune was against him, for by now an English force under Humphrey de Bohun and Richard de Lucy had been raised to drive out the invaders. William deemed it prudent to retire, and was followed north by the English. They had burnt Berwick and were preparing to devastate as much of Scot- land as they could, when news of Leicester's invasion reached them. It was now Richard de Lucy's turn to be cautious, and he arranged a truce with the Scottish king until January 13, 1174. The young king had achieved his planned effect, and the Scots were saved from probable defeat.

Robert of Leicester had landed in Suffolk, at Walton, on September 29, and had at once been joined by Hugh Bigod, earl of Norfolk. Having dismissed the ships, they set about the siege of Walton castle, which successfully resisted them. Robert there-

fore moved to Haughley, which he took on October 13, and
went from there to Framlingham. Here his Flemish troops did
considerable damage to the Bigod lands, and he himself quarrelled
with Bigod's wife. As a result, he was forced to move off towards
Leicester, which he hoped to relieve, without waiting the few
weeks necessary for contingents to arrive from other parts of
England to reinforce him. He did not get far with his plans, for the
royal officers had gathered a new army at Bury St Edmunds, where
Lucy and Bohun had been joined by the earls of Cornwall, Gloucester and Arundel. Henry himself considered that his English
supporters were perfectly capable of dealing with the situation, and
did not stir from Normandy.[21]

His trust proved fully justified: for in a battle near Fornham, on October 17, the earl of Leicester's army was completely
shattered. The English feudal cavalry overcame the smaller contingent of horse opposing them, and the Flemish footsoldiers,
who had marched through Norfolk so boldly and full of confidence, singing: 'Hop, Hop, Willekin, England is mine and
thine,' were powerless against the mounted knights. Scattering in
confusion, they were slaughtered by the local peasantry wielding
scythes and pitchforks. This was the first pitched battle on English
or Norman soil in Henry's reign; and its decisive results show why
the full hosts of France and the Angevin empire, although frequently drawn up in preparation, never dared to fight. The outcome was certain only in one respect: that one side would gain
almost total victory. Both the earl and countess of Leicester, and
all the knights accompanying them, were taken prisoner; any
surviving Flemings were drowned in the Fen dykes, although their
army had far outnumbered the English host. The victors of
Fornham followed up their success by assembling forces to hold
the earl of Norfolk in check at Colchester, Bury St Edmunds and
Ipswich. Bigod, feeling that resistance was vain, bought a truce
until June 4, 1174, with the added condition that his Flemish
troops be dismissed. The south of England was once again secure,
and although the rebels were strong in the north and midlands,
there was no immediate danger, since they were unable to find an
army. The garrisons of the earl of Leicester's castles were the only
forces of any serious military value in the field. Hence prepara-

tions could be made against the day when the Scottish truce was
due to expire.[22]

The next year, 1174, opened peacefully: a truce was arranged with
the French until the end of March. Neither side was interested in
a winter campaign, and this arrangement merely regulated the
length of the interval. A similar truce, also to the end of March,
was negotiated with the Scots by Bishop Hugh of Durham. Henry
remained in Normandy during this time, intending to continue
his defensive policy on the renewal of hostilities. There he received the archbishop of Tarento, who had been sent by the pope to
attempt to arrange a peace. Louis still resisted such overtures, and
the legate had to return with nothing to show for his labours.
    The first attack of the spring campaign came from the
Scots, who descended once more on the border castles, only to
meet the same successful resistance at Wark. At the suggestion of
Roger de Mowbray, who was now assisting him with a band of
Flemish soldiers, William then moved west to Carlisle. Robert de
Vaux was in charge of this garrison, and the Scots at first attempted
to bribe or intimidate him. Failing in both these methods, part of
the army was left to starve out the town, while the remainder, led
by William, took Liddell, Appleby,[23] Warkworth and Harbottle
before rejoining the siege. Finding himself short of provisions,
Vaux was forced to promise to surrender at Michaelmas if help
did not come by then. William withdrew satisfied, having taken
the necessary hostages, and set about the siege of Prudhoe. However, the northern magnates had by this time organised an army;
William was forced to retreat to avoid a battle, and tried his hand
at Alnwick instead. Here again, he sent part of the army under
Duncan of Angus and Richard de Morville to ravage the country,
while the rest carried on the siege. Warkworth town was sacked
and its inhabitants massacred; but before more damage was done,
a dramatic stroke of fortune ended the Scottish invasion. The
army from Yorkshire had followed William northwards. Some of
the knights, perhaps impatient of the slow progress of the footmen, rode on ahead to Alnwick in a small band. Among the four
hundred or so knights were Odinel d'Umfraville, William

d'Estuteville, William de Vescy, and Ranulf Glanville, the leaders of the expedition. When they arrived near Alnwick, they decided to make a reconnaissance of the situation. A sudden mist descended; and they wandered helplessly all night, only to find themselves, at dawn on July 13, before the very walls of Alnwick. William and his knights were enjoying a leisurely breakfast and preparing for the day ahead. The Scottish king, noticing the small group approaching, assumed that it was Duncan and his band of raiders returning. Only when the English raised their war-cry did he discover his mistake. By then the attack was launched. In the ensuing struggle, William's horse was killed under him, and he surrendered to Ranulf Glanville. Roger de Mowbray fled; and the remaining Scottish nobles were either killed or, like their king, taken captive to Newcastle.[24]

Three hundred miles to the south, the same dawn broke on the kneeling figure of Henry before Becket's tomb in Canterbury Cathedral, and slowly brought light to the gloom of the crypt where he had passed the night in prayer and fast, smarting from the scourging he had undergone at the hands of the monks on the previous days. He had been in England for four days, since the focus of the war had moved there. There had been some desultory fighting in France: he had taken Saintes in Poitou in May, and reduced Ancenis in Anjou about June 11. The young king had decided to attempt a more general revolt in England, sending support to the king of Scotland.* His followers continued to do what they could: Bigod had burnt Norwich, Ansketill Malory had carried out a successful raid on Northampton, and earl Ferrers had taken Nottingham. On the other side, Henry's bastard son, Geoffrey, had dealt severely with Roger de Mowbray's castles, and Richard de Lucy had laid siege to Huntingdon. Hence the young king decided that his personal presence was required in England, and on June 24, 1174, he arrived at Gravelines to cross the Channel. This came to his father's notice, who at once left for Barfleur with the more important of his prisoners and a force of Brabantines. A westerly wind enabled him to cross, while his son was forced to remain inactive at Gravelines, hoping for a change in the weather.

* This arrived too late, and the 500 Flemings were dispersed by Hugh of Durham.

Landing at Southampton, he went to Canterbury where he offered his prayers for the first time before the shrine of his dead friend and opponent, doing due penance for his part in Thomas' death, who was now a fully recognised saint.

The news of William the Lion's capture was not long in coming, and the coincidence between the actual occurrence of this momentous event and Henry's night of prayer was soon remarked, and the two events firmly linked as cause and effect. Five days later, Henry was in London, at the palace of Westminster. It was evening, and the king, suffering from a slight fever, had gone to bed early, when a messenger arrived. The chamberlain was unwilling to admit the man, although his news seemed urgent. The noise of arrival had been heard by the king, who presently asked who it was. On being told that the messenger came from Ranulf Glanville, Henry at once feared the worst and ordered his immediate admittance. The news quickly proved to be of a very different kind. Henry was naturally delighted; rewarding the messenger for his hard ride south, he roused his barons to share his rejoicing.[25]

The following day he took action against the remaining rebels, moving first to Huntingdon, which fell on July 21, and thence to Seleham, near Framlingham, where four days later he received Hugh Bigod's surrender of the castles there and at Bungay on condition that the Flemish mercenaries were given safe-conduct home. This event was marred for Henry by a personal mishap: the horse of one of his close companions, the Templar Tostes de St Omer, grew restive and kicked the king on the shin, causing a painful wound which later gave trouble.[26]

Thereafter the revolt collapsed as quickly as it had sprung up. At Northampton, Bishop Hugh of Durham, who although otherwise loyal, had been compromised by the arrival of his nephew in the north with a Flemish force, took the precaution of surrendering his castles to the king in order to obtain his nephew's safe return home. The earl of Leicester's castellans at Leicester, Mountsorel and Groby surrendered the strongholds from which they had continued to defy the king even after their master's imprisonment. Roger de Mowbray and earl Ferrers likewise sought the king's mercy. When Henry sailed for Normandy on August

7—just under a month after his arrival in an atmosphere of impending disaster and intense crisis—he left England completely at peace. Even the riots in London, a by-product of the breakdown of public order, had been quelled, and there was no question of further trouble from the barons.

The young king was still at Gravelines when the news of his father's arrival and of the capture of William of Scotland reached him. Realising that there was now little point in carrying out his plans, even though it meant abandoning all his costly preparations, he joined Louis again, and with him proceeded to the siege of Rouen in a desperate attempt to strike a serious blow at his father's position by seizing the Norman capital. This city, lying in the protection of the Seine and the hills, was too well protected to offer an easy prize, especially as one bridge remained in the citizens' hands. The French army watched impotently as victuals were brought into the city each day. Louis' only hope was a frontal assault, but a month's endeavours brought him no nearer to success. In accordance with the custom of the times, on St Lawrence's day, August 10, 1174, a truce was proclaimed for twenty-four hours. The citizens naturally took advantage of this to leave the city in which they had been confined for so long, and on the bank opposite to Louis' camp held all manner of sports, including a tournament. This was too much of a temptation for Louis' magnates, who urged a surprise attack. The king was unwilling to commit such treachery, but his nobles answered: 'With an enemy there can be no question of deceit or valour.' At last he yielded and the army was ordered to assemble in strict silence. However, this movement was observed by a monk within the town, who at once rang the great bell of the church to recall his fellow-citizens. When Louis' army reached the walls, they were repulsed with heavy losses, and the French king retired disheartened both by this defeat and by the unnecessary stain on his honour. The following day, Henry reached Rouen, and on August 12 sent his Welsh troops into the surrounding forests to cut off the French provision trains. He prepared for an attack on the French from within the city, filling a ditch which had been dug between the French camp and the walls so that two hundred men could advance abreast over it. At this,

Louis ordered his siege-engines to be burnt to prevent them from
falling into English hands. A skirmish ensued, and a truce was proposed by the archbishop of Sens and Theobald of Blois on the following day. That night, however, Louis judged discretion the best
course, and retired with his army, not halting until he reached
French soil. Once more, fear of a pitched battle was all too evident
in his actions.

On the following day, the French envoys returned to propose a meeting on the understanding that Henry in the meanwhile was free to proceed against his son Richard in Poitou. This
was agreed, and the English king went southwards. Richard was in
no mood to resist his father, who was now triumphant everywhere.
The expedition became a pursuit; castle after castle was abandoned
as Henry advanced. Eventually, on September 23, having heard of
the truce between Louis and the young king on one side and Henry
on the other, Richard came to his father, in guise of deepest
penitence, and submitted to him. Henry, who could never find it
in his heart to be angry with his sons for long, forgave him, and
peace was made.

The outcome of the conference between Henry, Louis, and the
young king, held between Tours and Amboise on September 29,
1174, was now scarcely in doubt. It remained for Henry to be as
generous or as harsh as he wished, within certain limits. He gave
nothing that he had not been prepared to give earlier; and the final
settlement was less favourable to his sons than the terms offered a
year before. A general amnesty and restitution was the first provision of the treaty, William of Scotland and the earls of Chester
and Leicester being the only exceptions. All oaths taken in the
course of the revolt were annulled, and homage was done by the
sons as before the rising, only the younger Henry being excused
because of his royal status. The benefits conferred on the three
sons were less than his former offer: the young king received two
castles in Normandy and £15,000 in Angevin currency annually;
Richard was awarded two Poitevin castles 'which could not harm
the king', and half the revenues of Poitou; and Geoffrey received
half the dowry of Conan's daughter. The question which had

originally sparked off the revolt was settled in Henry's favour:
the young king was to allow John to have Nottingham, Marlborough, and estates in Normandy and Anjou to the value of
£2,000 annually, with five castles. Finally, all estates forfeited by
the rebels were to be returned by the king. Of Eleanor, nothing
was said. Henry, by his treatment of her, showed that he felt her to
be largely responsible for the rebellion: she was to remain under
close surveillance for several years to come. The king's sons had
not gained the essential element of political power which really
interested them, and Louis had gained nothing for a costly war.
After all, Henry was the victor, and could hardly be expected to
increase the price he had to pay in the very hour of triumph as
insurance against the possibility of further troubles. Besides, he
had lost much for his part as well: the drain on the exchequer had
been considerable, and the disruption of the administration would
take some time to repair. He had had to abandon all external
diplomacy and any designs he may have had for the extension of
his empire. To this extent, Louis had gained a costly respite from
the threatening growth of Angevin power.

The settlement with William of Scotland proved harsh.
The Scottish king was still at Falaise when terms were arranged.[27]
He had to do homage for Scotland to Henry, and all his vassals
made a direct oath to the English king. In addition to giving his
brother David as a hostage, he had to surrender the five main
castles of Scotland—Edinburgh, Jedburgh, Roxburgh, Stirling and
Berwick—and the Scottish Church was to be subject to the jurisdiction of that of England. Henry seems to have been chiefly concerned to prevent further trouble from this quarter, and was in no
mood to remember assistance in the past from William's grandfather, David.

The great rebellion was at an end. Its causes, however, remained as sources of irritation which produced a continuous sore
on the body politic. As an isolated episode, the events of 1173–4
are striking enough. Yet they have never earned a place in the
popular memory, for the simple reason that they are paralleled
several times in the remaining years of Henry's reign on a smaller
scale. Henry paid dear for his one failing: his inability either to
apply ruthlessly to his sons a policy which was intrinsically reason-

N

able, or to make adequate terms with them. It was essential for the Angevin empire to be ruled by one absolute monarch if it was to survive the machinations of its enemies. Henry could neither bring himself to delegate that power in an efficient and equitable manner, nor to encourage the princes' interest in affairs other than high politics.

9

The Years of Peace

Easter again! The time of year that I like best;
Its flowers and showers and birdsong in the leafy woods
Rejoice my heart; but better still the gay pavilions,
The sward bedecked with glistening shields and polished arms,
The keen-edged swords and lances flashing in the fray!

Look there! A splendid sight! The common soldiers hunt
The frightened peasants fleeing with their precious goods,
While just beyond, see now, a castle's strength assayed,
Its palisades destroyed, a host camps by its moat!
The walls are battered down with rams and mangonels,
Besiegers scale the breach, the ramparts swarm with life
As helms are broken by the axes' blows, swords cleave
Through painted shields! A sortie issues down below,
A charge! Knights falling, horses running riderless,
And death to all! No prisoners now, no quarter shown!

Ah, such a life's the kind of life I'd lead;
No wine, no food, no sleep for me, if I can fight
And watch death walk with fire and sword in hand.[1]

THUS BERTRAN de Born, lord of Altaforte, soon after the great rebellion. His fame and influence were magnified by Dante, who put him in the *Inferno* as a sower of sedition and schism.[2] His mood was that of many of the barons of Aquitaine. Because they preferred Henry's distant authority to the presence of Richard, they had for the most part remained loyal to the king. When the elder Plantagenet was victorious, he still found there was much to be done. Many castles had been strengthened for war and, whether they belonged to his own supporters or not, constituted a grave menace to the peace. Richard was sent back to the south, with a mandate from his father to the Poitevins commanding them to obey his son in all things, and Henry at once set about the task of reducing all those castles—probably the majority—whose owners refused to comply with the king's orders that they should be returned to the state they were in fifteen days before the outbreak of war.

The aftermath of war brought problems of different kinds elsewhere. In Normandy, the disruption of the administration during the two previous years kept Henry and the young king occupied. On February 24, 1175, they held a conference with Louis at Gisors, and visited Rouen two days later; from there Henry went south to Anjou, having destroyed the fortifications added to the barons' castles, and received renewed homage from Geoffrey and Richard. Soon after March 23, Henry returned north to Caen and summoned his eldest son, who was still at Rouen, to go with him to England. Louis' agents, however, had been at work; they had advised the young king against going to England, because, so they said, his father intended to imprison him there. They were believed, and the king's order was met with a curt refusal. Henry grasped the source of his suspicions and adopted a conciliatory tone, which achieved the desired effect. In another of the theatrical scenes of repentance which are the only glimpse of Henry's family life during these years, the young king was reconciled with his father at Bur-le-Roi on April 1, weeping and protesting his innocence and loyalty as he did homage for his lands in England and France. Henry allowed him to go to see Louis immediately afterwards, while he himself stayed at Valognes, perhaps to give Geoffrey his instructions for the government of Brittany. At Easter, the two kings were together at Cherbourg. Here they were visited by count Philip of Flanders, who had taken the cross on Good Friday, and who wished to settle his affairs before departing for the Holy Land. A gift of £1,000 revenue from lands in England was confirmed by the two kings,

and in return Philip surrendered the charter he had received from
the young king at the outset of the rebellion.

Whatever Henry had been doing during these months, he now
felt that matters were sufficiently well organised for him to leave
for England. The two kings finally left Normandy from Barfleur
on May 8, 1175, and landed at Portsmouth the next day. It was to
be Henry's longest visit to the island since his coronation, and one
of the most fruitful. Within ten days of landing, a council of the
clergy was assembled at Westminster to regulate the condition of
the Church under the king's aegis. Peace had at last been achieved
for England's clergy with the election of Richard of Dover to the
see of Canterbury, confirmation of this having been obtained
from the pope in April 1174. A gentle and saintly man, Richard
of Dover was able to work out the implications of the settlement
of Avranches without crossing Henry's path. This particular
council was chiefly concerned with the moral state of the clergy,
and attempted to deal with the English practice of married priests.
The old quarrel between York and Canterbury flared up again to
mar an otherwise peaceful and successful piece of work; but although the kings remained throughout the council they do not
seem to have taken a direct hand in its business. On May 28,
Henry left for a second pilgrimage to Canterbury, accompanied by
his son, to give thanks to the saint for his intervention against the
rebels. This was the young king's first visit to the tomb of the
man who had once been his mentor, and it is interesting to reflect
that he had never attempted to use Becket's martyrdom as a rallying-cry against his father; partly for this reason it was now the
king and not his son who could offer thanks.

As always in Henry's lands, the general peace was disturbed
by minor troubles. The great lords might be quiet, but lesser
barons found new quarrels. At Gloucester on June 30, 1175, the
two kings held a council on Welsh affairs with Rhys ap Griffith
and other Welsh princes. Now that the border was fairly peaceful,
the marcher barons had taken to calling in the Welsh to fight in
their own private quarrels, or inciting them to attack others; a
weakness inherent in the system. Henry could only warn them and

require them to cease this civil war; to weaken them would lay the
western counties open to renewed Welsh attacks. The earl of
Gloucester and William de Braose, particular offenders in this
respect, were especially bound over to observe the settlement, the
former having already been required to surrender Bristol castle.

Immediately afterwards, the two kings returned to Woodstock where a further council was held. Apart from a great deal of
ecclesiastical business, Henry announced some political decisions,
aimed at preserving the newly established peace. Although a
general amnesty had been proclaimed, the king forbade any of his
former enemies to come to court without being personally summoned, and they were not to remain there longer than required,
or arrive by night. He was as much concerned to keep away those
who had been a bad influence on his son as to prevent quarrels at
court. A general edict was issued that no one living east of the
Severn should wear arms, neither bows nor pointed knives, and
that anyone so doing should be arrested. This was intended to
prevent any kind of violence; but since such weapons were used in
hunting and could also be carried in self-defence, the edict soon
became a dead letter.[3] As a warning to malefactors and to em-
phasise his determination to stamp out lawlessness, Henry ordered
that four knights who had murdered a forester should be hanged,
instead of paying the usual fines.

At the beginning of August 1175, the king was at Northampton, attending to a different aspect of the same question.
During the revolt, the forest laws had been disregarded on a large
scale, sometimes on the king's orders, but more often by private
individuals. Henry wanted both to reassert his foresters' authority
and to also use this as a source of lucrative fines. He therefore
instituted a series of sworn inquests by jury into all crimes against
the forest law committed during the anarchy of the two previous
years. Even the justiciar, Richard de Lucy, protested against this,
saying that he himself had been ordered to take game in the royal
forests by the king, but his intervention was without result. The
financial yields recorded by the exchequer were not remarkable,
about 100 offenders paying £2,093 in 1176.[4] Yet Henry was in a
sense justified by his obstinacy. There was a large backlog of expenses to be paid off from the rebellion, and forest fines were a

legitimate part of the royal revenue. The king was quite prepared to court unpopularity if fiscal considerations made it necessary.

The last echoes of the rebellion were dispersed at a great ceremony at York on August 10, when the two kings met William of Scotland to implement the terms of the treaty of Falaise. In York minster, the procession of notables of Scotland came to the two kings and made formal profession of obedience and allegiance; among them were king William and his brother David, all the Scottish bishops and abbots, and many Scottish barons. The bishops swore in addition to be responsible for king William's keeping of his oath, and to render obedience to the English Church. For the rest of Henry's reign, the northern border was to enjoy an almost complete peace, and no serious contest between English and Scots was to occur for more than a century. As in Ireland Henry's political settlement proved durable. His successors had a just pretext for retaliating against any Scottish disturbances to the extent of total conquest, since full homage had been duly paid. He ensured that so long as the English had no major military commitments elsewhere, that threat alone would be sufficient to hold them in check.

Henry returned south to continue the series of administrative assemblies, holding a council at Windsor on October 6. Messengers from France had brought good reports of the progress of both Richard and Geoffrey in the reduction of rebellious castles: Richard had taken Chatillon in the Dordogne after an eight weeks' siege. Envoys also arrived from the king of Connaught, who wished to make peace with Henry. This was satisfactorily reached, and the king could now turn, for the first time in nearly twelve years, to consider possible reforms in English finance and justice. This he did during the autumn, amusing himself in the intervals by hunting in Savernake forest and in Gloucestershire, and only coming east to receive the legate Hugh Pierleone at Winchester on October 31. Rumour had it that the king was considering a divorce, and that this was the reason for the legate's visit. It seems out of character for Henry even to have entertained the idea. A politician of his skill would not lose a quarter of his domains in the way that Louis of France had done, for had he divorced Eleanor, she would have become once again independent ruler of Aquitaine. He may

have hoped to arrange a settlement which would allow him to
retain the lands that formed her dowry, leaving her a specified
revenue from them. The story is probably no more than a popular
conjecture from the all too apparent rift between king and queen.
The legate would probably have complied with any of Henry's
requests; for his reputation for being more interested in bribes
than spiritual welfare was universal.[5] Henry obtained one important concession, already mentioned, from him: that the clergy
should be tried for offences against the forest law in secular courts.

After Christmas, which he spent with his eldest son at Windsor,
Henry had his scheme for revising the judicial machinery ready,
and on January 25, 1176, he put it before a great council at Northampton. Ever since the last decade of his grandfather's reign,
travelling justices had supplemented the normal county courts by
hearing cases in which the king had a direct interest, either financial or deriving from prerogative. But these justices in eyre had
held their commissions occasionally and without any systematic
organisation; some counties may never have known the institution,
and others had been visited only at long intervals, quite often
because there was very little business to be done there. The institution was primarily a temporary measure when pressure on the
royal court became too great, and it was being used with increasing
frequency. Henry's proposals were simple. In view of the larger
volume of business, the office of itinerant justice was to become a
regular feature of the administration, six groups of three justices
being responsible for between four and eight counties each.

This change was the result rather than a concomitant of a
new promulgation of the Assize made at Clarendon ten years
earlier.[6] A similar system had been used to enforce it when it was
originally issued. There had, however, been no continuous series
of visits such as is found after 1176. The reissue of the Assize was
a substantial enough undertaking to require new machinery, and
it was considerably expanded both in substance and detail in the
light of experience and new circumstances; indeed, it falls into
three separate parts.

The new Assizes are set out as instructions to the itinerant
justices; but they involve a great deal more than mere rules for

procedure or even than the duties laid down at Clarendon. The repression of crime with which the 1166 document was chiefly concerned remained the main object of the operation. The justices were to make inquiry of local communities whether any crimes had gone unpunished since the king came to the throne, and the procedure to be followed in such cases when discovered was laid down. Each community was to appoint representatives who would give evidence on oath as to crimes committed: an institution known as the 'jury of presentment'. All such cases fell within the king's justice, and he was to have all profits. Nor were any franchises (exempted areas) to escape this visitation. Detailed provisions were made for dealing with those known to have a bad record, with fugitives and with vagabonds. A general review of the system of frankpledge, under which groups of men stood surety for the good behaviour of individual members of a community, was to be carried out, and for this and for the pursuit of criminals the sheriffs were again authorised to enter franchises.

Some of this had been enacted in 1166. In addition, the justices were to carry out what amounted to a general survey of the realm; they were to inquire into escheats, church revenues, forfeit lands and wardships, which were due to the crown; they were to deal with all revenues due, castle guard duties, outlaws and arguments over fiefs; they were to take the barons' homage on the king's behalf. They were furthermore required to enforce two legal procedures relating to the land law not mentioned earlier, which became known as the assizes of novel disseisin and mort d'ancestor. Both were aimed at settling disputes over property which might arise between lord and tenant, and could not reasonably be tried in the lord's court, or between tenants of two different lords. Only now did these contingencies warrant special machinery. Novel disseisin was a method of dealing with recent seizures of land, on whatever pretext; it was to apply to all such incidents since the king had made peace with his son. It ensured that the possessor of the disputed lands was not deprived of them before judgement was given, and was probably first enacted in 1166, for in that year the first fines for the offence were paid to the exchequer. The other assize was completely new, and concerned the rights of heirs. The legal heir was to take possession of the land, even if the inheritance was for any reason contested by the lord or by any other, under the maxim that a dead man surrenders his seisin to the living man (le mort saisit le vif). Once again, Henry was using his rights as overlord to clarify matters otherwise all too liable to local influences and inconclusive lawsuits.

The council ended with an attempt to deal with the thorny problem of the subjection of the Scottish Church. Henry desired this for political reasons, but the two English archbishops disputed as to which archdiocese should hold this obedience. This quarrel degenerated, at a later church council in March, into an open fight between the retainers of York and Canterbury, in which the archbishop of York was hurt. Henry was not interested in interfering in such squabbles so long as they remained internal, and in August the archbishops finally declared a five-year truce.

Family matters once more came to a head in March, when the young king applied to his father for permission to go on pilgrimage to the shrine of St James at Compostella in north-west Spain.[7] The king saw that this rather uncharacteristic request was prompted by impatience with his company—the two kings had been together for the best part of two years—and by the schemes of the young king's intimates to remove him from his father's side. The young king obtained his request in part only, for he was not allowed to go further than Normandy. He departed about March 22, but was delayed for some days at Porchester. As a result, he was still in England for Easter, and spent the feast with his father at Winchester. Richard and Geoffrey had landed two days before and joined the gathering. Richard had much to discuss with his father, for a new revolt, headed by Wulfgrim of Angouleme and his brothers, had broken out in Poitou. Henry saw an opportunity of dissuading his eldest son from his pilgrimage and the latter agreed to go to his brother's aid instead. Even so, the young king, when he landed in France at Barfleur on April 20, 1176, went at once to see Louis of France and did not reach Poitou until the end of the following month. One other family problem had been settled since Christmas: the death of Henry's uncle, Reginald of Cornwall, had at long last enabled him to provide suitably for

John and, later in the year, a marriage was arranged for him with
the eldest daughter of the earl of Gloucester, which improved his
position considerably.

Soon afterwards Henry himself publicly announced his intention of going on crusade to the Holy Land. He accordingly sent
messengers to Philip of Flanders, who was about to make his way
there, asking him to put off his departure until he could join him.
Informed circles, however, suggested that his real motive was a
fear that Philip had designs on the crown of Jerusalem, which
was in the hands of the Angevins.[8] Henry would have a strong
claim to it on the death of the ruling king, and was unwilling to
see it go elsewhere. In other matters, his foreign politics flourished:
envoys arrived from William of Sicily seeking the hand of Henry's
third daughter Joanna, and, the princess being to the Sicilians'
liking, the match was arranged. Joanna was sent south on July 27,
suitably escorted and with appropriate gifts, to the young king in
Normandy, who conducted her to Poitiers, where they joined
Richard for the journey through Aquitaine. After a long and
arduous journey through Italy, the princess reached Sicily before
the end of the year, and the marriage was solemnised on February
13, 1177.[9]

Richard had meanwhile been active in Poitou in the suppression of the revolt of the count of Angouleme. He succeeded in
defeating his opponents about May 23, but it was not until after
midsummer and with his eldest brother's help that the rising was
completely crushed. Hostages were taken from the count for his
future good behaviour. Pleasure in this victory was marred for
Henry by news of the behaviour of the young king, who, as soon
as the war was over, began to make friends with his father's
enemies. When the vice-chancellor of the young Henry informed
his father, he was at first condemned to death as a traitor by his
master, and only the intervention of the bishop of Poitiers miti-
gated the sentence. It was this threat of renewed hostilities with
his son that moved Henry at a council at Windsor on September
25, 1176, to replace the baronial castellans throughout England by
his own men, taking all the castles into his own hands for the
moment. Even Richard de Lucy, his closest collaborator, was not
exempted and had to hand over his castle at Ongar.[10] Similar

measures were taken in Normandy, and the bishop of Winchester was sent there as justiciar to enforce this. Furthermore, the castles of the earl of Leicester, of Roger de Mowbray, and of Hugh Bigod, the ringleaders of the rebellion of 1173 in England, were dismantled; these included the fortresses at Leicester, Groby, Thirsk, Malzeard, Framlingham and Bungay.

At the beginning of November, more by coincidence than design, fresh tribute was paid to Henry's great prestige in Europe by the presence at Westminster, on the twelfth of the month, of embassies from Manuel Comnenus, the Greek emperor; from Frederick Barbarossa, the German emperor; from Henry of Saxony; from the archbishop of Rheims; from Philip of Flanders; and from the kings of Castile and Navarre. All of these appeared at a formal gathering, before which the ambassadors from Spain made a request which showed the esteem in which Henry's learning and statecraft were held. The two kings of Castile and Navarre had decided to refer a longstanding quarrel over their boundaries to the judgement of the king of England: a proposal to which Henry agreed.[11] Both the emperors had probably sent envoys in search of assistance, since they had each suffered severe military reverses, Manuel at Myrokephalon, and Barbarossa at Legnano, but Henry was loath to commit himself.[12]

If at the end of a busy year, Henry found himself at Nottingham with only Geoffrey and John, there was very little to give him cause for concern. Richard was master of Aquitaine, and Geoffrey had done well in Brittany, although there was a hint of trouble ahead in a dispute over the wardship of an important heiress, niece of Ralph de Déols, since the latter refused to surrender his guardianship of her and her lands. He himself had ordained well for England, and in the course of the year had journeyed widely throughout the realm enforcing the forest laws and inspecting the state of the land. At a council at Northampton on January 15 of the following year (1177), no great enactments seemed necessary: a few minor problems were despatched, and a messenger from Philip of Flanders was received. The count demanded the promised support for the crusade, and sought advice over Louis' suggestion of marrying his son and nephew to Philip's nieces. Henry answered the latter request by advising a delay until he himself could find suitable bridegrooms for them. The only major administrative operation of the year was an inquiry into the extent of the feudal services owed to the king, which was carried out by the sheriffs in accordance with instructions issued in council at Winchester on February 22.

At the same gathering, Henry issued orders for all his tenants-in-chief to be at London by May 8 to go on active service in Normandy. Matters had not been going entirely in his favour during the winter. Richard continued to be successful; but Ralph de Déols persisted in refusing to transfer his niece into the king's wardship, and the young king had been ordered to seize his estates. Since this involved the invasion of Berry and the taking of Chateauroux—lands to which Louis laid claim—renewed war with France seemed imminent. Henry actively encouraged this later in the year by laying claim to the dowry of Louis' daughters, the Vexin and Bourges, which, he said, had not yet been fully paid, ignoring his own failure to marry Richard to Alice as had been agreed.

Meanwhile, on March 13, 1177, the proceedings between Castile and Navarre opened in London. Before a huge crowd of noble envoys from both realms and most of his own magnates, Henry sat in Westminster Hall to hear the case. The envoys, unfortunately, spoke with a strong accent, which rendered their Latin difficult to northern ears, and Henry was obliged to request that their claims be put in writing. When this was done, the king pronounced judgement, finding both Sancho of Navarre and Alfonso of Castile* to some degree in the wrong, and commanding that restitution be made. The case was perhaps of little legal difficulty, but the choice of Henry as arbiter, and the execution of the judgement, added greatly to his stature among European rulers.[13]

Another foreign embassy arrived in Easter week, in the person of the count of Flanders, who sought leave from Henry at Canterbury to go on pilgrimage to Jerusalem without him. Henry, who seems to have had no real intention of going to the East at this period, readily granted the request, and gave him a small subsidy that he had asked for at the end of the previous year. Various

* Alfonso was Henry's son-in-law, having married Eleanor, his second daughter.

English barons, including the earl of Essex and Hugh de Lacy, joined him. The date of the assembly of the army for the expedition across the Channel was deferred until June 2, while Henry travelled to Wye for Easter. At a council at Winchester on his return, he once again changed the guardians of the English castles, replacing the holders by trusted members of his own household. Arrangements for a visit to Ireland by John were made, and this was followed up by the conference at Oxford at which John was made lord of Ireland and the administration was revised. Just as Henry was about to leave for France with the forces gathered at Winchester, news came of the return of Joanna's escort from Sicily. Wishing to hear from their own lips an account of their journey, Henry again postponed the departure of the army until July 1, and went to meet them. Meanwhile, Queen Margaret, who was expecting a child, was sent to Normandy to join her husband. However, she made her way, without Henry's permission, to her father at Paris. Here she gave birth to a son on June 19. The child, heir to the English throne after the young king, died three days later; there were no more offspring of the match.

It was not until August 17, 1177, that Henry finally embarked. A further council at Winchester on July 1 had agreed to wait for Louis' answer, and had taken special precautions against the castles of Hugh of Durham, who was suspected of an intrigue with Scotland. The king had then gone to Stansted near Portsmouth to spend a few days hawking on the Sussex downs.[14] But an old wound in his leg gave him trouble,[15] and he had returned to Winchester for treatment. Eventually, hearing nothing from Louis, he embarked and joined his eldest son in Normandy, reaching Rouen on September 11, in his company. Here they met Cardinal Peter, the papal legate, who threatened an interdict on Henry's whole empire unless Richard married Alice. A conference was rapidly arranged with Louis, and at Nonancourt on September 25 agreement was reached under the shadow of the cardinal's threat. The French and English kings agreed to go on a joint crusade and to become allies. The disputes over the Auvergne and Berry were reserved for arbitration, and elaborate arrangements for the mutual safety of the two kingdoms were made. Richard was to marry Alice, although no date was fixed for the ceremony.

Although the Berry question was *sub judice*, Henry was still free to pursue the kinsmen of Ralph de Deols who were illegally detaining the heiress. The young king was despatched to take immediate action. Henry, summoning the Norman host to Argentan on October 9, followed soon afterwards and rapidly disposed of the resistance, taking Chateauroux, capturing the heiress, and advancing into the Limousin to deal the final blow to the rebellion. Soon afterwards a conference was held at Gracay over the Auvergne question, which referred the matter to the tribunal on Berry appointed at Nonancourt. Henry then returned to Anjou, where he negotiated with the count of La Marche for the purchase of the latter's lands, since the count had no heir and wished to raise money to go on crusade. The agreement did not take full effect, since half the country was already in the hands of Henry's old opponents from Poitou, the Lusignans, and Henry had no opportunity of enforcing his rights. To round off this series of negotiations, Geoffrey and Richard contributed successes in Brittany and Aquitaine respectively. At the huge feast held at Angers that Christmas, Henry and his three sons could feel satisfied with the condition of the Angevin lands: internal order was secure, and all the domains were prosperous. A remarkable instance of the solidarity of Henry's empire was the issue of a general edict concerning forfeiture, applicable with equal force in Normandy, Anjou, Brittany and Aquitaine. No king since Charlemagne could have issued such a decree and seen that it was everywhere observed.

The year 1178 was the least eventful in the whole of Henry's reign. Apart from the sending, in conjunction with Louis, of a joint commission to suppress the Cathar heresy in Toulouse, and the appointment of new personnel in Normandy, little occurred in France before he left on July 15. The only major occasion during the rest of the year was a formal court at Woodstock on August 6, for the knighting of his son Geoffrey. The latter was the first to receive the honour from his father's hand, since the young king had been knighted by William the Marshal, his master-in-arms, and Richard by Louis, both during the rebellion of 1173-4. One reform was promulgated during the autumn, reducing the number of justices from eighteen itinerant officials to five permanently resident at court; experience had shown that too many hands at such work tended to lead to confusion and excessive severity. Any cases that were too difficult for the new tribunal could be referred immediately to the king. The itinerant justices, however, continued to visit the counties, but with lesser standing, and performing more administrative than legal work.

Christmas 1178 found the king and his sons apart once more; the young king was in Normandy, and Richard in Poitou where he continued to find rebels to suppress. The Poitevin barons were notoriously dissident, but their numerous revolts in face of Richard's continued success in the field suggest that his rule was harsh. The young king returned to England about March 11, 1179, and was with his father at Easter. Soon afterwards, a council was held at Windsor, an event noteworthy for the absence of Richard de Lucy, Henry's great collaborator. Feeling that his end was near, de Lucy had retired to the monastery of Lesnes, which he had founded in memory of Becket. At the council a new solution to problem of the administration of justice was put forward, by which England was divided into four circuits, each with five judges, an increase over the 1176 arrangement. Of the immediate fate of the central tribunal of 1178 little is known; it survived in some form both as a fixed court at Westminster, and as a body which assisted the justiciar during the king's absences. The chief catalyst in producing the change was the misbehaviour of the sheriffs, and it therefore seems that the judges were chiefly concerned with inquiries into their affairs, especially since three bishops (Winchester, Ely and Bath) were among those appointed, and clergy were not allowed to hear cases involving a blood-sentence (maiming or hanging) which a normal circuit would have involved.

The young king left his father to go into Normandy soon after May 20, in answer to a summons to the coronation of the son of Louis of France, Philip Augustus, now fifteen. Louis had cherished an ambition of securing the succession by having his son crowned during his own lifetime since 1172; and this was about to be fulfilled. But a little before the appointed date, Philip had lost his way out hunting, and wandered all night in the forest, catching a chill which became a dangerous fever. Louis, distraught with anxiety, hastened to the shrine of St Thomas, postponing the coronation. He landed at Dover on August 22 with a magnificent retinue, and was met by Henry. Together, the kings knelt before the tomb of Becket, who had been the central figure in both their lives for so many years. Louis made rich offerings and returned as swiftly as he had come, to find the prince well on his way to recovery. He accordingly fixed a new date, November 1, 1179, for the ceremony; but before this, he himself was paralysed by a stroke, and was absent on the day of the coronation. Henry's eldest son, himself a king, attending as the equal and not the vassal of the new ruler of France, held the crown over the head of Philip Augustus. Richard and Geoffrey were also present,[16] and the count of Flanders acted as swordbearer. In effect, Philip's reign began from the day he was crowned, for his father never recovered sufficiently to take an active part in the government again. Henry had perhaps been told by Gerald the Welshman of the prophecy made to him, then a student in Paris, on the night of Philip's birth in 1165: 'Tonight a child is born to us who will surely be a hammer to your king and curtail his power and lands.'[17] If he had remembered the saying, he might not have prayed so earnestly with Louis at Canterbury; for the new king was indeed to open a new era for France.

O

10

Absalom

THE FIRST action of the new king of France, in the early
months of 1180, was to dismiss his father's councillors. Louis,
paralysed and in no condition to take part in affairs of state, lay
helpless while his son followed the advice of Philip of Flanders,
who had returned from crusade, and had turned to diplomatic
affairs in earnest. However, the men thus deprived of their influence and position appealed to Henry for help against the count's
machinations. By the end of the winter the situation was such, in
spite of a conciliatory embassy which reached Paris on March 5,
1180, that preparations for war were necessary. The young king,
who had come to England to take an oath of obedience to his
father, returned to Normandy with Henry within a fortnight of
landing. Here they met the uncle of the new French king, Theobald of Blois, and other dissident French nobles who wished them to
intervene, and about the beginning of May both sides summoned
their forces. Philip Augustus did not improve chances of a reconciliation by going to Flanders just after Easter where he married
Isabella of Hainault, niece of the count of Flanders, despite the
latter's promise to Henry to take his advice over finding her a
husband. The count then designated Philip Augustus as his heir in
Flanders, with the result that Henry now had very real cause for
concern. Although no formal agreement had been made, the understanding of 1176, that the Flemish ruler, as an ally of Henry's,
would consult him on all major issues, was still regarded by the
Angevin as binding.

No actual fighting occurred, yet the tension continued un-
relaxed. Philip Augustus had arranged for the coronation of him-

self and his wife at Sens on June 8, Whit Sunday; but the count
of Flanders, fearing that something might intervene to prevent
this, persuaded his son-in-law to move the date forward to May 29
at Montmartre. In so doing, Philip Augustus offended another
French magnate, the archbishop of Rheims, for he had the ceremony performed by Guy of Sens. This added to the dissatisfaction
within his own realm, which was aggravated by a quarrel between
the young French king and his mother over the guardianship of the
castles which had formed her dowry. Louis had by now formally
transferred his powers to his son and surrendered his seal, and
could play no part in all this.

The Henry was anxious to settle these difficulties, for he saw no
benefit to be gained by war which could not be equally well attained by diplomacy. At a conference at Gisors on June 28, 1180,
he acted as mediator between Philip Augustus and his relatives,
arranging a settlement with the queen-mother in face of opposition
from the count of Flanders and the marshal of France. To ensure
peace, the count did homage to Henry in return for a subsidy of
1,000 marks per annum, promising to provide 500 knights to
serve for forty days when so required. Furthermore the treaty made
between Louis and Henry at Nonancourt was renewed, with
Philip Augustus' name in place of his father's, but omitting all
mention of the projected crusade. Shortly afterwards, on September 18, Louis died, and his son was now full master of France in
title as well as deed.

The remainder of the year was spent by Henry in Normandy;
a brief interview with Philip Augustus at Gisors to confirm the
peace took place on September 29. Otherwise, the Angevin
domains continued to reap the benefits of peace; even Poitou and
Brittany were relatively quiet. In the early part of 1180, at a
council at Oxford in March, Henry had ordered a reform of the
English coinage, both to encourage trade and to provide revenue
for the royal treasury. A moneyer from Tours was appointed to
carry it out by November 11. The resulting coins contained 95 per
cent of silver as opposed to 90 per cent in the old 'Tealby' pennies,
and the profits derived from coining them and exchanging the old
coins were put into the hands of royal officials, whereas previously
there had been numerous independent mints throughout the

country authorised to strike coinage.[1] The short cross pennies remained the only coins in circulation until 1247; once more, even in minor matters, Henry's work proved durable, and sterling began to assume increasing importance as a currency of international repute. Whether this entirely solved his financial problems seems doubtful, for the seizure of Roger of York's property on his death the following year can only be interpreted as a fiscal measure. The excuse given—that wills leaving goods to charity made by bishops after they fell ill were invalid—was pure cynicism on Henry's part.[2]

Just before the end of the year, further bad news arrived from Flanders. The count, having until now played a negative role, usually following Henry's advice, was beginning to grow restive, as events in the spring had shown, and he now broke yet again the agreement over the marriage of his nieces by giving the last two to the counts of Gelders and Louvain. After spending Christmas at Le Mans, Henry gave orders for a general assize of arms—a survey of equipment possessed by feudal tenants—throughout his continental domains. This was in preparation for measures against Flanders. All landowners whose property yielded more than £100 Angevin per annum were to equip themselves with horse and arms, the latter comprising a mailed tunic, shield, sword and lance. All other men were to accoutre themselves with leather jerkin, helmet and either lance or sword or bow and arrows; and all such equipment was to be passed from father to son.[3] These measures were at once imitated by Philip Augustus and Philip of Flanders; both realised that with so skilled an adversary their only hope was to hold him in check by copying his devices, rather than attempt to outmanoeuvre him. Louis had never seriously tried to compete with his mighty vassal, being a gentle and peace-loving man by nature; his son was of different mettle, and initiated a general policy in administration and finance based on that of Henry.

Neither side, however, was prepared for war. A conference at Gué St Remy on April 27, 1181, settled matters between France and England for the moment and even produced a closer understanding than before. Henry intended to leave for England immediately after this, going to Barfleur at once; but trouble in Flanders detained him. The count had quarrelled with the lord of

Clermont over the possession of a castle, and proceeded to besiege
it in spite of the French king's prohibition. The latter appealed to
Henry for advice. Acting once again as mediator, the English king
succeeded in making a temporary peace at Gisors before sailing for
England on July 26.

On landing, he at once made for Canterbury, where he paid
the by now customary visit to Becket's shrine. He then set out on a
comprehensive tour of the island, in the course of which he issued
an assize of arms on very similar lines to that in force in France, requiring in addition a general oath of loyalty.[4] This act withdrew
some military power and responsibility from the barons, and
broadened the scope of the king's claims on his subjects in this
sphere.

The increase of English influence, which threatened to develop
into an alliance which might cherish ambitions outside France,
still displeased Count Philip of Flanders. He therefore attempted
to persuade the German emperor to form an alliance with him.
This came to nothing, but did not damp the count's determination for action, and in November he proceeded to attack the eastern
borders of the French king's lands, obtaining the homage of the
count of Sancerre and the support of the duke of Burgundy and the
countess of Champagne. All that resulted was an apparent strengthening of the dreaded alliance; for Henry's three sons went to the
aid of the king of France and in a rapid winter campaign reduced
the count and his accomplices to submission.

Henry, who spent the Christmas of 1181 at Winchester,
tried to cross to France as soon as this news reached him. Contrary
winds, however, delayed him until March 3, when he was able to
cross from Portsmouth to Barfleur. Before leaving, he made his will.
His realms were at peace, his health unimpaired, so the reasons for
this were best known to himself. In it he made charitable bequests
to the religious causes and orders in which he had been especially
interested. Ten thousand pounds went to the crusaders; and general
gifts to all the religious houses of England and Normandy were
accompanied by special bequests to the abbeys of Cluny, Marmoutier, Marcilli, Premontré and Arroaise. An unusual clause was

the provision of sums to provide dowries for poor women; one is half-inclined to suspect that Henry had in mind the 'washerwomen' who had always attended his court on its travels, ministering to the king's amours rather than his linen.[5]

Although the king probably did not foresee it, he could hardly have chosen a more apt moment to make his testament, for the long years of peace were drawing to a close, and he was not to see England again with an easy mind. At first events were favourable: a permanent treaty was reached between France and Flanders at a conference on April 4, 1182. The count of Flanders had to surrender Amiens and the claim to the count of Clermont's homage, and renounce once more all alliances with Henry's sons dating from the time of the great rebellion. Otherwise matters were to remain as before the outbreak of hostilities.[6]

Henry then turned to deal with a problem which had been on his mind for some time. The emperor of Germany, Frederick Barbarossa, had long distrusted the king of England's son-in-law, Henry the Lion, duke of Saxony, and in 1179 had accused him of neglecting his duty during an invasion of Italy, with the result that Lombardy had been lost. Further, he had engaged in private war against the archbishop of Cologne, and had plotted against Frederick with the Byzantine emperor. The Saxon duke realised that he could not escape conviction at the royal court, and chose not to appear. As a result, on January 6, 1180, a sentence of forfeiture of his domains was pronounced against him. This was followed in November 1181 by a decree of seven years' banishment, since he refused to swear obedience to the emperor's son in the event of Barbarossa's death on crusade; Duke Henry held that the Holy Roman Emperor was chosen by election and not by the rules of hereditary succession. Henry Plantagenet had been unable to intervene in the previous sentence, but he now sent the earl of Aumale to plead for the duke, and was successful in obtaining the reduction of the sentence from seven years to one. The duke left Germany in July, bringing with him Matilda and his sons Lothar and Otto; the latter, in a strange reversal of fate, was to become emperor in 1198. He arrived in Normandy about the end of August, when he met Henry at Chinon, and here the Saxons remained, for their sentence of exile was renewed the next year. Only in 1185, after the pope had intervened on their behalf, did they return. Matilda came to England briefly in 1184, visiting her mother in her semi-confinement at Berkhamstead.[7]

Minor rebellions in Poitou and Brittany broke out in the latter part of the year. Ranulf Glanville, since 1180 justiciar of England and Henry's chief officer, conducted the campaign to suppress them. At the great court held at Caen at Christmas 1182, Henry's chief concern was not these minor troubles, but a recurrence of the old quarrel with his heir over the latter's part in the government. The young king had spent four years, between 1176-80, in a series of great tournaments in northern France, with no thought of politics, while his brothers Richard and Geoffrey were serving a hard apprenticeship in real warfare. His nature was better suited to such diversions than to more serious work. Universally popular, he was on the other hand too easily swayed by flatterers and bad counsellors.[8] During these years, the presence of William the Marshal—a man of no particular position but outstanding in character—had prevented him from getting into too much trouble. He had been the leading spirit of a chivalric movement reflected by the new romances of Chrétien de Troyes and the lais of Marie de France. In later days, William, telling his story to a poet who recorded it for us in vivid words, was to look back on these days as a high summer of knightly ideals, in contrast with the troubles of Henry III's reign:

> It was the young king who revived chivalry, for she was
> dead, or almost so. He was the door through which she entered,
> her standard-bearer. In those days, the magnates did nothing
> for young men; he set an example and kept men of worth
> about him. And when the men of high rank saw how he as-
> sembled all men of worth, they were astonished at his wisdom,
> and copied his example. The count of Flanders did likewise,
> and so horses and arms, lands and money were distributed to
> young men of valour. Nowadays the great have put chivalry
> and largesse in prison once more; the life of knights-errants
> and tourneys is abandoned in favour of lawsuits.[9]

The younger sons of great families had little share in their lands or wealth and, apart from a career in the Church, they could make their own way in the world only by such means as tournaments, with the accompanying profits from ransoms. The Marshal himself was in that position; and this was the positive contribution of chivalry, encouraged especially by the generosity of the count of Flanders. From this period also dates the evolution of formal rules for jousting (which survived into the sixteenth century), the use of enclosed lists, and the widespread employment of shields and devices. But this make-believe world also encouraged spendthrifts and loose living, and was no substitute for the harder training of real warfare. Here individual prowess and personal charm were more important than clear thinking and foresight; and here the young king was at home.

On his accession to the French throne, Philip Augustus discouraged tournaments in his realms, as Henry had done in his. With the count of Flanders now intent on playing politics seriously, the devotees of jousting found times difficult. The young king returned to real warfare for a time in 1181, helping the French against his erstwhile patron of Flanders; but by the end of the following year he was once more restive, given to visiting the court of France where the new king encouraged his dissatisfaction. Although Henry had all his sons with him at that glittering court held at Christmas 1182, storms were plainly brewing. The young king's return from France had cost Henry the promise of a large pension, but no mention had been made of any fief. William the Marshal had fallen into his master's disfavour; he was unable to win sympathy from either the young king or his father when he appeared and offered to do trial by battle at odds of three to one to disprove the slanders alleged against him. All he could obtain was a safe-conduct to the borders of Henry's lands.[10]

On New Year's Day, 1183, Henry attempted a new method of appeasement. Reversing his earlier policy, perhaps with hopes of appealing to his son's vanity, he made Geoffrey do homage to his elder brother. Richard was also asked to do so, but refused, because of a quarrel over a castle which he had built at Clairvaux. The young king claimed that this stood on land belonging to him, and Richard as strenuously denied the charge. The meeting broke up inconclusively, and Richard returned to Poitou, where he

fortified his castles in readiness for the now expected civil war.
Sent by Henry to quell Richard's pride, the young king found
allies in the Poitevin barons, who, always ready to stir up difficulties, accused Richard of misgovernment and encouraged his eldest
brother to invade Poitou on their behalf. This he did, assisted by
Geoffrey, and bitter fighting ensued. Even before this broke out,
Bertran de Born had written a political attack on both the young
king for not acting against Richard, and on the latter for misgovernment.[11] Although de Born is not quite accurate about the
reasons for the war, the contrasting characters of the brothers are
sharply drawn:

> A new sirventes, singer! Music ho!
> I'll cry abroad the young king's latest deed:
> His father ordered him to quit at once
> His claim against his brother Richard's lands,
> And he obeyed him! Henry, landless king,
> For it I crown you king of cowards!

> A coward surely, now you live like this
> On paid and promised money; not the peer
> Of heroes such as fought in other years.
> And, men of Poitou, he betrays your trust;
> He lies to you and leaves you penniless.

> Sir Richard may not want my good advice;
> But, heed it or not, I'll tell him this:
> Although your brother is no threat to you,
> You ought to treat your loyal liegemen well,
> And stop the pillage of their lands and crops,
> Don't take their castles on the least excuse!

> And then, for all I care, the younger king
> Can stay and joust at Flemish tournaments!
> If only Geoffrey, noble duke of Brittany,
> Had been the eldest of the English princes;
> For he's a better ruler than you both!

Henry, as he assessed reports reaching him in Normandy, realised that things were not likely to go well for Richard. He was unwilling to let the young king and Geoffrey make their own terms, and therefore came with a large army to Limoges which was the centre of his eldest son's operations. Arriving at Easter, he encamped for a protracted siege, blockading the town. A fierce contest ensued; Henry himself was twice shot at, and the young king did not scruple to use deceit to keep his father from aiding Richard against the rest of Poitou. Although Henry received him warmly when he came to offer submission, the young king, who had pretended to assume the cross, threw off this guise, attacked the party sent by his father to receive hostages, and declared openly for the Poitevin barons. Further attempts by Henry to win him back met with no success: the next mission sent to the young king under temporary truce were either killed or wounded in his presence by his partisans. Geoffrey behaved similarly; and soon afterwards, when he came to Henry to propose peace, this proved to be no more than a feint by which he was able, as he returned through the town, to plunder the abbey of St Martial of its most precious treasures in order to pay his Brabantine mercenaries.[12] Both brothers then left the town and carried fire and sword into other parts of Aquitaine, while Henry, fearing lest the revolt should spread to Normandy and England, ordered that the ringleaders of the 1173 rebellion should be placed under close surveillance. He himself remained before Limoges, which still held out.

The young king took Aixe on May 23. Undeterred by an excommunication issued against all disturbers of the peace by the Norman bishops on May 26—which in any case exempted him personally—he continued southwards in search of booty but fell sick at Uzerche. Recovering quickly, he found himself critically short of money, and made for the nearest shrine of importance, that of St Amadour at Rocamadour, which he plundered systematically, even replacing the sword of the Frankish hero Roland by his own. However, the sickness that had attacked him proved to be more than the passing effect of the summer heat. Retracing his steps, he was forced to halt again at Martel, where his condition grew so serious that he recognised the approach of death. Sending for his father, he lay in a fever of body and conscience. Henry was dissuaded from obeying his instinctive grief as a father and hastening to his son's side, lest the message prove to be a trick. Instead a bishop was sent, with a precious ring that had once belonged to Henry I as token of his mission. The prelate arrived just in time. On June 7, the young king, at last in earnest, made his confession, first in private and later before his assembled followers. For another four days he lingered on. He sent a messenger to his father to crave mercy for his supporters, for his mother, Queen Eleanor, and for his wife, Queen Margaret; and to request that his body be buried at Rouen. On June 11, lying on a bed of ashes with stones at his head and feet in token of deep repentance, he asked that the crusader's cloak he had once so lightly assumed should be put on him in high seriousness, and within a few hours he was dead.[13] At his side stood William the Marshal, who had received his master's forgiveness a few days before, and was now charged with accomplishing the vow to go on Crusade which death had prevented the young king from carrying out.[14]

'Nothing in his life became him like the leaving it'; and with the news of the younger Henry's death, the memory of his treacheries and sacrileges yielded in men's minds to the nobler image of his few virtues: his chivalry, charm and generosity. Even Bertran de Born laid aside his wonted vitriol to write an elegant and moving 'planh' in his memory:[15]

> Now every grief and woe and bitterness,
> The sum of tears that this sad century's shed,
> Seem light against the death of the young king,
> And prowess mourns, youth stands sorrowful;
> No man rejoices in these bitter days.
>
> All pride in battle, skill in song and rhyme
> Must yield to sorrow's humble threnody,
> For cruel death, that mortal warrior,
> Has harshly taken from us the best of knights:
> Beside him charity itself was mean,
> And in him every noble virtue shone.

So pray we all that God in his great grace
May grant His pardon to the young English king,
Who yesterday was most valiant knight;
Now he is fallen to the great lord Death
And leaves us naught but chagrin and despair.

Stories of the young Henry's last hours began to circulate; he was soon revered as blessed; it was said that such was the strength of his filial repentance that, when a bishop remonstrated with him for wearing a jewel in the hour of death, the one ring on his hand, that sent by his father, could not be removed. Cures were reputedly wrought by his relics, and a church was built in memory of one of these miracles. By the time the funeral cortège reached Le Mans, the young king's reputation was such that the citizens seized the body and forcibly interrèd it in the church of St Julian where his grandfather Geoffrey lay. Henry had to order its disinterment to comply with his son's wish to be buried at Rouen. The ceremony took place on June 22, 1183.[16] Whether Henry was present is not recorded; but if he were, his emotions must have been tempered by political considerations. If the speech reported to have been made by him to his son's followers is genuine, he was not afraid to say that his son's death was a cause for rejoicing as far as the good of his realm was concerned; but his private grief was deep.[17] When William the Marshal came to him and told him the news, he had said simply: 'I trust in God for his salvation'; and on being asked to pay his son's debts, he did so, commenting: 'He has cost me enough, but I wish he had lived to cost me more.'[18] The Angevins loved and hated with equal fervour, and Henry had been as full of kindness as his son had been of hatred. But both father and son knew well that public policy came before private quarrels, and hence Henry had seemed to be the one who lacked affection until the last weeks of his son's life. None of those close to the king could find much good to say of his son as a statesman, and such praise as they bestowed was for his manner rather than his deeds.

'Then the world became quiet "with the passing of Python".'[19] Limoges fell on June 24; Richard dispatched his brother's fleeing mercenaries with the aid of the king of Aragon. Geoffrey made his peace with the king and the new heir at Angers on July 3. The implications of the new situation had yet to be worked out. Henry showed at once, however, that he trusted Richard no more than his dead brother by confiscating all his castles in Poitou. That Henry now had a chance to remedy his earlier mistakes of policy regarding his heir was plain; it only remained to see how he used it. Richard was very different from his brother; a leader by force of character rather than charm, schooled in the harsh arena of the Poitevin revolts, he was at once more obstinate and a more skilled and clear-thinking opponent, almost a match for his father in energy and cunning. Peace might cost more than a few promises and a tearful reconciliation next time.

11

They that take the Sword . . .

FOLLOWING HIS eldest son's death, Henry put forward the new solution for the disposal of the Angevin empire after his own death at a meeting with his sons in Normandy in September 1183. Ranulf Glanville and John were summoned from England; Eleanor was released from custody for the first time in a decade, although she arrived too late for the gathering. Henry's response to the new situation was simple. Richard should hold the lands intended for his eldest brother—Normandy, Anjou and England—and be suzerain of Brittany, Aquitaine, Scotland, Wales and Ireland. Geoffrey should continue to hold Brittany, but with Richard as overlord; and John, previously without a major portion, should hold Aquitaine from Richard. No attempt was to be made to have Richard crowned.[1] Henry felt that this had been the root of much of the trouble with the young king, and now preferred to associate his heir with him in the government of his realms without a definite position and title, since coronation, as the young king had argued, could be regarded as a surrender of his own rights.

Unfortunately, Henry had failed to consult with Richard as to whether the arrangements suited him. There were powerful arguments in favour of Henry's disposition of his lands. Richard would hold the central block of territory, through which all communications to the outlying parts must pass, and would be in a strong position to crush any attempts at concerted revolt by John and Geoffrey. However, Richard did not see matters in this way. Less farsighted than his father, he considered only the immediate past and future. He was being asked to surrender his duchy of Aquitaine in exchange for a position with even less opportunities for action than that of the young king. Aquitaine had been his own preoccupation for the past ten years. However unpopular he was, all his restless energy had been directed towards the settlement of the duchy, whether suppressing the continual internecine wars between the barons, putting down rebellions against his own authority, or arranging more peaceful matters of finance and government. He felt an affection for these warm southern lands which the north could never replace for him; although Norman in physical appearance, with no trace of his mother's southern blood, at heart he was far closer to her and her country than to his father. It was this irrational feeling that Henry could not appreciate; his cold and calculating intellect was readier to find enthusiasm for an abstract justice than for the living people of his lands.

Richard, when faced with his father's demand, asked for three days' grace to consider the matter. He used this respite to escape to Poitou and gather forces to resist his father, sending a messenger to say that he would never surrender Aquitaine. This alone was serious enough. Richard appeared to be the young king's heir in rebellion as well as in lands and titles. But in addition there were difficulties with the French king as well. As soon as the news of the death of Henry's eldest son reached him, Philip Augustus at once reclaimed the dowry of Margaret, his half-sister, and widow of the young king. This comprised the vital border area known as the Norman Vexin, and Gisors, which Henry had held for twenty-three years. Henry replied by claiming that the Vexin had come to him through Eleanor, and sent her to visit this area in support of his argument. As for Gisors, it was his in any case, and Louis had quitclaimed him of all French rights over it except overlordship. He declared himself ready to take the matter to Philip's own court.

In the course of the autumn, however, both questions were settled without renewed cataclysms. Henry did not press the demand for the surrender of Aquitaine when he heard of Richard's action, and allowed him to retain the duchy for the meanwhile. But John had always been his favourite son, and it seemed inevitable that some provision would have to be made for him from the lands either ruled by Richard or to which he was heir. The Vexin problem was settled peacefully, at a conference near Gisors

on December 6, 1183. In return for Henry's actual homage to the
French king, which, although admitted in treaties, the English
king had never ceremonially performed, and an allowance of
£2,700 Angevin for Philip Augustus' half-sister, Henry was
allowed to retain these lands. As for Gisors, Philip, by an ingen-
ious move, used this as a source of future attacks on Henry by
making it the dowry of his other half-sister, Alice, to whom
Richard was betrothed. This match had been arranged at Nonancourt in 1177, but there had been no move on Richard's part to
solemnise the marriage. Alice had remained in the custody of her
prospective father-in-law at Winchester.

Henry's satisfaction with his great work in the sphere of government became evident during the two years of relative peace that
followed. In the hands of such experts in law and finance as Ranulf
Glanville, Walter of Coutances, and Richard Fitz-Neale in England, William Fitz-Ralph and William du Hommet in Normandy, and Stephen of Tours in Anjou—a group of administrators
without parallel in the western world—the government was efficient
and strong. The system by which they ruled was no stereotyped,
formal machinery, but could be adapted by its creator to the needs
of the moment. Now Henry felt that there was little more he
could do, and no major legislation appeared for the rest of his
reign. The Forest Assize of November 1184 was little more than
a reiteration of existing usages for the benefit of commissions of
inspection.[2] Otherwise, these last years were notable for two great
works (perhaps officially encouraged but inspired elsewhere) on the
government of England written by senior royal officials as a record
of legal and financial practice as they had known it: *De Legibus
Angliae* (On the Laws of England) attributed to the justiciar,
Ranulf Glanville, and *Dialogus de Scaccario* (Dialogue on the Exchequer) composed by Richard Fitz-Neal. From these two books
there emerges the first reasonably complete picture of the workings
of medieval secular government. Much of the structure had been
inherited by Henry, and his work had been to remove the an-
omalies and make good the defects. Nowhere in either book is
there any doubt as to the procedure in any particular case. The
regulations are laid down with a precision previously impossible,

and show a striking advance from the first systematic attempts at recording law made under Henry's grandftaher.

Reverting to his old role as mediator, Henry once again settled a dispute between Philip Augustus and the count of Flanders, at a conference at Choisy on June 5, 1184. The French king had married Isabella of Hainault on the understanding that he was to inherit the Vermandois if Philip of Flanders died without a male heir. But the countess of Flanders had died, and the count wished to marry the princess of Portugal. This revived his hope of a son and successor, and no provision had been made in the marriage treaty for this contingency. The French king therefore claimed that the count should hand over the Vermandois before he remarried. Although Henry had been responsible for arranging the match, he upheld the French claim and declared a truce for one year from midsummer.

Returning to England, events in Wales claimed his attention. Rhys ap Griffith was proving troublesome once more, and it was doubtful how long he would remain loyal to Henry, who therefore demanded his homage and assembled an army to bring him to submission. The mere threat proved enough, and Rhys appeared at Worcester in July 1184, where he did fealty and promised hostages, which however failed to appear. A further summons later in the year was no more effective. Henry was too preoccupied to take action for the moment, and let the matter rest.

Various embassies arrived at this time seeking Henry's favour. From Scotland, William the Lion sent to ask for the hand of Henry's granddaughter, Matilda of Saxony, a request which Henry granted subject to the pope's permission, because the two were related within the prohibited degrees. The archbishop of Cologne and Philip of Flanders came in August on pilgrimage to Canterbury, where Henry reconciled the archbishop with his son-in-law, Henry of Saxony. He arranged through the archbishop the betrothal of Richard to the emperor's daughter, completely disregarding the match with Alice confirmed at the end of the previous year. He perhaps intended that John should marry Alice, and was more interested in the possible alliance with the emperor than worried by repercussions which were bound to arise with

P

France. The matter was resolved by the death of Richard's new
fiancée later in the year. About the same time, Henry was successful in obtaining the emperor's pardon for Henry the Lion, through
an embassy headed by the archdeacon of Lisieux. The duke returned to Germany in the following year, taking Matilda and his
eldest son, but leaving his younger children with their grandfather.

The chief events of the remainder of the year were connected with ecclesiastical affairs. Both the sees of Canterbury and
York were vacant and, towards the end of November, Henry summoned an elective assembly to his court. In addition to the bishops,
the canons of York and the monks of Canterbury, this splendid
gathering included Richard, Geoffrey and John, Eleanor and
Matilda and her husband. Matters did not go smoothly with the
Canterbury election, the prior and monks claiming that the right
of election was theirs alone, and that the bishops had no business
to express an opinion. The result of the first meeting was a double
election, the prior and monks choosing Theobald of Ostia, the
bishops Baldwin of Worcester; and Henry had to apply some co-
ercion to obtain, a fortnight later, the unanimous choice of the
latter.[3] Meanwhile, formal peace had been made between his sons,
and Geoffrey left for Normandy with those responsible for its
defence. Henry evidently hoped that Richard and John, left with
their mother, might reach some agreement over her southern duchy.
But after another court at Windsor at Christmas 1184, at which
many magnates were present, Richard obtained leave to go back to
Poitou. No solution had been reached.

Early in the New Year, Henry received an important and
not entirely unexpected visitor from Palestine. The Angevin house
ruled there as well, Henry's grandfather Fulk having abdicated and
spent the last years of his life on crusade in the Holy Land, winning the crown of Jerusalem by marrying the only daughter of the
previous ruler. Hence in the crisis following Saladin's new invasions and the accession of Baldwin V, who was a leper, it was
natural that an appeal for help should be made to Henry. Heraclius,
patriarch of Jerusalem, and the grand master of the Knights
Hospitaller reached England in March 1185. Henry went to meet
them in Reading, where they presented him with letters from Pope
Lucius III urging a new crusade, and the patriarch made a moving

appeal for help against the infidels. At the end of his speech, he presented Henry with the keys and standard of Jerusalem, and the keys to the Holy Sepulchre. The king, however, declined to give an answer until he had taken the advice of his barons on the matter, which he did at a great council at Clerkenwell on March 18. The barons were doubtful about the project, advising him to stay at home, since this alone would provide for 'the safety of the realm' which he had sworn to preserve at his coronation. The king made no definite acceptance of this, but remained non-committal, leaving for France shortly afterwards.[4] He performed one important ceremony before his departure: the knighting of John at Windsor on March 31, before the latter went to Ireland.

In Henry's absence in England there had been fresh trouble on the eastern border of France between Philip Augustus and the count of Hainault, but this had been settled at the beginning of the year. The immediate problem was to suppress Richard's new disturbances. The Poitevin castles had been fortified by him; he had quarrelled with his brother Geoffrey, perhaps over the government of Normandy, and was carrying on a spasmodic civil war. As soon as Henry landed, he gathered an army to suppress this. Before the end of April, he had sent messengers to Richard, ordering him to surrender Aquitaine to his mother, who had just arrived in Normandy. This solution was an astute one; Eleanor, after the long emptiness of her years of captivity, was eager to take some part in the government even at her son's expense, and she still retained the affection of the barons of Aquitaine. Richard, on the other hand, had expected his mother's support. Knowing his own unpopularity, he realised that resistance was impossible. In May he yielded to his father's demand without opposition, transferring affairs to Eleanor and joining his father in Normandy. Henry, content with this triumph, at this point repeated his fatal mistake by failing to give Richard a position of responsibility, thereby reducing him to the inactivity which had finally so galled his eldest brother. Admittedly, Richard's conduct towards his father during the last year had revealed a lack of mutual trust and understanding hardly calculated to inspire Henry with confidence. But the king, for his part, must surely have seen that his son had been accustomed

for the past ten years to an active and energetic life, and was unlikely to remain quietly at his father's side. Nor can there be any
question that Henry was thinking of leaving Richard in charge
while he was on crusade. In an interview with Philip Augustus and
Heraclius, he had agreed to send men and money to Jerusalem, but
had refused to allow any of his sons, even John, to go as leader of
the expedition.

Uneasy peace prevailed throughout the summer. Henry
thought of returning to England at the beginning of the winter, a
ship being sent for him on November 1.[5] But after a conference at
Aumale on November 7, he felt that the situation was too pre-
carious for him to depart. Peace had been made between France
and Flanders on a permanent basis, with the adherence of the archbishops of Rheims and Cologne (who had taken part in the quarrel)
subject to the emperor's ratification. Although the emperor seemed
favourably inclined, the quarrel over Hainault had been settled at
the beginning of 1185 only to break out afresh. It was an area in
which four princes had an interest: Philip Augustus of France and
Philip of Flanders as claimants and immediate neighbours, Henry
and the emperor as being influenced by the outcome. Henry was
further hindered in his plans by an illness two days later, which
kept him at Belvoir castle for some weeks. Here Philip Augustus
came to visit him: a sign of the continuing friendliness between
the two kings, which had been apparent from Henry's several
successful mediations between the French monarch and his enemies. However, there still remained some outstanding obligation
which Henry had not yet settled. Perhaps because of these, perhaps
convalescing from his illness, Henry remained in Normandy all
winter, spending the Christmas of 1185 at Domfront. On March
10, 1186, at Gisors, the old questions of Queen Margaret's dower-
lands and Richard's betrothal to Alice were raised, and Henry repeated his promises of June 1183. The French king for his part
agreed to make no claims against Henry or his heirs over Gisors,
on the castle of which Henry had just spent £2,500 to make it
defensible.[6]

Before crossing the Channel, Henry provided against further
trouble on Richard's part by garrisoning Aquitaine with reliable
officers, and sending Richard himself to settle a new quarrel with

the count of Toulouse, giving him large sums of money for the purpose. Richard carried out a successful campaign, the count's appeals to France falling on deaf ears. For the moment, Philip Augustus was unwilling to interfere against Henry or his sons.

Henry landed at Southampton with Eleanor, on April 27, 1186, and spent almost a year in England. It was the last time of peace he was to enjoy. There was little business to occupy his attention: a large number of vacant bishoprics meant that a council had to be called at Woodstock in May to make elections, seven bishops and an archbishop for York being required. Some of the sees had not been filled for some time: York had been vacant since the death in 1181 of Roger Pont L'Eveque, Becket's old opponent; while Carlisle had had no bishop since 1157. The difficulties over the Canterbury election in 1184 had prevented the other archbishopric from being filled; and Carlisle remained vacant after this council, in fact until 1204.

Scottish affairs also came before the council. William the Lion had been having difficulty over a revolt in Galloway, and came south to seek Henry's aid. Henry first arranged a marriage alliance with him, by which William was to marry Henry's second cousin Ermengarde, the fate of Matilda of Saxony, his previous fiancée, not being recorded. Henry followed this by preparations at the beginning of July for an expedition to Galloway, the first military action in the north that he had led in person. However, the leader of the rebellion, Roland thought better of his conduct on hearing of the king's approach, and coming to Carlisle, made due submission.[7] By July 15, Henry was back in Worcestershire at his hunting-lodge at Feckenham. On September 5, 1186, the marriage of William and Ermengarde was celebrated at Woodstock. The rare event of a royal wedding between adults was commemorated with great splendour, the feasting lasting for four days.[8]

The autumn brought news which made Henry's peace uneasy. In August, Geoffrey of Brittany had visited Philip Augustus in Paris. There he had begun to plot against his father: the first sign that Philip was preparing to return to Louis' old policy of exploiting the innumerable petty quarrels that arose among the Angevins. But this threat vanished with Geoffrey's death on

August 19. Involved in a melée at a tournament, he had fallen
from his horse. Refusing to surrender, he was trampled on and
died from internal injuries. Philip Augustus had sent for all the
best doctors in Paris, but their skill was of no avail, and it was
given out that the prince had died of a fever similar to that which
had carried off his elder brother.[9] He was buried with all the outward signs of deep mourning before the altar of Notre Dame. The
French king was the only person who really seemed to care for
him; and it was said that he had to be restrained from leaping into
the grave.[10] Henry was not deeply moved by the news, and it
caused no great stir. Geoffrey, though skilled in military affairs,
eloquent and astute, never won men's hearts or admiration as his
elder brothers had done; he took after his Angevin grandfather, in
whose dry and ambitious nature these three qualities predomin-
ated.

    Geoffrey's death appeared at first to solve more problems
than it created. As a precaution, John was recalled from a proposed
expedition to Ireland, but the matter was not formally discussed
at Marlborough on September 14 when the prelates and some
magnates gathered to make elections to the sees of York, Salisbury
and Exeter, which had not been filled in March. Philip Augustus
was not going to be baulked of his opportunity to make trouble,
and demanded as overlord the wardship of the heiress of Brittany,
Geoffrey's daughter. Henry's ambassadors, Ranulf Glanville,
Walter of Coutances and the earl of Essex, succeeded in obtaining
a truce until January 18, 1187. Before they returned Henry
decided in council at Reading on October 9 to try to prolong the
truce until Easter.

    However, at the end of November, a small incident on the
Norman frontier provoked a major crisis. The constable of Gisors,
inspecting the state of the border in the course of his duties, came
across workmen on Philip's orders building a castle at Vaux near
Gisors. When the constable took an armed force to stop the work,
a riot ensued and the lord of Vaux was killed. The constable, feeling his position unsafe, transferred the custody of the castle to
reliable officers and took refuge with Richard. Philip was furious,
and ordered the imprisonment of all English and Normans to be
found within his domains. Henry retaliated in like manner, and

started to levy Welsh troops. Neither side was quite ready for war, and soon afterwards reparation was made. A further embassy was now sent to France, consisting of Glanville, the bishop of Rochester, and two knights, who were told by Philip Augustus that Normandy would only be safe if Richard desisted from harrying the count of Toulouse. The French king was now bent on attacking and reducing the Angevin power, as his subsequent actions showed, and the outbreak of hostilities was now only a question of time.

Henry was not anxious to engage Philip Augustus in war; more ruthless by far than his father, the French king had adopted the tactics which brought Henry such rich rewards: the use of larger forces of mercenaries in swift campaigns striking at the enemy's weakest places instead of the gradual progresses from siege to siege. Nor could Henry be sure of Richard's loyalty. Still without any great share in the government, the Toulouse expedition could not occupy him for much longer. Hence, as soon as he could in the New Year, 1187, Henry crossed to France. Leaving Dover on February 14, he was within sight of the port of Wissant, when the wind changed and forced him to return. On February 17, he managed the crossing, although many of his retinue were lost in a storm on the voyage from Shoreham to Dieppe. He at once went to Aumale, where Richard and John, Walter of Coutances and the earl of Essex, met him to report on the situation. At Philip Augustus' suggestion the kings met at Gué St Remy on April 5. The French demands proved too much for Henry. Philip was clearly eager for war, and held diplomatic weapons which Henry found hard to counter. He had also raised a revolt among the discontented Breton barons, and had high hopes of assistance from an imperial army in Lombardy. Henry could only retaliate by obtaining the service of the count of Flanders. On or about May 17, 1187, the dreaded conflict started. Henry had divided his army into four parts: Richard, John and his bastard son Geoffrey of Lincoln commanded three of these, and William earl of Essex the fourth. The campaign opened with the French king seizing Issoudun and Gracay, while Richard occupied Chateauroux. The

headquarters of the latter's army was at Déols, which the mercenaries pillaged. Hearing of the French successes, Richard gave
orders to burn Déols and the abbey, lest they should be used as a
base for an attack on Chateauroux. However, this sacrilege was
prevented by a strange incident that night. A group of frightened
townsfolk had gathered to pray before the statue of the Virgin
outside the south door, when mercenaries sacking the town before
it was burnt came and jeered at them in their habitual godless
fashion; for all who fought for pay were under formal sentence of
excommunication. One of them threw a stone at the statue, breaking the arm of the infant Jesus, which, to the terror of the onlookers, began to flow with blood, while the impious soldier was
struck dead. News of this miracle reached Chateauroux, terrifying
Richard's men. The prince countermanded his orders for the burning of town and abbey. The next evening, the statue was seen to
move and tear its veil. Richard himself, inspecting it afterwards,
was prepared to testify to this.[11] Meanwhile, Philip Augustus had
encamped nearby, and Henry had joined his sons. In view of the
miracle, and—a weightier consideration—the danger of a pitched
battle, negotiations were opened. These dragged on for three
weeks, but at last, on June 23, two cardinals, who had come from
England with Henry, were able to persuade the kings to make a
truce for two years, Philip Augustus returning such conquests as
he had made.

First efforts on Henry's part to win back Richard only led
Henry nonetheless returned home with a heavy heart. For
as soon as peace was made, Richard had gone to visit the French
king and had struck up a close friendship with him, 'eating from
the same dish and sleeping in the same bed',[12] each taking keen
delight in the other's company. This bore a close resemblance to
the friendship of the young king and Louis, which, though less
ardent, had resulted in the same strong influence of the French
king over the English heir. Philip Augustus had further cause for
rejoicing, for on September 3 Queen Isabella gave birth to his first
son, named Louis after the child's grandfather.

First efforts on Henry's part to win back Richard only led
to the latter's arrival at Chinon in the king's absence, from which
castle he carried off the treasure of Anjou before returning to
Philip Augustus. Besides this, he took a crusader's oath and as-

sumed the cross, without his father's consent. Rumours had reached him that Henry was considering making John heir to all his domains except Normandy and England. Although there was no good reason whatever for such action, Richard may have believed this in view of Henry's fondness for his youngest son. Reconciliation proved the rumours false. When Richard met his father at Angers, he was well received and no demands were made of him beyond renewing his homage. Either about this time or before his expedition to Toulouse in 1185, he had been reinstated in Aquitaine, for as soon as the meeting was over, he left for the south to suppress a revolt by the Lusignan family, who had always been among the leaders of the discontented barons. His father meanwhile took two rebel castles in Brittany, and by marrying the earl of Chester to his daughter-in-law, Constance (Geoffrey's widow), left the government of the province in strong hands.

The situation vis-à-vis France remained critical. The Lusignan rebels were reputed to be subsidised by Philip Augustus and after Christmas Henry had to meet him near Gisors to answer repeated demands that the betrothal of Richard and Alice be fulfilled. They were joined by the archbishop of Tyre, bringing fresh tidings of disaster from Palestine. Following a battle at Hattin, Guy, king of Jerusalem, and many notables had been captured, and the True Cross had fallen into the infidels' hands. An urgent appeal was made to both monarchs for immediate assistance. As a result of the archbishop's pleading and mediation, Henry and Philip Augustus agreed to take the cross and to swear a truce until they returned from crusade. Henry was the first to put on the surcoat bearing a white cross borne by the English crusaders; Philip assumed the red cross surcoat of the French contingent, and shortly afterwards the count of Flanders followed their example adopting a green cross for his men. It was arranged that a tithe should be levied throughout England and France to pay for the expedition. At last it seemed that the Third Crusade, so long advocated, was about to set out.[13]

Henry soon demonstrated that his intentions were serious. Two days later, on January 23, 1188, at Le Mans, he issued instructions for the collection of the crusading tithe by the local clergy as assessed by the Templars and Hospitallers, and an ordin-

ance relating to the property and debts of those taking the cross
followed. At the end of the month, he crossed to England, where,
at Geddington on February 11, a great assembly was held to discuss the crusade. Archbishop Baldwin of Canterbury opened the
proceedings with an eloquent exhortation to those present to join
the expedition, and this was followed by the promulgation of
measures similar to those taken in Normandy. The Jews were also
forced to make large contributions, and the richer merchants of
London, York and other great towns were taxed with particular
severity. The king remained in southern England until June, making arrangements for his departure.

Richard's activities in Poitou had been successful in the previous
year, but he now had to take steps to crush a new rebellion by the
Lusignans, which he did with especial harshness, for a close friend
of his had been murdered at the beginning of the revolt. This was
scarcely over when the old quarrel with Toulouse broke out afresh.
Count Raymond had captured some Poitevin merchants in his
lands; he brutally blinded and castrated some, killed others and
imprisoned the rest, in revenge for Richard's action in previous
years. Retaliation came swiftly: the prince soon had the whole
region of Quercy under his control, and took prisoner the count's
minister Peter Seilun, on whose advice the outrages had been
committed. Raymond replied by seizing two English knights returning on pilgrimage from Compostela. Richard refused to surrender Peter in exchange for them, nor would he ransom them,
knowing that the Church would take action against an attack on
pilgrims. Philip Augustus, however, had been watching events
closely, and ordered the count to return the knights for this reason.
The count refused, and Richard, without asking the French king,
at once invaded Toulouse itself.

　　Henry had been waiting for news with growing anxiety, but
hardly expected Philip Augustus' reaction to the invasion to be so
strong. Messengers from the French king arrived in England complaining of Richard's conduct, especially excesses in ravaging the
count's lands. Although the king realised that Philip was bent on
renewed war, he replied mildly, saying that Richard had acted

without his advice. This soft answer was not enough to turn away Philip's wrath. Richard had meanwhile sent word to Henry by the archbishop of Dublin that Philip had encouraged the invasion of Toulouse because of the count's resistance. Henry attempted pacification by sending Baldwin, archbishop of Canterbury, to mediate. All was to no avail, for on June 16, 1188, the French king took Chateauroux in Berry, with other baronial castles. He had now broken the truce and had no intention of going on crusade until he had humbled the Angevins.

In so dangerous a crisis, Henry could not remain absent. Accordingly he embarked at Portsea with a force of Welsh mercenaries on July 10, landing at Barfleur the following day. He had left England for the last time; but no such thought could have entered his mind, for he had been far harder pressed on many occasions before now; he was only fifty-six and his strong constitution had stood up remarkably well to the incessant travelling and restless activity of his life. Other thoughts occupied his mind. Although the crisis might not be uncommonly serious, he now faced an adversary as resolute as himself and even more ruthless. For his part, he had had no need to destroy the French kingdom to gain his ends, and there were many good reasons for not doing so. Philip Augustus found himself in a position where all his ambitions were checked by Henry's presence; and he had now deliberately set out to undermine the Angevin power, regardless of ethics or dangers.

The war itself reflected the new nature of the rivalry of Angevin and Capetian dynasties. Fought with the utmost vigour on both sides, the talks which punctuated it were totally uninfluenced by the personal considerations of Henry's old friendship with Philip Augustus and his father, which until now had been evident even in the bitterest moments of dispute. Richard drove the French king out of Berry in August; but Normandy was invaded by another French force under the bishop of Beauvais, which burnt the castle of Aumale. The other combatants moved north to the borders of Anjou, near Blois, where each gained minor successes. Henry made a last effort to secure peace, asking for reparation and threatening to renounce his homage to the French crown. The latter demanded

the Vexin area and Berry in reply; the ambassadors, Walter of
Coutances and William the Marshal, returned empty-handed.
Henry thereupon invaded French territory from Normandy and
advanced to Mantes, burning various border towns in the hope of
finding Philip Augustus there, while Richard returned to Berry.
Threatened from both north and south, the French king in turn
made proposals for peace. From September 30 until October 2,
the two kings talked at the great elm-tree in the valley between
Gisors and Trie, where such meetings between the French and
Norman rulers traditionally took place. Henry and his men sat in
the tree's shade while Philip Augustus and his party sweltered in
the full heat of the late summer sun. When the talks proved fruitless and Henry had departed, the enraged French king gave orders
for the tree to be hewn down,[14] in token of his determination that
any future parleys should only consist of dictation of terms to the
Angevins.

But Henry was able to score a major diplomatic triumph
before war could be resumed. Philip Augustus' two chief allies,
the counts of Flanders and Blois, who had advised him against
making war, refused to bear arms against any christian prince
until after the crusade. Philip Augustus had to seek peace again. A
conference at Chatillon on October 7 broke down when the French
king, having agreed to mutual restoration of conquests, suddenly
demanded the castle of Pacy-sur-Eure as a guarantee. He then reopened hostilities by taking Palluau, near the mouth of the Loire.
But the costs of the campaign were growing heavy and the season
late; he therefore led his Brabantine and German mercenaries back
to Berry, where instead of paying them as promised, he confiscated
their equipment and dismissed them. Richard now decided to see
what he could gain by the dissensions between Philip Augustus
and his father, and turned his hand to diplomacy. He offered to
submit to the judgement of the king of France in the Toulouse
question, without consulting his father. This action, weakening
his hand in any bargaining, angered Henry greatly. Richard also
disbanded his mercenaries, saying it was for the sake of peace,
although cost was the real consideration.

The kings met again at Bonsmoulins on November 18, and
once again the proposal of mutual restitution was made. This time

it was Richard who objected. In return for the valuable lands of Quercy and Cahors, worth 1,000 marks a year, he was to receive the two castles of Chateauroux and Issoudun held by the French king, which were enfeoffed to vassals and brought in no revenue. He turned to his father, and demanded that he be given Alice in marriage. Persistent rumours, probably put about by Richard, whispered that Henry had seduced the girl and was keeping her as his mistress.[15] These were given official status after Henry's death when Richard no longer wished to wed her, and used them as an excuse, which was accepted by Philip Augustus. But Henry was too astute to commit such a gross political blunder for the sake of a passing whim, especially as the princess was reputedly 'a very ugly woman'.[16] To make sure that his father would not give way, Richard added a demand which Henry had refused to concede when made earlier by Philip: that homage be done to him as the Angevin's heir. This Henry could not allow, lest he appear to be yielding to French pressure.

Richard now conformed to the pattern of his family. Disdaining ties of kinship and long-term prospects for the sake of short-term political ambitions—although he did not imply any transfer of allegiance from one lord to another—he did homage to the king of France for all the lands his father held, excepting his father's tenure of those lands during his lifetime and the homage which he owed to his father. In return, Philip Augustus restored Chateauroux and Issoudun to him. Faced with this desertion—the most serious rebuff since the revolt of 1173—Henry had no choice but to make a truce until January 13, 1189, and prepare for the worst. Richard's move, although in itself little more than a manoeuvre to retain the lands in Quercy whose return Philip Augustus would otherwise have demanded, was made more damaging by his departure with the French king at the end of the conference. Henry sent William the Marshal and Bertrand de Verdun after his son, to find out why he had left. Failing to overtake him at Amboise, they learnt that Richard had just departed after spending the entire night issuing letters of summons to his men. They could only return and report his treason to the king.

Henry had two determined adversaries now, one attacking his

empire with the object of fragmenting it, the other intent on extracting as large a concession of power within it as he could get.
Their aims thus complemented each other. Richard, as heir to his
domains, had considerable support from those within Henry's
lands who bore the king no particular affection and were anxious
to gain good standing with Richard as king-to-be. There were
some conspicuous absentees from the Christmas court at Saumur;
and when renewed fighting broke out in January, the Bretons went
over to Richard and Philip *en masse*.

One last hope for peace remained: the Church's concern for
the crusade. A papal legate, John of Anagni, was despatched from
Rome with a commission to make peace between France and
England, so that the crusade might proceed. He was authorised to
use excommunication against all disturbers of the peace except the
kings themselves. Henry was forced to postpone two proposed
meetings because he had fallen ill during the winter, the first prolonged illness he had suffered; but the parties concerned eventually
met in conference at La Ferté Bernard. Here Philip Augustus,
Richard, Henry and the legate met about June 4, 1189, with
various prelates and magnates, four archbishops being there to
assist the legate. Neither side was prepared to give way. Philip
Augustus and Richard demanded the same terms as before, with
certain elaborations equally unacceptable to Henry. Richard was
to marry Alice at once, and to be recognised as his father's successor
in England, a precaution against any attempt to leave the kingdom
to John. Both kings were to go on crusade, and Richard and John
were to come with them. Henry rejected the last two conditions.
John of Anagni used the ultimate weapon he possessed: threatening Philip with an interdict. All he earned for his pains was a taunt
from the French king that he was in the pay of England. Henry
and the legate rode away with bitterness in their hearts, one knowing that there was little to be done but trust in his Angevin luck
and cunning, the other aware that the failure of his mission had
postponed the crusade to an indefinite date.

Almost at once, the French forces swept into Maine and down
towards Anjou, taking castle after castle.[17] La Ferté Bernard itself
was the first to fall; and hardly any resistance was offered by the

castellans of Bonnétable, Beaumont and Ballon. Here, on June 9, the invaders halted for three days. Henry was only fifteen miles away at Le Mans. A mere handful of supporters were with him. Even John was elsewhere. But Le Mans was his birthplace. If the lords of Maine were prepared to betray him, he could still trust in the citizens. Swearing never to leave them, he received in return their assent to withstanding a siege if necessary. Henry had only a few mercenaries to conduct the defence, and no immediate hope of relief.

On Sunday, June 11, the French army advanced as expected. Henry sent out William the Marshal and three other knights, lightly armed, to reconnoitre. A thick mist lay on the river Huisne below the town, and they were able to crouch behind a bank and observe the large army passing by at close quarters. They returned and reported to Henry, who made a sortie, broke down the only bridge, and put stakes in all the fords. Feeling secure from attack, he withdrew again to the citadel, while the French encamped near the wood of Le Parc. After giving orders that if the French attacked the suburbs outside the walls were to be burnt, the king retired for the night. The following day, he rose and heard mass early; then he rode out to inspect the situation. With a show of bravado, he went unarmed, and ordered William the Marshal and other knights to follow his example. The small party noticed that the French were sounding the river beside the broken bridge. Henry's luck had at last run out, for the enemy had discovered an old ford which had not been blocked. The Angevin contingent hastily withdrew, hotly pursued by the French. William the Marshal had to conduct a spirited defence of the east gate to cover their retreat, and the suburbs were fired. Once again, Henry's plans went astray. As he went back into the town, he saw that the wind had blown the flames inside the walls, and three or four fires were soon raging. Seeing no hope of extinguishing them, he decided on drastic action. Recalling the earl of Essex and William the Marshal from beyond the gate, he gave orders for a retreat towards Fresnay, twenty-four miles to the north on the Alençon road, with about 700 knights. Finding himself in flight for the first time in his life and overwhelmed by the defeat, Henry looked back on the flames which consumed his birthplace, and vented his despair in bitter blas-

phemy: 'Since thou, O God, to crown me with confusion and increase my dishonour, hast basely taken from me this day the city
I have loved best in all the world, wherein I was born and bred and
my father lies buried, and the body of St Julian lies entombed, I
also will surely recompense Thee as far as I am able, by withhold-
ing from Thee that which Thou lovest best in me.' Richard followed in hot pursuit of his father. William the Marshal turned
to cover Henry's retreat for the second time that day, and found
himself face to face with the unarmed prince. Richard cried mercy:
'By God, marshal, do not kill me; it would not be a good deed,
because I am unarmed.' The marshal smiled grimly, and saying, 'I
shall not kill you: I leave that to the devil', plunged his spear into
Richard's horse. Confusion ensued among the prince's followers,
and the delay enabled Henry to reach Fresnay in safety, while the
rest of his men went on to Alençon. Almost all the mercenaries
were killed save for a small band who held one of the towers of Le
Mans for another three days. But at Alençon the Norman host was
assembled, and Henry's prospects seemed to have improved.

The Norman barons, however, were reluctant to attack, in
view of the size of Philip's host and Henry's losses at Le Mans.
The king had to change his plans. Racked once more by a recurrence of his illness of the winter, he reached the little hill-top
town of Sainte-Suzanne on June 13, on his way to Anjou. Travelling south, he reached the castle of Chinon by the end of the
month. He relied now on his bastard son, Geoffrey, who had been
chancellor of England for the past six years, to see that his orders
were carried out. He had given instructions that the Norman
castles were only to be surrendered to John, and that a levy of
Welsh mercenaries was to be brought from England.

Philip Augustus, who had shown no interest in pursuing
the king, turned to secure the chief strongholds of Anjou. He
reached and captured Tours, defended by a handful of knights, on
July 3. Henry had apparently decided to leave Chinon for Angers,
for on July 2 the count of Flanders and the duke of Burgundy
found him at Saumur. They had come to persuade him to make
terms. On his barons' advice, he agreed to meet Philip Augustus
and painfully made his way east to Ballan, not far from Tours,
where, in the throes of fever caused by blood poisoning from a

wound in his heel, he sheltered in a commandery of the Knights Templar. The French king arrived at Coulombières,* the agreed meeting place. There he was told that Henry was seriously ill; but Richard refused to believe this, and said openly that it was a feint. His father was forced to go and meet them, although almost at the end of his strength. As soon as he arrived, Philip saw that his opponent was not in a fit state to sit on horseback, and offered him a cape to sit on. Henry refused, and remained in the saddle. The day was still and clear. As the two kings talked, a flash of summer lightning struck near them, and thunder rolled and echoed along the Loire valley. Henry reeled in his saddle and had to be supported while he listened to his enemy's demands. These were similar to the terms advanced four weeks earlier. The full humiliation of his situation penetrated to Henry's dimmed senses. He was to do homage to Philip Augustus; to surrender Alice; to make his barons swear fealty to Richard; to join with the French king the following Lent to go on crusade; to pay an indemnity of 20,000 marks; to surrender castles in pledge to Richard and Philip Augustus. His adversaries had won. He was sick and tired to death, in no mood to fight back against overwhelming odds as he had done in the past, at the beginning of his career, and at its height, when his sons rebelled. Even so, as he gave the kiss of peace to Richard, he muttered: 'God grant that I may not die until I have had my revenge on you.' He made only one request: that lists of the allies of each party be drawn up and exchanged. Roger Malchat, his sealkeeper, was sent to Tours to see to this, while Henry wearily retraced his steps to Chinon.[18]

That night, in the castle high above the valley of the Vienne, overlooking the slate-roofed houses beneath and the forests beyond the river in which he had so often hunted, Henry tossed and turned on his sickbed, tended by his bastard son Geoffrey of Lincoln and by William the Marshal. Sensing that he might not recover now, he thanked Geoffrey for his services, saying that he had been the most faithful of his sons: 'If, God willing, I recover from this sickness, I will certainly give you all that a father should, and

* Now Villandry.

Q

make you among the most powerful and greatest men in my domains. What I cannot repay now, should I die, may God repay you.' He gave him a gold ring with the device of a panther, asking him to send it, with another ring, to the king of Castile, his son-in-law.[19] Later Roger Malchat entered and Henry asked at once to hear the names on the list of his enemies. The first name resounded louder than the thunder earlier in the day. John, his favourite, for whose share in the inheritance he had fought so long had joined his brother and the French king. Turning his face to the wall, he groaned, and cried: 'Now let everything go as it will; I care no longer for myself or anything else in the world.'[20]

The end came quickly, on the following day, July 6. Henry had himself carried into the chapel, and laid before the altar, where he received extreme unction. His last words, before speech failed him, were 'Shame, shame on a conquered king'.[21] He lay in a coma for some while. Then, when the few remaining barons had gone elsewhere, he lost his last battle to death. The attendants, knowing that his desperate state meant that there would be none of the traditional rewards for them, stripped the body, plundered all they could find, and left the despoiled corpse to be found by William the Marshal soon afterwards. One of the knights, William de Trihan, had to take off his cloak to cover the corpse, and even the faithful marshal was hard put to it to arrange matters as befitted a royal funeral.[22] Sceptre, ring and crown were hastily found or made. The corpse was carried in state from the castle, down the winding path into the town's narrow streets and across the bridge over the Vienne, quiet and cool in the sunlight. The cortège moved slowly through the rolling forest south of the river, until, in the heat of noon, they reached the abbey of Fontévrault, where the nuns awaited their royal patron.

That night, Richard came there alone. He went straight to the choir where his father lay in state, surrounded by the nuns praying for the repose of his restless soul. His footsteps echoed from the high walls as he strode down the aisle; then he stood motionless and outwardly unmoved before the bier for a moment, 'as long as it takes to say a paternoster', before turning to look into his father's face for the last time: a face changed by illness and marked by the bleeding that had accompanied death. He knelt briefly, then rose and left the church as swiftly and silently as he had come.[23] Next day, Bishop Bartholomew of Tours laid the king to rest before the altar. It was where the king had wished to be buried, though he had once named Grammont as his resting-place. Here in the cool air beneath the high domed roof of the granite church among the Angevin hills he lies today.

Epilogue

THE FIGURE of Henry in his last hours, a fallen prince, bereft of outward majesty, alone with death, contrasts sharply with the triumphs of his lifetime. Was he really a doomed fugitive, or was the tide about to flood in his favour once more, when the fatal illness struck him down? He had emerged victorious from desperate straits many times before, and the speculation is not an idle one. The coalition of Philip Augustus and Richard which overthrew him was short-lived, and against the background of intrigues between Henry's sons and the French king which had gone on for two decades, their sudden victory seems almost a political accident. Henry had always been a match for each of them individually; what overcame him was a swift and determined campaign which caught him not only unawares but also sick. The bare fact of Henry's death in defeat must stand; but he was far from vanquished. His work and much of what he had fought for survived him. His legacy was not merely the empire he had created, but also his government and laws, and the traditions he had helped to foster.

Richard parted from Philip Augustus very shortly after his father's death, and the old dichotomy of Angevin and Capetian began to revive. Henry's empire survived the initial test of the transfer of power to a new ruler, and it soon became clear that the old king had succeeded in making a state, which unlike its contemporaries, was to a great degree independent of the central figure in it. Its structure could hardly have been put to severer tests than those it was to experience in the next ten years. With Richard's absence on crusade, the king was for the first time missing from the governments on both sides of the Channel, beyond easy recall, and it was left to his subordinates to rule in his name. They remained loyal to him even in the days of his captivity in Germany. This was due solely to the high degree of organisation and to the concept of responsibility built up by Henry; and for the same reason, Richard's domains held out against Philip Augustus' continual erosions in his absence. The detailed history of these years, however, is less a postscript to Henry's reign than a pointer forward to new developments. Only in the troubles with the regency in England was there a reminder that absolute integrity could not yet be secured without the personal presence of the king to overawe his servants and subjects.

If at the end of Richard's reign the empire was intact, Henry's successor had not treated his subjects lightly. William of Newburgh recalled in this connection Rehoboam, Solomon's son, who, when the Israelites complained of the latter's grievous yoke, answered: 'My father chastised you with whips, but I shall chastise you with scorpions.' Heavy taxation for the crusade, and then for the king's ransom, had raised discontent among rich and poor alike. Nor had the alliance with France for the crusade endured. Richard died at Chalus engaged in nothing more than a petty internal quarrel over treasure trove, but he had been fighting Philip Augustus at intervals for the previous five years. He had had to deal with the rebelliousness of his brother as well; but that was now past, and John had shown promising signs both in the council chamber and on the field of battle of being a worthy heir to his father's talents.

Yet within six years of Richard's death, by the spring of 1205, almost all the Angevin lands oversea lay within the power of the French king, only Poitou holding out for John. Chateau Gaillard, Richard's proud fortress on the Seine, built to defy French invaders with great cost and much loving care, had fallen the previous year. Rouen had succumbed to a bold venture by Philip Augustus while John sat idle in England; and the Bretons had risen to drive out their alien rulers. In the course of the latter revolt, John had made a major error of judgement in ordering the murder of Arthur of Brittany. This crime not only aroused the Bretons and gave them a rallying-cry, but also provided Philip Augustus with a legal pretext for seizing John's lands. On the slenderest of evidence, he summoned John, as his vassal, to answer at his court for Arthur's disappearance. John could not make out a case—the only possible reply would have been to produce Arthur alive—and chose not to answer, thereby incurring the customary penalty of forfeiture of his lands. Why he then failed to resist the French king's attacks, but threw himself energetically into the business of government in England, as the official records amply attest, must remain a mystery. It seems that his fatal flaw was not the infamy and cowardice attributed to him by Victorian historians but a total inability to act in moments of crisis. Now that he was faced with a threat of overwhelming proportions, his activities in England smacked of a desperate optimism, with a blind eye turned to events elsewhere. Nor could he inspire his men in the same way as his elder brothers Henry and Richard, and there were no leaders of sufficient stature among his men in Normandy capable of doing that for him.

Once the crucial period from 1203 to the spring of 1205 was past, there was little left that could be done. John's expedition in 1205 to relieve the defenders of Poitou was impressive in its preparations; but the loyalty of the barons was doubtful, and at the last moment the king was dissuaded from going. Only in the next year did he reach Poitou, where he regained most of his mother's inheritance; but the failure of an expedition in 1212 and the defeat of a great coalition of Philip Augustus' enemies at the battle of Bouvines in 1214 meant that any hopes of reconquering more than this small fragment of the lands which his father had ruled were gone for good.

The fate of Henry's lands must be told to complement the history of their acquisition. Since an empire created by one man rarely outlasts his lifetime, especially when it is as disparate and lacking in natural frontiers as that of Henry, it is not on this evidence that judgement should be passed on Henry's achievements—even if, in passing, we note the fateful permanence of his work of conquest in Ireland.

When Henry came to the English throne, disorder and poverty prevailed throughout the kingdom. The barons had oppressed the countryside, ravaging the crops, sacking the villages, in order to maintain their private armies. Henry himself had connived at this so long as it furthered his cause. As a result, almost a quarter of the country was in no fit state to pay the taxes due in the first year of his reign. The conquest of England in 1066 had caused far less damage than these internecine wars. 'In every shire a part of the inhabitants wasted away and died in large numbers from famine, while others went with their wives and children into a grim self-inflicted exile. Villages widely famed could be seen standing empty, because the people of the countryside, men and women, young and old, had left them; fields whitened with harvest as the year drew on into autumn but those who should have cultivated them had fallen prey to famine and its companion, pestilence.'

Beyond the purview of the chronicler, matters were in still worse case. The judicature organised by Henry I had fallen into almost total decay; the general visitations of the kingdom on which general good order depended had vanished, and local justices struggled to keep what control they could, or became a law unto themselves. The king's central court might still function, except during the period of Stephen's captivity, but its writs were all too often worthless. The exchequer's old vigilance over the royal finances was reduced to a task of raising what money it could, while every baron in a position to do so had set up his own treasury, whose officers were not bound to legal methods of gathering wealth. No wonder men shouted 'Long live the king' with such enthusiasm as Henry made his way to London to be crowned; for he bore with him the promise of both past and future: a return to the peace and safety of his grandfather's time.

Thirty-five years later, these same men would for the most part have agreed that the promise had been fulfilled beyond all expectation. It was fifteen years since the barons' swords had been unsheathed against the king, and that brief revolt had quickly succumbed to Henry's loyal followers. For at Fornham and Alnwick it was not the king himself, but his deputies, who had upheld law against the forces of chaos. In this lay the key to Henry's success. He had gathered about him a body of men prepared to support him in face of revolt and unpopularity in carrying out his business. His grandfather had created methods of maintaining order, but had found only a few men to implement it, men who aroused the barons' enmity to far too great a degree, especially since they were all churchmen. Henry, like every other medieval ruler, had employed churchmen, but from the very beginning of his reign had also found literate laymen to carry out his work: men with no other qualifications save intelligence and loyalty to the king's aims.

By such means, Henry had revived and augmented his grandfather's laws and institutions, and had developed them to a new perfection. The exchequer and the courts had grown from rudimentary or dislocated systems to the most complex and efficient of their kind in Europe: a secure basis for further evolution. Little of Henry's actual methods survive to the present day; but on the other hand almost all our legal and fiscal institutions appear in their first effective incarnation during his reign. An example is Henry's development of the jury: from a flexible device that could be turned to various ends with varying success, he made it by the end of his reign an exact instrument in the enforcement of law. It had been used as a method of obtaining sworn evidence on anything from murder to the extent of a freedman's strip of land, and hence as means of presenting a man for trial or of answering a royal inquest on service owed. By 1189, a new function, that of hearing and weighing evidence in cases where there was nothing conclusive against the accused, had appeared. This system had distant origins in Saxon procedure; Henry's genius brought it out when the need arose and made it a permanent part of our legal code. He had enforced law more strictly, while making the law itself more humane, by abolishing trial by ordeal, and forbidding the ancient custom of looting shipwrecks.

With the restoration of order, England's prosperity grew. Henry never exploited this wealth for his own ends, taking no more than was necessary, and practising a strict economy in the expenses of government. 'He never laid any grievous burden on his realm of England or on his lands overseas, until the recent tithe for the crusade, which was also levied on other countries', wrote a chronicler at the time of his death. 'He never laid any tribute on churches or monasteries on pretext of necessity like other monarchs, but even preserved their immunity from tolls with religious fervour. He abhorred bloodshed and the sacrifice of men's lives, and strove diligently to keep the peace, whenever possible by gifts of money but with armed force if he could not secure it otherwise.'[1] Under his rule, England knew longer years of peace, fewer summonses to the feudal host, than she was to enjoy for centuries to come; even the turbulent Welsh respected Henry's firm hand, and there had been only one call to go overseas, compared with the crusades and expeditions to recover lost lands of succeeding reigns. The local lords could look after their estates undisturbed by the repercussions of matters of state; the merchants could journey safely through the land from fair to fair with their precious loads of spices, silk and other luxuries from distant lands; the city-dwellers could ply their trade free from wars and rumours of war.

A similar picture of prosperity, on a lower level, can be drawn for Henry's lands in France. The barons here had never been tamed to the same degree as in England, and disturbances had been almost continuous somewhere in his vast territories. Yet only a few towns and castles had been seriously affected; any mercenaries who got out of hand were quickly restrained by the king, or if not in his employ, were crushed by him or his barons. Henry's laws and edicts held good over a far greater area than those of the French king; he was the first ruler since the days of Charlemagne's sons who could issue and enforce general edicts throughout three-quarters of what is now France. The first examples are the assizes of 1177–80. Yet he was wise enough not to irritate local pride by destroying the different customs of the various regions. Nor did his work fail with the expulsion of the English power in the following century. Philip Augustus, realising its value, had already begun to copy it in France, introducing an imitation of the Assize of Arms shortly after its promulgation in Normandy in 1184; and when he gained control of the Norman government, he not only continued the system of local government built up by Henry and his predecessors, but introduced more measures based on it into his French domains.

Yet Henry's reign was not all sweetness and light; and when the ill-will and crossed ambitions of some of his subjects are discounted against his great reforms, there still remains a residue of violence and hatred to be explained. Henry was the greatest statesman of his age, and his failing was one common among rulers. Accustomed to great power from his youth upwards, he could brook no personal challenge to that authority: hence stemmed the quarrel with Becket and the strife with his sons which make up the darker side of the picture. This was the inherited trait that gave his contemporaries their evidence of the demonic origins of the house of Anjou. The Plantagenets and their forebears had always stood first for their own power and then for that of their family; and to this extent they were as selfish and pernicious as any independent-minded baron in the wars of Stephen's reign. Henry had other weaknesses as well: a hasty temper, a streak of impiety and cunning: but these scarcely affected his course and purpose in affairs of state.

Henry was a lover of power, a miser when it came to parting with a vestige of authority; and in the use of that power his greatness lies. That he chose to devote both his power and his energy to a better ordering of the affairs of his realm, rather than to frivolous wars and crusades or to exploitation and tyranny, in an age which knew no ethics of devotion to the state, and no concept of the welfare of the people, was his outstanding virtue. Those he had ruled remembered him after his death with more affection than he had enjoyed in his lifetime. Let us return to William of Newburgh:

> Ungrateful men and those bent on evil courses talked incessantly of the wickedness of their own monarch and would not endure to hear good spoken of him. To such men in particular the hardships of the days that followed alone brought understanding. Indeed, the evils that we are now suffering have revived the memory of his good deeds, and the man, who in his own times was hated by many, is now declared everywhere to have been an excellent and beneficial ruler.[2]

Richard rides in state outside Parliament, Becket was for long Christendom's most popular saint; Henry is remembered only as their opponent. Such is the irony of popular history. How they came to acquire these attributes is a matter for the gleaner of myths and legends; but it is no reason for ignoring the achievements of England's greatest medieval statesman, one who earned

this simple epitaph from the same thoughtful historian who had
known his times:[3]

> In his exalted position in the state, he was most diligent
> in defending and promoting the peace of the realm; in wield-
> ing the sword for the punishment of evildoers, he was a true
> servant of God.

APPENDICES

I. THE CHRONOLOGY OF THE COUNCIL OF CLARENDON, 1164

The chronology of the Council of Clarendon is not very clear. We have several authorities, all of them imprecise. Two of them—Herbert of Bosham and Gilbert Foliot—were definitely eye-witnesses, while both Ralph de Diceto and Gervase of Canterbury were writing long after the event.

The information available is as follows:

OPENING DATE	DURATION	CLOSING DATE
Herbert of Bosham (Materials, iii 279)		
Not given	At least two days; constitutions prepared overnight.	Not given
Ralph of Diceto (i. 312)		
January 25	Long negotiations.	Not given
Gilbert Foliot (Materials, v 527–9)		
Not given	Three days; then customs written down and signed.	Not given
Official copy of constitutions (Materials, v 71–9)		
Not given	Not given.	January 29
Gervase of Canterbury (i. 176–80)		
January 13	Not given.	Not given

Miss Norgate (*England under the Angevins*, ii 44–5) ingeniously incorporated Gervase's date, making the council run from January 13 to January 30, with an adjournment from January 16 to 25; but to do so she had to ignore the remarks of the two eye-witnesses about the writing down of the constitutions, which, according to her, caused this hypothetical adjournment. It is far more probable that Gervase is wrong, since the other statements resolve themselves to within a day or so. The course of events would seem to have been thus:

January 25: Council assembles
January 26: Thomas gives his assent (or following day)
January 27: Henry orders writing out of the customs

January 28: Customs presented to Thomas

January 29: Agreement in modified form without seal of archbishop accepted by Henry.

Hence the three days referred to by Foliot would be the discussions from January 26 to 28, and Ralph de Diceto's opening date would harmonise with the closing date on the official copy.

II. THE ASSIZE OF CLARENDON

In *The Governance of Medieval England from the Conquest to Magna Carta*, Richardson and Sayles make some major criticisms of the accepted text of this document (pp. 438–49). They argue that only three paragraphs of the document formerly accepted *in toto* as the Assize of Clarendon are suited to the circumstances of 1166, and give these in a reconstructed form. The old accepted text, with its remarkable style, is, according to them, the work of a private writer, which explains the curiously autocratic formula 'the king wills' with which seven of the twenty-two clauses begin. There are hence three stages in the evolution of the texts. *Firstly*, there was the original Clarendon text (reconstructed by Richardson and Sayles, p. 441); *secondly*, there was the expanded Northampton assize of 1176 (in Roger-Benedict, i. 108–11); and *thirdly* came the private memorandum of this latter text (in Roger-Benedict, ii clxix–cliv), which derives from the Northampton text and is later than 1176. The new version of the enactment at Clarendon runs as follows:

If any man shall have been accused, by the oath of twelve knights of the hundred (and if no knights are present by the oath of twelve lawful freemen) and by the oath of four men from each vill of the hundred, of murder or theft of robbery, or of sheltering men who have done any of these things, or of forgery [or counterfeiting] or of arson, he will go to the ordeal by water and, if he fails therein, he will lose one of his feet.

And if he is cleared by the ordeal by water, he shall find sureties for his conduct and shall remain in the kingdom, unless he was accused of murder or any other grave felony by the whole community of the county and the lawful knights of the district, for which, if he was thus accused although he endured trial by water safely, he shall nonetheless leave the kingdom within forty days, and shall take his chattels with him, saving the right of his lords, and shall forswear the kingdom subject to the king's mercy.

No one shall harbour in his house in town or vill any stranger for more than one night if he is unwilling to be responsible for him at law, unless that guest has a reasonable and valid excuse which the host shall show to his neighbours. And when he departs he will do so publicly in the presence of his host's neighbours and by light of day.

The main point which Richardson and Sayles seek to make is well established by their arguments. On the other hand, it is debatable whether they have not excised too much in order to re-create this approximation of the original text. Some of the business allotted to the justices in 1176 (cf. the 1176 instructions), and the lack of evidence for such business being carried out can be explained by the various circumstances which curtailed the carrying out of the visitation. As the 1176 text stands, the clauses of instruction would seem to have undergone an internal rephrasing to suit new needs; bearing this in mind, the clauses on jurisdiction over all cases involving half a knight's fee or less, the inquiries into escheats, churches, marriages, and custody of castles, and the instructions to commit thieves to the sheriffs' care might all be restored to the 1166 text without contravening any surviving evidence. What is quite certain is that Henry's legal reforms and attempt to introduce a greater degree of order were not made as dramatically as it had hitherto seemed. The old picture of a radical programme brought in with little preparation and then re-enacted as necessary has been replaced by the idea of a gradual development strongly influenced by the lessons of experience.

III. THE CHRONOLOGY OF HENRY'S LAST DAYS

There are eleven nearly contemporary authorities who refer to the events of June and July 1189. Their evidence, never comprehensive, is often conflicting; and the course of the last days of Henry's life can be reconstructed only by piecing together fragments from various writers. The account given by each is summarised below, and an attempt at resolving the discrepancies offered.

1. Three writers who may have been eye-witnesses of the events. *William the Marshal* is known to have been present at the siege of Le Mans and at Chinon, and was responsible for Henry's burial. His account was recorded by another writer from his verbal reminiscences about thirty years later, and contains no dates. It serves to establish a sequence of events.

Conference between La Ferté Bernard and Nogent le Rotrou; Henry goes to Ballon (8345–60).
Philip takes La Ferté Bernard.
Henry goes to Le Mans (8361–8).
Philip takes Ballon and Montfort-le-Rotrou.
Philip attacks Le Mans; Henry retreats to Fresnay (8399–8887).
Henry leaves Fresnay for Alençon.
Henry leaves Alençon for Sainte-Suzanne, and then goes to Chinon (8888–9012).
Philip requests an interview, between Tours and Azay.
Henry arrives at Ballan; the interview takes place. (9013–78)

Henry goes to Chinon, and the list of rebels is brought that evening. (9078–9112)

Fever grows worse, death follows rapidly.

On the other side, both *Guillaume Lebreton* and *Rigord* may have been with Philip Augustus as he advanced through Henry's lands. Guillaume Lebreton wrote two versions of the story, one a prose chronicle, the other a poem in praise of Philip, the *Philippide*.

In the prose chronicle (190), Philip takes La Ferté Bernard and Montfort-le-Rotrou, then besieges and takes Le Mans. He goes on to take Tours, and has a parley with Henry at Colombières. A few days later, Henry dies at Chinon.

The *Philippide* differs in the addition of a few more details: Philip assembles his army at Nogent-le-Rotrou in May (89), takes La Ferté Bernard and Le Mans. Henry flees to Alençon, pursued by Richard (90). Philip takes Tours while Henry is at Chinon; the two kings meet at Colombières, and Henry dies three days later (93).

Rigord's account was originally written thirteen years before Guillaume's first draft, in 1196, and was revised in 1206. It gives more dates, but these are open to question.

Philip takes Nogent-le-Rotrou (94), La Ferté Bernard and four other castles, and then Le Mans. Henry flees to Chinon. Philip is before Tours on June 23. Twelve days after the capture of Tours, Henry dies, on July 6. (Hence Tours fell on June 25.)

2. The next group consists of writers who may have been eye-witnesses, or who were definitely in close contact with the court at the time. The first of these is Henry's old enemy, *Gerald of Wales*, who has left two accounts. In his book *De Principis Instructione*, where the king's fate is held up as a dreadful example, the substance of his account is as follows:

Sunday June 4 marks the opening of hostilities. Philip invades Maine, and Henry goes to Le Mans, which is burnt. Henry passes the following night at Fresnay.

Philip invades Touraine and takes Tours.

On Friday (date unspecified), a conference takes place near Azay. Henry goes to Chinon.

On Thursday, seven days after the beginning of the fever, Henry dies.

In the life of Henry's illegitimate son, Geoffrey, Gerald gives more details, but omits some of his previous statements.

On the day after the burning of Le Mans, Geoffrey goes to Alençon with the army (369). He rejoins Henry at Savigny, with a hundred knights. Tours is captured, and a conference takes place at Azay. Henry makes peace on the following day, goes to Chinon, and dies on the seventh day of his illness (372).

Gervase of Canterbury was certainly not present himself in France, but other members of his convent had sought an interview with Henry over a protracted lawsuit of theirs only a few days before his death, and were probably still in the neighbourhood.

On Friday June 9, a conference was held near Le Mans (446), and within three days, the town was burnt (Sunday June 11). About Thursday June 29, Henry submits and makes peace. Soon afterwards, the Canterbury monks find him at Azay (448), and on Thursday July 6 he dies at Chinon (449).

3. The last three writers all had connections with the court, and their accounts may well be based on the experiences of those who had been with Henry.

Roger of Howden is now known to have written not only the chronicle that bears his own name, but also the anonymous document for long attributed to Benedict of Peterborough, which is in many ways a draft for his other work. The *Roger-Benedict* version, written about three years after the time of Henry's death, gives the following sequence:

Before Sunday May 28, a conference is held near La Ferté Bernard (ii. 66). Later, Philip takes La Ferté Bernard, Montfort, Maletable, Beaumont and Ballon, and waits for three days. On a Sunday, Philip arrives at Le Mans. On Monday, Le Mans is burnt and Henry flees to Chinon. Philip takes a series of castles, Montdoubleau, Les Roches, Montoire, Chartre, Chateau du Loir, Chaumont, Amboise, Rochecorbon, arriving at Tours on Friday June 30. On Sunday July 2, the count of Flanders and the duke of Burgundy go to Saumur to meet Henry. Monday July 3 marks Philip's capture of Tours. Peace is made with Henry, who dies at Chinon on Thursday July 6 (ii. 71).

The later version runs in almost identical terms, except that the conference between Tours and Azay is inserted about June 29. A list of the rebels is given to Henry then, and he goes straight to Chinon thereafter.

Ralph de Diceto, dean of St Paul's, was writing about the same time as Howden, but his information seems to have been less detailed, and his chronology is always a little erratic.

On Monday June 12, Le Mans is burnt (ii. 63). About June 22, the tower near the north gate, which had held out, surrenders (a detail also found in William the Marshal). On Wednesday June 28, Henry submits, at a place between Tours and Azay, and he dies at Chinon on Thursday July 6.

William of Newburgh has almost nothing to add in the way of detail. His brief account describes Philip Augustus as laying siege to Angers, which seems at best improbable, since it is not mentioned anywhere else, and would have entailed a march along the Loire passing within a few miles of Chinon.

Such are the recorded facts; what fixed points, generally agreed, can be found? The most important is the exact date of Henry's death, Thursday July

R

6. At the other end, it is generally agreed that a conference was held at La Ferté Bernard, and the date is given as between May 28 and June 9. The siege of Le Mans is better documented, and the agreed date for its capture is June 12.

From this, we can obtain the following sequence by a process of selection and rejection:

On June 4, a conference was held at La Ferté Bernard.
The three eye-witnesses agree that Philip's campaign started immediately after this conference, and to account for more than a week between La Ferté Bernard and the siege of Le Mans is difficult. The time may have been even shorter.
The conference breaks up without result, and Philip, in the course of the next day or two, takes La Ferté Bernard, Montfort, Maletable, Ballon and Beaumont.

On this *Roger-Benedict*, *William the Marshal*, *Lebreton* and *Rigord* agree.

Henry goes to Ballon and thence to Le Mans.

William Marshal provides the detail of Ballon; most authorities mention or imply Henry's presence at Le Mans before the siege.

Philip appears before Le Mans on Sunday June 11; the town is burnt on the following day.

The date comes from *Gervase of Canterbury*, *Roger-Benedict* and *Ralph de Diceto*; *William the Marshal* confirms that Philip arrived the day before the town fell.

Henry flees to Fresnay; his army goes on to Alençon. His son Geoffrey rejoins him at Savigny.

William the Marshal, and *Gerald of Wales* name Fresnay; the former and *Lebreton* say that Henry went on to Alençon, but *Gerald of Wales* gives a more circumstantial account, which seems more probable, and which would explain why the others were under the impression that the king had gone to Alençon.

Henry continues to Sainte-Suzanne, while Philip proceeds to the siege of Tours.

The detail of Sainte-Suzanne is added by *William the Marshal*; the siege of Tours is generally mentioned. There is a difficulty over the dating of its capture, which is only satisfactorily resolved by *Roger-Benedict*, who places it on Monday July 3. If we accept *Rigord*'s date of June 25, the French king's activities between then and the conference at Colombières a few miles away, on July 4, have to be explained.

Henry meets Philip at Colombières, between Tours and Azay, on July 4, having received the duke of Burgundy and count of Flanders at Saumur on July 2.

William the Marshal, who was certainly at Chinon, is our most important witness for the very last days of Henry's life. He implies that the meeting at Colombières—*Lebreton* names the place—took place not more than two days before Henry's death, since the list of rebels was brought that evening, and Henry died very soon after reading the list, either the same day or the day after. The exact interval is not precise, but would seem to preclude the interval of a week implied by other writers, notably, *Diceto* and *Gervase*. *Lebreton* agrees that the interval was brief—he says three days; and *Roger-Benedict* puts forward a plausible sequence of events, dating the conference on the 4th, and Henry's death on the 6th. His later revision of the conference to June 29 was probably on the influence of another writer, rather than an eye-witness. *Gerald of Wales* gives no definite help; but since Henry died on the seventh day of the fever, and he was already very ill at Colombières, the gap between the two events is again narrowed to at most four days. Regarding Henry's death, as we have observed, this vital event is universally recorded as taking place on July 6.

BIBLIOGRAPHY

The bibliography that follows makes no claim to completeness, but is intended as a useful guide to works on the period. The section of the list on Art, Architecture and Military Background is a selection only, and some purely technical authorities have been omitted from the first part.

Names or titles printed in capitals indicate the abbreviation by which the work is cited in the Notes.

SOURCES

ADAM OF EYNSHAM: *The Life of St Hugh of Lincoln.* Ed. and tr. D. L. Douie and H. Farmer. London, 1961–2.

ANCIENT CHARTERS. Ed. J. H. Round, Pipe Roll Society Publications, vol. 10. London, 1888.

BATTLE ABBEY: *Chronicon Monasterii de Bello.* Ed. J. S. Brewer. Anglia Christiana Society. London, 1846. (New edition: ed. Eleanor Searle. Oxford 1980)

BERMONDSEY: *Annales Monasterii de Bermundesiea,* See Monastic Annals.

BRUT Y TYWYSOGION: *The Chronicles of the Princes.* Ed. and tr. Rev J. W. ab Ithel. Rolls Series 17, London, 1860.

BURTON: *Annales Monasterii de Burton.* See Monastic Annals.

CHRONIQUES de ST MARTIAL de Limoges. Ed. H. Duplès-Agier. Société de l'Histoire de France. Paris, 1874.

CHRONIQUES DES COMTES D'ANJOU et des Seigneurs d'Amboise. Ed. L. Halphen et R. Poupardin. Paris, 1913.

DENHOLM YOUNG: *Charters.* See Translations.

DUNSTABLE: *Annales Prioratus de Dunstaplio.* See Monastic Annals.

ETIENNE DE ROUEN: *Draco Normannicus.*
   In: *Chronicles of the Reigns of Stephen, Henry II and Richard I,* vol. II. Ed. R. Howlett. Rolls Series 82. London, 1886.

FEET OF FINES 1182–96: Pipe Roll Society Publications, vol. 17. London, 1894.

GERALD the Welshman (Giraldus Cambrensis): Opera. Ed. J. S. Brewer, J. Dimock, and G. F. Warner. Rolls Series 26. London, 1861–97.
> Vol. I: *De Rebus a se gestis, Invectionum libellus, Symbolum electorum*, etc., 1861.
> Vol. II: *Gemma ecclesiastica*, 1862.
> Vol. IV: *Speculum Ecclesiae, Vita Galfredi*, 1873.
> Vol. V: *Topographica Hibernica, Expugnatio Hibernia*, 1867.
> Vol. VI: *Itinerarium Kambriae, Descriptio Kambriae*. 1868.
> Vol. VIII: *De Principis Instructione Liber*, 1891.

GERVASE OF CANTERBURY: *The Historical Works*. Ed. W. Stubbs. Rolls Series 73. London, 1879–80.

GESTA STEPHANI: *The Deeds of Stephen*. Ed. and tr. K. R. Potter and R.H.C. Davis. Oxford 1976.

GUERNES DE PONT-SAINTE-MAXENCE: *La Vie de Saint Thomas le Martyr, poème historique du xiième siècle*. Ed. E. Walberg. Oxford, 1922.

GUILLAUME LE BRETON: *Oeuvres de Rigord et de Guillaume le Breton, Historiens de Philippe Auguste*. Ed. H.-F. Delaborde. Société de l'Histoire de France. Paris, 1885.

HEREFORDSHIRE DOOMSDAY 1160–70: Pipe Roll Society Publications.

HENRY OF HUNTINGDON: *History of the English*. Ed. T. Arnold. Rolls Series 74. London, 1879. New ed? (Ed. & tr. Diana Greenway, Oxford 1998?).

L'HISTOIRE DE GUILLAUME LE MARECHAL: Comte de Striguil et de Pembroke, Regent d'Angleterre de 1216–19. Ed. Paul Meyer. Société de l'Histoire de France. Paris, 1901.

JOCELIN OF BRAKELOND: *Chronicle concerning the acts of Samson, abbot of the monastery of St. Edmunds*. Ed. and tr. H. E. Butler. London, 1949.

Holyrood: *A Scottish Chronicle known as the Chronicle of Holyrood*. Ed. M. O. Anderson. Scottish History Society. Edinburgh, 1938.

JOHN OF HEXHAM: *Continuation of Simeon of Durham*.
> In: *Symeonis Monachi Opera Omnia: Historia Regum. Eadem historia ad quartum et vicesimum annum continuata per Joannem Hagulstadensem*. Ed. T. Arnold. Rolls Series 83. London, 1885.

JOHN OF SALISBURY: *The Letters of John of Salisbury*. Ed. and tr. W. J. Millor and H. E. Butler, rev. C. N. L. Brooke. London, 1955.
> *Memoirs of the Papal Court*. Ed. and tr. M. Chibnall. London, 1956.

JORDAN FANTOSME: *Metrical Chronicle*.
> In: *Chronicles of the Reigns of Stephen, Henry II and Richard I*, vol. III. Ed. R. Howlett. Rolls Series 82. London, 1886. New ed.

MARGAM: *Annales de Margam:* See Monastic Annals.

MATERIALS for the History of Thomas Becket, Archbishop of Canterbury. Ed. Rev. J. C. Robertson (vols. I–VI), J. B. Shephard (vol. VII). Rolls Series 67. London, 1875–85.
> Vol. I: *William of Canterbury* (life and miracles).
> Vol. II: *Benedict of Peterborough* (miracles); *John of Salisbury; Alan of Tewkesbury; Edward Grim* (lives).

Vol. III: *William FitzStephen; Herbert of Bosham* (lives).

Vol. IV: *Anonymous lives.*

Vol. V–VII: *Letters.*

MELROSE: *The Chronicle of Melrose* (facsimile edition). Ed. A. O. and M. O. Anderson. London, 1936.

MONASTIC ANNALS: Ed. H. R. Luard. Rolls Series 36. London, 1864–9.

Vol. I: *Annales de Margan. Teokesberia, Burton.*

Vol. II: *Annales Monasterii de Wintonia, Waverleia.*

Vol. III: *Annales Prioratus de Dunstaplia, Annales Monasterii de Bermundeseia.*

Vol. IV: *Annales Monasterii de Oseneia, Chronicon Thomae Wykes, Annales Prioratus de Wigornia.*

NIGEL LONGCHAMP: See Translations.

OSENEY: *Annales Monasterii de Oseneia.* See Monastic Annals.

OTTO OF FREISING: See Translations.

PETER OF BLOIS: *Epistolae.* Ed. J. A. Giles. In: J. P. Migne, Patrologiae Cursus Completus. vol. 266. Paris, 1855.

PIPE ROLLS:

The Great Rolls of the Pipe, 1155–8. Ed. Rev. J. Hunter. London, 1844.

The Great Roll of the Pipe, 1158–88. Pipe Roll Society Publications, vols. 1–9, 11–13, 15–16, 18–19, 21–2, 25–34, 36–8. London, 1884–1925.

The Great Roll of the Pipe. 1189–90. Ed. J. Hunter. London, 1844.

POLYDORE VERGIL: *Polydorii Vergilii Urbinatis Anglicae Historiae libri vigintisex.* Basle, 1455.

RALPH OF COGGESHALL: *Chronicon Anglicanum.* Ed. J. Stevenson. Rolls Series 66. London, 1875.

With Thomas Agnellus: *De morte et sepultura Henrici Regis Angliae Junioris,* etc.

RALPH OF DICETO: *Historical Works.* Ed. W. Stubbs. Rolls Series 68. London, 1876.

RALPH HIGDEN: *Polychronicon, with English translations of John Trevisa.* Ed. Rev. J. R. Lumby. Rolls Series 41. London, 1882–5.

RALPH NIGER: *The Chronicles.* Ed. R. Anstruther. Caxton Society. London, 1851.

RECUEIL D'ANNALES Angevins et Vendômoisis. Ed. L. Halphen. Paris, 1903.

Contains: *Annales de St. Aubin, Annales de Vendôme, Annales de St. Serge d'Angers.*

RECUEIL DES ACTES de Henri II Roi d'Angleterre et Duc de Normandie concernant les provinces françaises et les affaires de France. Ed. L. Delisle. Paris, 1919.

RECUEIL DES CHRONIQUES de Touraine. Ed. A. Salmon. Tours 1854.

RECUEIL DES HISTORIENS des Gaules et de la France (vols. xii, xiii, xviii). Par des Réligieux Bénédictins de la congregation de St. Maur. Paris, 1764 ff.

RICHARD FITZ-NEALE: *Dialogus de Scaccario.* Ed. and tr. C. Johnson. London, 1950.

RIGORD: *Oeuvres.* See Guillaume Le Breton.

ROBERT OF TORIGNI: *Chronicle.*

In: *Chronicles of the Reigns of Stephen, Henry II and Richard I*, vol. IV, Ed. R. Howlett. Rolls Series 82. London, 1889.

ROGER-BENEDICT: *Gesta Henrici Secundi Benedicti Abbatis. The Chronicle of the reigns of Henry II and Richard I, A.D. 1169–92, known commonly under the name of Benedict of Peterborough.* Ed. W. Stubbs. Rolls Series 49. London 1867.
  (Now attributed to Roger Howden. See Stenton, *EHR* LXVIII 1953, 574–82.)

ROGER HOWDEN: *Chronica.* Ed. W. Stubbs. Rolls Series 51. London, 1868–71.

ROGER WENDOVER: *The Flowers of History.* Ed. H. O. Howlett. Rolls Series 84. London. 1887–9.

ROTULI NORMANNIAE: *Magni Rotuli Scaccarii Normanniae sub Regibus Angliae.* Ed. T. Stapleton. London, 1840.

The SONG OF DERMOT and the Earl. Ed. and tr. G. H. Orpen. Oxford, 1892.

SUGER: *Vie de Louis le Gros.* Ed. and tr. (into French) H. Waquet. Paris, 1929.
  Vie de Louis le Gros suivi de l'histoire du Roi Louis VII. Ed. H. Molinier. Paris, 1887.

THOMAS SAGA Erkibyskups: a life of Archbishop Thomas Becket in Icelandic, Ed. and tr. F. Magnusson. Rolls Series 65. London, 1875.

THOMAS AGNELLUS: *De morte et sepultura Henrici Regis Angliae Junioris.* See RALPH OF COGGESHALL.

WALTER MAP: *De Nugis Curialium.* Ed. M R. James. Anecdota Oxoniensia xiv. Oxford, 1914. (Ed. and tr. C. N. L. Brooke. Oxford 1998).

WAVERLEY: *Annales Monasterii de Waverleia:* see Monastic Annals.

WILLIAM OF MALMESBURY: *De Gestis Regum Anglorum; Historia Novella.* Ed. W. Stubbs. Rolls Series 82. London, 1887–9.
  Historia Novella. Ed. and tr. K. R. Potter. London, 1955.

WILLIAM OF NEWBURGH: *Historia rerum Anglicarum.*
  In: *Chronicles of the Reigns of Stephen, Henry II and Richard I*, vol. I, 101–293. Ed. R. Howlett. Rolls Series 82. London 1886.

WILLIAM OF TYRE: see Translations.

WORCESTER: *Annales Prioratus de Wigornia:* see Monastic Annals.

TRANSLATIONS

English Historical Documents *(EHD)* 1042–1189. Ed. D. C. Douglas and G. Greenaway. London, 1953.

Gerald the Welshman: *The Autobiography of Giraldus Cambrensis.* Tr. H. E. Butler. London, 1937.
  The First Version of the Topography of Ireland by Giraldus Cambrensis. Tr. J. J. O'Meara. Dundalk, 1951.
  Concerning the Instruction of Princes. Tr. J. Stevenson. London, 1858. (Predates the Rolls Series edition—not textually reliable.)

Greenaway, George. ed. and tr. *The Life and Death of Thomas Becket, Chancellor of England and Archbishop of Canterbury.* Based on the account of William FitzStephen his clerk with additions from other contemporary sources. London, 1961.

Hutton, Rev. W. H., ed. and tr. *S. Thomas of Canterbury: An account of his Life and Fame from The Contemporary Biographers and Other Chroniclers.* London, 1889. (Superseded by Greenaway.)

John of Salisbury: *The Statesman's Book: being the Fourth, Fifth and Sixth books, and selections from the Seventh and Eighth books of the Policraticus.* Ed. and tr, J. Dickinson. New York, 1927.

Frivolities of Courtiers and Footprints of Philosophers: being a translation of the First, Second and Third Books and selections from the Seventh and Eighth Books of the Policraticus of John of Salisbury. Tr, J. Pike. Minnesota and Oxford, 1938.

Melrose: *The Chronicle of Melrose.* Tr. J. Stevenson. (Church Historians of England IV pt. I.) London, 1858. (Unreliable.)

Nigel Longchamp: *A Mirror for Fools, or, The Book of Burnel the Ass.* Tr. J. H. Mozley, Oxford, 1961.

Otto of Freising: *The Deeds of Frederick Barbarossa,* by Otto of Freising and his continuator Rahewin. Tr. C. C. Meirow. Columbia University Press, 1953.

Roger Howden: *Annals.* Tr. H. T. Riley. London, 1853 (Predates Rolls Series edition—textually unreliable.)

William of Tyre *A History of Deeds done beyond the Sea.* Tr. E. A. Babcock and A. C. Krey. Columbia University Press, 1943.

There are also English translations in the following editions cited under Sources: Adam of Eynsham, Brut y Tywysogion. Gesta Stephani, Henry of Huntingdon, Jocelin of Brakelond, John of Salisbury (Letters and Memoirs of the Papal Court), Jordan Fantosme, Richard Fitzneale, Song of Dermot, Thomas Saga, Walter Map, William of Malmesbury.

SECONDARY AUTHORITIES

A. GENERAL

BEMONT, Charles: 'La Bulle Laudabiliter'
In: Mélanges d'Histoire du Moyen Age offerts a M. Ferdinand Lot. pp. 41–53. Paris, 1925.

CHARTROU, Josèphe: L'Anjou de 1109–51: Foulque de Jérusalem et Geoffroi Planta-genet. Paris, 1928.

DUGDALE, William, and DODSWORTH, Roger; Monasticon Anglicanum. London, 1817-30.

DUGGAN, Charles: Twelfth-century Decretal Collections and their importance in English history. University of London Historical Studies XIX, London, 1963.

EYTON, Rev. R. W.: Court, Household and Itinerary of King Henry II, instancing also the chief agents and adversaries of the king in his government diplomacy and warfare. London, 1878.

HALL, Hubert: Court Life under the Plantagenets (Reign of Henry II). London, 1899.

HALPHEN, Louis: 'Les entrevues des rois Louis VII et Henri II durant l'exil de Thomas Becket en France.'
In: Mélanges d'histoire offerts à M. Charles Bémont. Paris, 1913.

HASKINS, Charles H.: Studies in the History of Medieval Science. London, 1960.
'Henry II as a Patron of Literature.'
In: Essays in Medieval History presented to Thomas Frederick Tout. Ed. A. G. Little and F. M. Powicke. Manchester, 1925.

HASSALL, Arthur ed: Historical Introductions to the Rolls Series by William Stubbs, D.D. London, 1902.

KING, Edmund, ed.: The Anarchy of King Stephen's Reign. Oxford 1994.

LEBRETON, Charles: La Pénitence de Henri II Roi d'Angleterre et le concile d'Avranches en 1172. Saint-Brieuc, 1884.

LUCHAIRE, Achille: Histoire des institutions monarchiques sous les premiers Capétiens. Paris, 1883.

MICHEL, Francisque: Deux années du règne d'Henri II Roi d'Angleterre (1173–4). Poitiers, 1841.

NORGATE, Kate: England under the Angevin Kings. London, 1887.

ORPEN, Goddard H.: Ireland under the Normans 1169–1216. Oxford, 1911.

POOLE, Austin L.: From Domesday Book to Magna Carta 1087–1216. Oxford, 1950.

POOLE, Reginald L.: 'The Early Lives of Robert Pullen and Nicholas Breakspear.'
In: Essays in Medieval History presented to T. F. Tout. Ed. A. G. Little and F. M. Powicke. Manchester, 1925.

RAMSAY, Sir James H.: *The Angevin Empire, or The Three Reigns of Henry II, Richard I, and John*. London, 1903.

RICHARD, Alfred: *Histoire des Comtes de Poitou, 778–1204*. Paris, 1903.

STENTON, F. M.: *Norman London, An Essay*, with a translation of William FitzStephen's description by H. E. Butler and a Map of London under Henry II by M. B. Honeybourne. annotated by E. J. Davies. Historical Association Leaflets 93–4, 1934.

STUBBS, William: *Seventeen Lectures on the study of medieval and modern history and kindred subjects*. Oxford, 1886.

   Historical Introductions: see Hasnall, Arthur (above).

B. GOVERNMENT

ADAMS, George B.: *Council and Courts in Anglo-Norman England*. New Haven and Oxford, 1926.

AMT, Emilie.: *The Accession of Henry II in England. Royal Government Restored*. Woodbridge and Rochester NY, 1993.

BOUSSARD, Jacques.: *Le Gouvernement d'Henri II Plantagenet*. Paris, 1956.

BROOKE, Z. N.: *The English Church and the Papacy from the Conquest to the Reign of King John*. Cambridge, 1931.

CHENEY, C. R.: *From Becket to Langton: English Church Government 1170–1213*. Manchester, 1956.

FOREVILLE, Raymonde: *L'Eglise et la Royauté en Angleterre sous Henri II Plantagenet (1154–89)*. Paris, 1943.

HARDEGEN, Friedrich.: *Imperialpolitik Konig Heinrichs II von England*. Heidelberg. 1905.

HASKINS, Charles H.: *Norman Institutions*. London, 1960 (reprint).

HOYT, Robert S.: *The Royal Demense in English Constitutional History 1066–1272*. New York, 1950.

PETIT-DUTAILLIS. Charles: *The Feudal Monarchy in France and England from the Tenth to the Thirteenth Century*. London, 1936.

POWICKE, Sir Maurice. *The Loss of Normandy 1189–1204. Studies in the history of the Angevin Empire*. Manchester, 1960 (reprint).

RICHARDSON, H. O., and SAYLES, G. O.: *The Governance of Medieval England from the Conquest to Magna Carta*. Edinburgh, 1963.

ROUND, J. H.: *Feudal England: Historical Studies on the Eleventh and Twelfth Centuries*. London, 1909.

   Geoffrey de Mandeville: A study of the Anarchy. London, 1892.

   The Commune of London and other studies. London, 1892.

TOUT, T. F.: *Chapters in the Administrative History of Medieval England*. Manchester, 1920.

WOLFF, Ilse: *Heinrich II von England als Vassall Ludwigs VII von Frankreich*. Breslau, 1936.

C. BIOGRAPHY and Literary Tradition

ABBOTT, E. A.: *St Thomas of Canterbury. His Death and Miracles.* London, 1898.

BARLOW, Frank.: *Thomas Becket.* London 1986.

BERINGTON, Rev. J.: *The History of the Reign of Henry the Second and of Richard and John his Sons; With the Events of the Period from 1154 to 1216.* Dublin, 1790.

BRADBURY, Jim.: *Philip Augustus, King of France 1180-1223.* London 1998.

BROWN, Paul A.: *The Development of the Legend of Thomas Becket.* Philadelphia, 1930.

CARTELLIERI, Alexander.: *Philipp II August Konig von Frankreich.* Leipzig and Paris, 1899–1900.

CHIBNALL, Marjorie.: *The Empress Matilda: Queen Consort, Queen Mother and Lady of the English.* Oxford 1991.

CROUCH, David.: *William Marshal: Court, Career and Chivalry in the Angevin Empire.* London and New York 1990.

DARK, Sidney.: *St Thomas of Canterbury.* London, 1927.

DUBY, Georges.: *William Marshal: The Flower of Chivalry.* London and New York 1986.

GILLINGHAM, John.: *Richard the Lionheart.* London 1978
    Richard Coeur de Lion: Kingship, Chivalry and War in the Twelfth Century. London 1994.

GREEN, Mrs J. R.: *Henry the Second.* London, 1892.

HELTZEL, Virgil B.: *Fair Rosamond: A Study of the Development of a Literary Theme.* Evanston, 1947.

HODGSON, C. E.: *Jung Heinrich, König von England, Sohn König Heinrichs II, 1155–83.* Jena, 1906.

HUTTON, W. H.: *Thomas Becket, Archbishop of Canterbury.* London/New York, 1949.

KELLY, Amy: *Eleanor of Aquitaine and the Four Kings.* London/New York, 1932.

KNOWLES, Dom David: 'Archbishop Thomas Becket—a character study.'
    In: *The Historian and Character.* Oxford, 1963: 98–112.
    The Episcopal Colleagues of Thomas Becket. Cambridge. 1960.

LABANDE, Edmond-René: *Pour une image veridique d'Aliénor d'Aquitaine,* Poitiers 1952. (Offprint from *Bulletin de la Société des Antiquaires de l'Ouest* (4e série—tome II) 1952.)

LYTTELTON, Lord George: *The History of the Life of King Henry the Second.* Dublin, 1768–72.

MACKIE, J: Duncan.: *Pope Adrian IV.* Oxford and London, 1907.

MAY, Thomas: *The Reigne of King Henry the Second, written in seaven bookes.* London, 1633.

MOORE, Olin H.: *The Young King, Henry Plantagenet (1155–83) in History, Literature, and Tradition.* Ohio, 1925.

MORRIS, John: *The Life and Martyrdom of Saint Thomas Becket, Archbishop of Canterbury.* London and New York, 1885.

PAIN, Nesta: *The King and Becket.* London/New York, 1964.

PAINTER, Sidney: *William Marshal, Knight-Errant, Baron and Regent of England.* Oxford, Baltimore, 1933.

NORGATE, Kate: *Richard the Lion Heart.* London, 1924.

RADFORD, Lewis B.: *Thomas of London before his Consecration.* Cambridge, 1894.

ROBERTSON, J. C.; *Becket, Archbishop of Canterbury: A Biography.* London, 1859.

ROSSLER, Oskar: *Kaiserin Mathilde, Mutter Heinrichs von Anjou, und das Zeitalter der Anarchie in England.* Berlin, 1897.

SALZMANN, L. F.: *Henry II.* London, 1917.

SPEAIGHT, Robert: *Thomas Becket.* London/New York, 1989.

VOSS, Lena: *Heinrich von Blois Bischof von Winchester 1129–71.* Berlin, 1932.

WALBERG, E.: *La tradition hagiographique de Saint Thomas Becket avant la fin du XIIe siècle: études critiques.* Paris, 1929.

WARREN, W.L.: *Henry II.* London 1973.

WARREN, W. L.: *King John.* London, 1961.

WEBB, Clement C. J.: *John of Salisbury,* London, 1932.

D. ART, LITERATURE AND MILITARY BACKGROUND

ARMITAGE, Ella S.: *The Early Norman Castles of the British Isles.* London, 1912.

BORENIUS, Tancred: *St Thomas Becket in Art.* London, 1932.

CLAPHAM, A. W.: *Romanesque Architecture in Western Europe.* Oxford, 1936.

HILL, R. T., and BERGIN, T. G.: *Anthology of the Provencal Troubadours.* Yale/ Oxford, 1941.

THE HISTORY OF THE KING'S WORKS, ed. R. A. Brown.
    I, II: *The Middle Ages,* by H. M. Calvin and A. J. Taylor, HMSO, London/New York, 1963.

HOLLISTER, C. Warren, ed.: *Anglo-Norman Political Culture and the Twelfth-Century Renaissance.* Woodbridge and Rochester, NY 1997.

LOT, Ferdinand: *L'Art Militaire et les Armées au moyen age.* Paris, 1946.

OMAN, Sir Charles: *A History of the Art of War in the Middle* Ages (2vv.). London, 1924.

THOMAS, L.: *Poésies Complètes de Bertran de Born.* Toulouse, 1888.

VERBRUGGEN, J. F.: *The Art of Warfare in Western Europe.* Woodbridge & Rochester, NY, 1997.

ARTICLES

Abbreviations:

    BEC   Bibliothèque de l'Ecole des Chartes
    DAGM   Deutsches Archiv für Geschichtc des Mittelalters
    EHR   English Historical Review
    TRHS   Transactions of the Royal Historical Society

Barlow, Frank; 'The English, Norman and French Councils called to deal with the Papal schism of 1159.' *EHR* LI, 1936: 264–8.

Boussard, Jacques; 'Les Mercenaires au XIIe siècle: Henri Plantagenet et les origines de l'armée du métier.' *BEC* CVI, 1945–6: 189–224.

Brooke, Z. N.; 'The effect of Becket's murder on papal authority in England.' *Cambridge Historical Journal* II, 1926–8: 213 –28.
    and C. N. L. 'Henry II. Duke of Normandy and Aquitaine.' *EHR* LXI, 1946: 81–9.

Brown, R. A.: 'Royal Castle-Building in England 1154–1216.' *EHR* LXX, 1955: 353–98.
    'A List of the Castles 1154–1216.' *EHR* LXXIV, 1959; 249–80.

Cartellieri, Alexander; 'Die Machtstellung Heinrichs II von England.' *Neue Heidelberger Jahrbücher* VIII, 1898: 269–83.

Cheney, Mary: 'The Compromise of Avranches in 1172 and the spread of Canon Law in England.' *EHR* LVI, 1941: 177–97.

Davis, H. W. C.: 'The Anarchy of Stephen's Reign.' *EHR* XVIII, 1903: 630–40.
    'Simonsfeld: Jahrbücher des Deutschen Reiches unter Friedrich I' (Review). *EHR* XXIV, 1909: 772.
    The Chronicle of Battle Abbey.' *EHR* XXIX, 1914: 426–34.

Davis, R. H. C.: 'What happened in Stephen's reign, 1135–54.' *History.* XLIX, 1964, 1–12.
    Geoffrey de Mandeville.' *EHR* LXXIX, 1964.

Delisle, L.; La pretendue célébration d'un concile a Toulouse en 1160.' *Journal des Savants* 1902 45–51.

Duggan, Charles: 'Henry II and the Criminous Clerks.' *Bulletin of the Institute of Historical Research,* 1962, XXXV; 1–28.

Fawtier. R.: 'L'histoire financière de l'Angleterre au Moyen Age.' *Le Moyen Age,* 1928: 48–67.

Galbraith, V. H.: 'A New Charter of Henry II to Battle Abbey.' *EHR* LII, 1937: 67–73.

The Literacy of the Medieval English Kings.' *Proceedings of the British Academy* XXI, 1935: 213–15.

Gray. J. W.: 'The Ius Praesentandi in England from Clarendon to Bracton.' *EHR* LXVII, 1952; 481–509.

Grundmann, Herbert: 'Rotten und Brabanzonen: Soldner-Heere im 12. Jahrhundert.' *DAGM* 5, 1941–2: 419–92.

Haskins, Charles H.: 'England and Sicily in the Twelfth Century.' *EHR* XXVI, 1911: 433–47, 641–65.

Hubert, Jean: 'Le Miracle de Déols et la trève conclue en 1187 entre les rois de France et d'Angleterre.' *BEC* XCVI, 1935: 285–300.

Hunt, R. W.; 'English Learning in the Late Twelfth Century.' *TRHS* XIX, 1936: 19–42.

Huygens, R. B. C.: 'Dialogus inter Regem Henricum Secundum et abbatem Bonnevallis; un écrit de Pierre de Blois réédité.' *Révue Bénédictine* 68, 1958: 87–112.

Johnson, Charles: 'The Reconciliation of Henry II with the Papacy: A Missing Document.' *EHR* LII. 1937: 465–7.

Jollife, J. E. A.: 'The Camera Regis under Henry II.' *EHR* LXVIII, 1953; 1–21, 337–62.

Lapsley, G. T.: 'The Flemings in Eastern England in the Reign of Henry II.' *EHR* XXI, 1906: 509–13.

Lillie, Rev. H. W. R.: 'St Thomas of Canterbury's Opposition to Henry II.' *Clergy Review* VIII, 1934; 261–83.

Maitland, F. W.: 'Henry II and the Criminous Clerks.' *EHR* VII, 1892: 224–34.

Poole, Austin L.: 'Henry Plantagenet's Early Visits to England.' *EHR* XLVII. 1932: 447–52.
    'Die Welfen in die Verbannung.' *DAGM* 2, 1938: 129–48.

Poole, Reginald L.; 'Henry II, Duke of Normandy.' *EHR* XLII. 1927: 569–72.

Powicke, F. M. 'The Angevin Administration of Normandy.' *EHR* XXI, 1906: 625–49: XXII, 1907: 15–42.

Ramsay, Sir J. H.: 'Chroniclers' Estimates of Numbers and Official Records.' *EHR* XVIII, 1907: 625–9.

Richardson, H. O.: 'The Chamber under Henry II.' *EHR* LXIX, 1954: 596–611.
    'The Letters and Charters of Eleanor of Aquitaine.' *EHR* LXXIV. 1959: 193–213.
    'Richard Fitzneal and the Dialogue de Scaccario.' *EHR* XXIII, 1928: 161– 71, 321–40.

Stenton, Lady F. M.: 'Roger of Howden and Benedict.' *EHR* LXVIII, 1953: 574–82.

Vacandard. E.: 'Le divorce de Louis le Jeune.' *Révue des questions historiques* 47, 1890: 408–32.

Vasiliev, A. A.: 'Manuel Comnenus and Henry Plantagenet.' *Byzantinischer Zeitschrift* 29, 1929–30: 233 ff.

White, C. H.: 'The Career of Waleran Count of Meulan and Earl of Worcester (1104-66).' *TRHS* XVII. 1934: 19–49.

NOTES

Prologue

[1] Stenton, 34-5.
[2] Fitzneale, 6.

1: *The Troubled Land*

Sources: Gervase of Canterbury, i, 92-140 (usually in error on chronology: *vide* *EHR* XLVIII, 1952, 447-52); Gesta Stephani, 1-137; Henry of Huntingdon, 243-80; Melrose, 33; Recueil d'Annales, 9-11; Robert of Torigni, 104-54; William of Malmesbury, ii, 527-96, or ed. Potter; William of Newburgh, 29-60.

Secondary Authorities: Chartrou, 26-66; Delisle, 120-2; Green, 7-8; Norgate, England under the Angevins, i, 1-96, 261-377; A. L. Poole, From Domesday Book to Magna Carta, 128-66; Rossler, 1-377; Round, Geoffrey de Mandeville; Salzmann, 1-5; Voss, 1-122.

Articles: Davis, *EHR* XVIII, 1903, 630-41.

[1] According to Henry of Huntingdon (254) he died of eating lampreys against his doctors' orders. The place was St Denis-le-Fermont.
[2] Rossler, 417-20, discusses this at length. He produces considerable evidence in favour of the two being twins; some of it is dubious in isolation, but it amounts to a persuasive argument. On the other hand, the Handbook of British Chronology places William's birth after Matilda's, without citing any authority.
[3] Norgate, I, 258-60.
[4] Chartrou, 29.
[5] Now in the Musée du Tessé at Le Mans.
[6] Boussard, 99-112.
[7] Gerald, Opera, viii, 301.
[8] Ibid., viii, 309.
[9] *EHD* II, 199-200; Anglo-Saxon Chronicle (Peterborough) s.a., 1139.
[10] Chartrou, 39.
[11] Haskins, Studies in the History of Medieval Science, 20-42.
[12] Poole, *EHR* XLVII, 1932, 447-52.
[13] Chartrou, 224.
[14] Boussard, 287, 298, 335.

¹⁵ Margan, 14 gives the date as October 31, 1147, which would mean that
Henry made his request while Robert was still alive; but from what we know
of Robert's character he is unlikely to have refused assistance, and the episode
probably refers to his son.

2: *The Winning of a Kingdom*

Sources: Arnulf of Lisieux, xxvii-xxix; Chroniques des Comtes d'Anjou, 130;
Gerald, Opera, viii, 160-1 (tr. *EHD* 382-3); Gervase of Canterbury, i,
140-60; Gesta Stephani, 137-54; Henry of Huntingdon, 280-92; John of
Hexham, 322-32; John of Salisbury, Memoirs, 52-3, 61-2; Meaux, 131;
Melrose, 33; Ralph of Diceto, i, 291-300; Recueil des Annales, 12-13, 97,
100; Recueil des Chroniques, 135; Robert of Torigni, 155-82; Roger of
Howden, 211-14; Suger ed. Molinier, 161-6; Suger ed. Waquet, 281-5;
Waverley, 234; William of Newburgh, 87-95; William of Tyre II, 180-96.

Secondary Authorities: Chartrou, 65-76, 244; Foreville, 3-79; Green, 9-14;
Haskins, Norman Institutions, 158-64; Kelly, 1-81; Labande; Luchaire II,
265-7; Norgate, England under the Angevins, i, 377-407; A. L. Poole,
From Domesday Book to Magna Carta, 150-66; Richard, 90-115; Rossler,
377-434; Salzmann, 5-13.

Articles: Z. N. and C. N. L. Brooke, *EHR* LXI, 1946, 81-9; Davis, *EHR* XVIII,
1903, 630-41; R. L. Poole, *EHR* XLII, 1927, 569-72.

1 Gervase of Canterbury gives the correct date for this expedition, although he
does not mention that of 1147, unless his account of the recall of Henry dated
1146 (i. 131) belongs to 1147 rather than the end of the 1142 expedition.
2 John of Hexham, 323, Gesta Stephani.
3 Gesta Stephani, 147-8; this might have taken place at the beginning of the
expedition since Henry landed on the south coast, but there is no other reason
for rejecting the order of events given in the Gesta.
4 Z. N. and C. N. L. Brooke, *EHR* LXI, 1946, 89, give as Henry's chancellors
for this period:
    to 1150, Richard de Bohun (Geoffrey's chancellor).
    1150 to Sept. 1151, William de Vere or William Fitzgilbert (Henry as
    duke of Normandy).
    Sept. to Dec. 1151, Richard de Bohun (Henry as count of Anjou and duke
    of Normandy).
    Dec. 1151 to at least 1153, William de Vere or William Fitzgilbert.
5 Chartrou, 73.
6 William of Newburgh, 93.
7 John of Salisbury, Memoirs, 61-2; Gervase of Canterbury (i. 149) also com-
mends silence as to rumours circulating about Eleanor's conduct in the East.
8 But see Louis' letter (Recueil des Historiens, xv, 514) to Abbot Suger, in
which he describes an incident in which Eleanor's ship was separated by a
storm from the rest of his fleet, yet shows no feeling whatsoever.

[9] Kelly, 74–5.

[10] Labande, 17–18; Recueil des Historiens, xiv, 21.

[11] Labande, 19–20.

[12] Recueil des Chroniques, 135.

[13] John of Salisbury, Memoirs, 52–3; Gervase of Canterbury, 149.

[14] Gervase of Canterbury, i, 149.

[15] Richard, 112.

[16] Meaux, 131.

[17] Details of the revolt are given in full in Robert of Torigni, 165–9; Richard, 113; Boussard, 11; Norgate, England under the Angevins, i, 395–4.

[18] It seems unlikely that Henry would have made the long and arduous voyage direct to Bristol, especially since the south coast was favourable to him. Hence it is more plausible to suggest that he landed in the Weymouth Bay area as in 1142, and made his way overland to Bristol. But see Z. N. and C. N. L. Brooke, art. cit.

[19] On the other hand, Henry of Huntingdon (285–6) attributes Stephen's withdrawal to the weather and the flooded river.

[20] Gesta Stephani, 155; Richardson and Sayles, 252, n. 5, for order of events.

[21] Richardson and Sayles, 253–5.

3: A Prince among Princes

Sources: Adam of Eynsham, 62–3, 73–4, 85–6, 116–8; Arnulf of Lisieux, xxvii–lii, Gerald, Opera, i, 42, 52, 57; viii, 261, 312–3 (trs. in Autobiography 60, 72, 81, 106, 110–11); v, 303–6, viii, 158–63, 214–15, 304, (trs. in EHD 386–8, 380–6); Gerald, Topography, last chapter; John of Salisbury, Letters, 31–2; Policraticus II, 21–2, 32, 166; Materials, iii, 2–13, 26–8, vi, 72, 455–6; Nigel Longchamp 45–8; Peter of Blois, ed. 197–202; Ralph Higden, viii, 52–5, 58–9; Ralph Niger, 167–70 (for unfavourable view); Walter (trs. Tupper, 297–9, 302–3); William Newburgh, 280–6.

Secondary Authorities: Berington, 445; Bloch, 42–2, 49, 54; Delisle, 351–505 (personnel of Henry's court); Dugdale, 522, 532, 543, 546–7, 548, 551, 1008–9; Haskins, Studies in the History of Medieval Science, 20–42; 113–29, and 'Henry II as a patron of Literature,' 71–7; Heltzel, 1–14, Kelly, 150–1, 192–3; Knowles, Colleagues of Becket, 1–52; Mackie, passim; A. L. Poole, From Domesday Book to Magna Carta, 232–62; R. L. Poole, Early lives of Robert Pullen and Nicholas Breakspear, 61–70; Stubbs, Seventeen Lectures, 115–55; Webb, 6–21, 139–58.

Articles: Haskins, EHR XXVI, 1911, 433–47, 641–65; A. L. Poole, Deutsches Archiv für Geschichte des Mittelalters, 2, 1938, 129–48.

[1] See especially Pipe Roll 23 Henry II 1176–7, 198 and 201, where £500 was spent on furs, robes and clothes for the king's use.

S

[2] Walter Map, 237 (tr. Tupper, 297); Gerald, Opera, viii, 214–15; Peter of Blois, Ep. LXVI in Migne, Patrologia Latina, ccvii, 197–8.

[3] Gerald, Opera, viii, 304 (tr. EHD, 384).

[4] Orpen, 254.

[5] Walter Map, 237 (tr. Tupper, 297).

[6] Peter of Blois, Ep. XIV, tr. W. L. Warren, p. 23–4.

[7] Materials, III, 49 (tr. Greenaway, 76).

[8] Haskins, 'Henry II as patron of literature', 76.

[9] PR 2 Henry II 1155–6, 46; 3 Henry II 1156–7, 84, 90, 102; and successive years.

[10] PR 16 Henry II 1169–70, 146—'Hamelin owes one Norway hawk and one gerfalcon for having his suit heard.'

[11] Adam of Eynsham, 116–8.

[12] Walter Map, 241 (tr. Tupper, 302).

[13] Brown, EHR LXX, 1955, 353–98, LXXIV 1959, 249–80; Armitage.

[14] History of the King's Works, 80.

[15] Rotuli Normanniae, 110–11.

[16] Map in History of the King's Works, 85, text 81–7.

[17] History of the King's Works, 910–18 (Clarendon), 1009–17 (Woodstock), 491–3 (Westminster).

[18] Pipe Roll, 25; Henry II, 1179–80, p. 125.

[19] History of the King's Works, 1015–16.

[20] Gerald of Wales, Expugnatio Hiberniae 303, tr. EHD, 386.

[21] Materials, vi, 72.

[22] There is an interesting note of the king's regular almsgiving in the Hereford-shire Doomsday 1160–70, probably compiled by Thomas Brown, the king's almoner.

[23] Dugdale, Monasticon, 543, 546, 547, 548, 551; and Pipe Rolls, passim.

[24] Adam of Eynsham, 35–6.

[25] Ralph de Diceto, i. 407.

[26] Materials, vi, 455–6.

[27] Roger-Benedict, ii, 160–1.

[28] Guernes de Pont-Sainte-Maxence, 11, 301–35.

[29] Heltzel, 1–14; Ralph Higden, viii, 54.

[30] Gerald of Wales, Opera viii, 214–51.

[31] Materials, III, 24–5 (tr. Greenaway, 44–5).

[32] Haskins, EHR XXVI, 1911, 433–47, 641–65.

[33] Smythe, 39–40.

[34] See biographies in Knowles, Colleagues of Becket; Cheney ch. x.

[35] Nigel Longchamp, 45–8.

[36] See Mackie (Adrian IV), and Webb (John of Salisbury).

[37] Haskins, 'Henry II as Patron of Literature'.

[38] R. S. Loomis, Tristram and the House of Anjou: Modern Languages Review, xvii, 1922, 24–30.

[39] John of Salisbury, Policraticus, I, 166.

[40] Pipe Roll, 12 Henry II, 1165-6 (£1 to Maurice 'fabulator' p. 32); 23 Henry II, 1176-7 (£3 per annum to Henry the harper, p. 165); 21 Henry II, 1174-5 (payments for bears and bearwards, p. 29).

[41] Pipe Roll, 22 Henry II, 91.

[42] Hall, Court Life under the Plantagenets, bases his reconstruction on this.

[43] Richardson and Sayles, 156-70, 194-8, 221-8, 240-5.

[44] Boussard, 285-308.

4: The New Order

Sources: Arnulf of Lisieux, xxx-xxxi; Brut y Tywysogion, 185-95; Gerald, Opera vi, 130, 137-8; Gervase of Canterbury, i, 161-9; Holyrood, 131; Monastic Annals, i, 47, ii, 56, iv, 380; Otto of Freising, 178-9, 261, 324; Ralph de Diceto, i, 300-5; Recueil d'Annales, 14-15, 71; Recueil des Historiens, xii, 121; Robert of Torigni, 183-211, 317-27; Roger Howden, 213-8; William of Newburgh, i, 101-26 (tr. *EHD*, 322-30, 334) and 158-9 (1160 marriage treaty confused with 1169 peace). Denholm Young (coronation charter).

Secondary Authorities: Boussard, 401-26; Eyton, 1-59; Foreville, 79-106; Green, 21-38; Haskins, Norman Institutions, 162-70; Hoyt, 95; Hutton, 1-50; Kelly, 91-112; Mackie, 109-18; Norgate, England under the Angevins, i, 407-506; Radford, 2-152; Richard, 121-33; Salzmann ,14-49; Voss, 123-4; Wolff, 6-32.

Articles: Barlow, *EHR* LI, 1936, 264-8; Brown, *EHR* LXX, 1955, 353-98; *EHR* LXXIV, 1959, 249-80; Davis, *EHR* XVIII, 1903, 630-41; Delisle, *Journal des Savants*, 1902, 45-51; Ramsay, *EHR* XVIII, 1903, 625-9.

[1] Davis, *EHR* XVIII, 1903, 630-41.

[2] Translation in Denholm Young (pages not numbered).

[3] Foreville, 55.

[4] Morris, 23.

[5] Chronicle of Battle Abbey, 72-127.

[6] Robert of Torigni, 177, Ralph de Diceto, 297, i, 297.

[7] Brown, *EHR* LXXIV, 1959, 249 ff.

[8] Round, Geoffrey de Mandeville, 418-9.

[9] Webb, 96-7; Mackie, 109-18; Bémont, 41-53. Gerald, Opera v, 316 (tr. *EHD*, 776-7).

[10] Voss, 123-4.

[11] Materials III, 29-31 (tr. Greenaway, 45-7; Hutton, 23-5).

[12] Boussard, *Bibliothèque de l'Ecole des Chartes* CVI, 1945-6, 189-224.

[13] Otto of Freising, 178-9, 261.

[14] Hardegen, 20-2.

[15] Barlow, *EHR* LI, 1936, 264-8; Delisle. *Journal des Savants*, 1902, 45-51.

[16] Otto of Freising, 324.

266 HENRY PLANTAGENET

5: *The Central Problem*

Sources: Arnulf of Lisieux, xxxii–xlvii; Brut y Tywysogion, 199–207; Etienne de Rouen, 725–42; Gerald, Opera vi, 143; Gervase of Canterbury, i, 169–203; Holyrood, 141; Materials, I, 1–49, II, 299–314, 323–45, 353–406, III, 13–76, 155–357, IV, 1–64, 80–109, 186–90, 201–12, 266–352, V, 1–316 (II, 373, tr. *EHD* 708; IV, 299, tr. *EHD*, 716 and Greenaway, 63; IV, 27 tr. *EHD*, 716–7 and Greenaway 64–5); Melrose, 36–7; Ralph de Diceto, i, 305–29; Robert of Torigni, 211–29; Roger Howden, 219–23; Thomas Saga, i, 1–313; William of Newburgh, 131–47 (chs. XVI, XXIV, tr. in *EHD*, 332–4).

Secondary Authorities: Adams, 127–78; Boussard, 427–50; Eyton, 59–91; Foreville, 107–70; Green, 82–126; Halphen, 152–3, 159; Hodgson, 6–7; Hutton, 51–140; Kelly, 113–29; Knowles, Colleagues of Becket, 53–96; Salzmann, 50–64.

Articles: Davis, *EHR* XXIV, 1909, 772; Gray, *EHR* LXVII, 1952, 481–509; Maitland, *EHR* VII, 1892, 225–35; Duggan, *Bulletin of Institute of Historical Research*, XXXV, 1962, 1–28.

[1] Materials, III, 181 (tr. Greenaway, 51; Hutton, 26–7).
[2] Foreville, 19–22; Z. N. Brooke, The English Church and the Papacy, 59–193.
[3] Materials, III, 182.
[4] Materials, III, 37–41 (tr. Greenaway, 55–7).
[5] Pipe Roll 10 Henry II, 1163–4.
[6] Boussard, 436–7; Richardson and Sayles, 66–8, 87–91.
[7] Boussard, 535–40; Ramsay, 65 ff—but see Fawtier, *Le Moyen Age*, 1928, 48–56.
[8] Maitland, *EHR*, VII, 1892, 224–34; Duggan, *Bulletin of Institute for Historical Research*, 1962, XXXV, 1–28; Lillie, *Clergy Review*, VIII, 1934, 261–83; Foreville, 136–51.
[9] Roger of Pont-L'Eveque had been Becket's rival in the household of Theobald and had preceded him as archdeacon of Canterbury; Gilbert Foliot had opposed Becket's election whether from disapproval of Thomas or disappointment at not being chosen himself (cf. Materials, v, 512–20, 522–44).
[10] The letters concerning the Becket controversy up to the archbishop's flight are in Materials, v, 1–133.
[11] See Appendix 1.
[12] See note 8 above; and Greenaway, 68–72; *EHD*, 718–22; Hutton, 50–9, for translations. Also: Richardson and Sayles, 306–10; Davis, *EHR* XXIV, 1909, 772; Z. N. Brooke, English Church and the Papacy, 202–12.
[13] The accounts of the Northampton council are reasonably straightforward: William FitzStephen and Herbert of Bosham provide complementary eyewitness accounts (Materials, III, 49–70, 296–312; tr. Greenaway, 75–91, *EHD*. 724–33; Hutton, 66–86).

[14] The most important source for the years from 1166-9 are the letters: those from October 1164 until April 1166 are printed in Materials, V, 134-316.
[15] See Appendix II.

6: *This Low-born Clerk*

Sources: Arnulf of Lisieux, 72-3, 122-3 (tr. *EHD*, 741, 770-1); Etienne de Rouen, 675-724, 753-6; Gervase of Canterbury, i, 203-32; Histoire de Guillaume le Maréchal, I, vv. 1636-1904, III, 25-8; Materials, I, 49-136, II, 1-19, 314-22, 345-52, 406-50, III, 77-154, 357-534, IV, 65-79, 109-44, 190-200, 352-408, V, 316-544, VI passim, VII, 1-470 (III 449, 465-7, tr. in *EHD*, 751-2, 755-6 and Greenaway, 129, 136-7); Meaux, i, 191; Melrose, 37-8; Otto of Freising, 338; Polydore Vergil, 215-16; Ralph de Diceto, i, 329-345; Ralph Niger, 92-5; Recueil d'Annales, 37, 103; Recueil des Historiens, xii, 442, xiii, 679; Robert of Torigni, 229-49; Roger-Benedict (from 1169), i, 3-14; Thomas Saga, i, 313, ii, 241; William of Newburgh, 154-65 (tr. in part *EHD*, 334-42).

Secondary Authorities: Boussard, 427-35, 451-9; Eyton, 91-153; Green, 127-54; Halphen, passim; Hardegen, 13-20; Hutton, 141-271; Kelly, 129-49; Knowles, Colleagues of Becket, 96-139; and The Historian and Character, 98-128; Norgate, England under the Angevins, ii, 57-79, 120-8; Salzmann, 84-100.

See also Abbott, Brown, Dark, Morris, Robertson, Speaight and Walberg for various views of Becket and the legends about him.

[1] Boussard, 428-9.
[2] Halphen, 159.
[3] These letters, known from their opening words as 'Loqui de Deo', 'Exspectans expectavi', and 'Desiderio desideravi', are given in Materials, v, 266-8, 269-78, and 278-82 (tr. Greenaway, 109-111; Hutton, 120-1).
[4] Materials, v, 282-542 (parts tr, Hutton, 124-67).
[5] Materials, vi, 82-162 (parts tr, Hutton, 176-9).
[6] Materials, vi, 206-7 (tr, Hutton, 179-80); dated June 17, 1167. Alexander had previously (April 5, 1166) warned the archbishop of York and the other English bishops against usurping Canterbury's rights of coronation (Materials, v, 323).
[7] Etienne de Rouen, 711.
[8] Walter Map, 238 (tr. Tupper, 298-9; *EHD*, 389).
[9] Materials, vi, 269-70 (tr. Hutton, 183-7).
[10] Materials, vi, 306-7.
[11] Histoire de Guillaume le Maréchal, I, 1636-1904, III, 25-8.
[12] Materials, iii, 419-27 (Herbert of Bosham) (tr. Greenaway, 123-7; Hutton, 189-98), and ii, 506-13.
[13] Gervase of Canterbury, i, 208.
[14] Materials, vi, 537-9.
[15] Materials, vi, 558-84.

[16] Materials, vi, 599 (tr. Hutton, 199–200).
[17] Materials, vii, 23–32; Hardegen, 17–20.
[18] Materials, vii, 70–5.
[19] Gervase of Canterbury, i, 214–15.
[20] Materials, iii, 448–51 (tr. Greenaway, 129–30; Hutton, 202–4), vii, 161–7.
[21] Gervase of Canterbury, i, 219.
[22] Polydore Vergil, 215–16.
[23] Roger-Benedict, i, 6.
[24] Materials, iii, 465–7 (tr. Greenaway, 136–7).
[25] Roger-Benedict, i, 6–7.
[26] Ibid. i, 9.
[27] Materials, iii, 114 (tr. Greenaway, 140).
[28] Materials, ii, 429.
[29] Arnulf of Lisieux, 122–3 (tr. EHD, 770–1, part in Greenaway, 161).

7: *The Western Edge of the World*

Sources: Brut y Tywysogion, 188–207, 210–19; Gerald, Opera, v, 227–88, 316 (tr. EHD, 776–7), vi, 62, 130, 137–43, 227; Gervase of Canterbury, i, 233–7; Materials, vii, 440–85; Ralph de Diceto, i, 346–53; Robert of Torigni, 249–52; Roger-Benedict, i, 14–30; Roger Howden, ii, 18–35; Song of Dermot, 19–203, 209–17; William of Newburgh, 165–9 (chronology confused).

Secondary Authorities: Boussard, 458–69; Eyton, 153–69; Green, 154–69; Kelly, 176–7; Norgate, England under the Angevins, ii, 82–119, 128–34; Orpen, i, 80 ff., ii, 1–110; A. L. Poole. From Domesday Book to Magna Carta, ch. ix; Salzmann, 101–21; Warren, 33–7.

[1] Robert of Torigni, 249; Boussard, 460.
[2] Recueil des Historiens, xiii, 679; Vasiliev, Byzantinischer Zeitschrift, 29, 1929–30, 233 ff.
[3] Voss, 130.
[4] On the Welsh expeditions see Brut y Tywysogion, 188–207, 210–19 and Gerald, Itinerarium and Descriptio Kambriae in Opera vi.
[5] Gerald, Opera, vi, 62.
[6] Brut y Tywysogion, 212–15.
[7] See chapter IV, note 9.
[8] Orpen, i, 254.
[9] Ibid., i, 261.
[10] Gerald, Opera, v, 281–3, gives the text of the Constitutions.
[11] Gerald, Opera, vi, 287–8.
[12] Roger-Benedict, i, 162–5.
[13] Ibid., i, 339.

8: *The Great Rebellion*

Sources: Chroniques de St Martial, 58; Gerald, Opera, viii, 163–5; Gervase of Canterbury, i, 237–51; Histoire de Guillaume le Maréchal, i, 2079–384, iii, 30–5; Holyrood, 153, 156–8; Jordan Fantosme (part repeated in *EHD*, 374–6); Materials, vii, 471–516; Melrose, 40; Ralph de Diceto, 351–98; Recueil des Chroniques, 139; Recueil des Historiens, xii, 442–3 (Geoffrey of Vigeois); Robert of Torigni, 253–66; Roger-Benedict, i, 30–81; Roger Howden, ii, 35–69; William of Newburgh, 170–98.

Secondary Authorities: Boussard, 469–88; Brooke, English Church and the Papacy, 211, ff.; Eyton, 169–85; Foreville, 329–72, 389–401; Green, 170–84; Hodgson, 21–49; Kelly, 178–88; Lebreton; Michel; Norgate, England under the Angevins, ii, 79–81, 134–68; Richard the Lionheart, 13–17; Painter, 30–6; Richard, 169–80; Richardson and Sayles, 309–12; Salzmann, 122–44; Wolf, 85.

Articles: Boussard, *Bibliothèque de l'Ecole des Chartres* CVI, 1945–6, 203–10.
Brooke, *Cambridge Historical Journal*, II, 1926–8, 213–28.
M. Cheney, *EHR* LVI, 1941, 177–97.
Gray, *EHR* LXVII, 1952, 481–509.
Johnson, *EHR* LII, 1937, 465–7.
Lapsley, *EHR*, XXI, 1906, 509–13.

[1] Materials, vii, 481–2, 501–2, 506–8.
[2] Materials, vii, 513–16 (De reconciliatione regis).
[3] See Lebreton's pamphlet for the exact details of the ceremony and the evidence about it.
[4] Johnson, *EHR* LII, 1937, 465–7.
[5] Materials, vii, 519.
[6] Gerald, Opera, vii, 170–2; Ralph Niger, 168.
[7] Materials, vii, 519.
[8] Foreville, 373–88; Richardson and Sayles, 294–5, 357–8. Gerald's explanation (Opera, iv, 75–6), that Henry's absence abroad was the real reason for his inability to interfere, scarcely holds water.
[9] Brooke, English Church and the Papacy, 211; M. Cheney, *EHR* LVI, 1941, 177–97.
[10] Richardson and Sayles, 295–8.
[11] M. Cheney, *EHR* LVI, 1941, 189.
[12] Ibid., 191; Gray, *EHR* LXVII, 1952, 481–509.
[13] Brooke, English Church, 212: *Cambridge Historical Journal*, II, 1926, 213–28.
[14] Robert of Torigni, 255.
[15] Melrose, 40.
[16] According to Geoffrey of Vigeois (Recueil des Historiens, xii, 442), Raymond of Toulouse had also encouraged Richard and Eleanor to revolt against Henry.
[17] Richard had held Aquitaine since 1170, apparently at his mother's wish (Recueil des Historiens, xii, 442; Geoffrey of Vigeois).

[18] Ralph de Diceto, i, 371.
[19] Michel's pamphlet covers the events of these two years in good detail but without valuations of evidence: Norgate, England under the Angevins, ii, 135–67 is reliable on dubious points of chronology.
[20] Robert of Torigni, 259.
[21] Ralph de Diceto, i, 377–9 is the most reliable authority for the details of this episode.
[22] Jordan Fantosme gives a full description of the Scottish campaign.
[23] Jordan Fantosme, 365–73; William of Newburgh, 188.
[24] Roger Howden, ii, 64.
[25] William of Newburgh, 198; Roger-Benedict, i, 96–9.
[26] Gervase of Canterbury, i, 293.

9: The Years of Peace

Sources: Adam of Eynsham, 62–3, 73–4, 85–6; Chroniques de St Martial, 188; Gerald, Opera, viii, 166–87, 293; Gervase of Canterbury, i, 251–95; Histoire de Guillaume le Maréchal, i, 2385–3424; Meaux, 209; Pound, 42; Ralph de Diceto, i, 398–440, ii, 3–6, iii, 35–44; Recueil des Historiens, xiii, 683 (Anonymous of Laudun); Robert of Torigni, 266–91; Roger-Benedict, i, 81–251, 263–6; Roger Howden, ii, 71–201; William of Newburgh, 203–23.

Secondary Authorities: Boussard, 489–583; Cartellieri, 1–36; Eyton, 185–237; Green, 184–9; Haskins, Norman Institutions, 175 ff; Henderson, 39–45; Hodgson, 49–58; Kelly, 189–202; Norgate, England under the Angevins, ii, 169–219: Richard the Lionheart, 17–39; Painter, 36–46; Richard, 180–202; Salzmann, 145–58.

Articles: Boussard, Bibliothèque de l'Ecole des Chartes CVI, 1945–6, 210–12.
Haskins, EHR XXVI, 1911, 433–47, 641–65.
Vasiliev, Byzantinischer Zeitschrift, 29, 1933.

[1] Thomas, 133–5 (author's translation).
[2] Dante, Inferno, Canto, XXVIII, 118–42.
[3] Roger-Benedict, i, 92–3.
[4] A. L. Poole, From Domesday Book to Magna Carta, 33–4.
[5] Gervase of Canterbury, i, 256; Meaux, 209; Gerald, Opera, viii, 232.
[6] Richardson and Sayles, 439–44. (See Appendix II.) The text is given in Roger-Benedict, i, 108–11; Roger Howden, ii, 89–91. Other treatments of the subject (e.g. Bousard, 494–510), while of value on details are unreliable because they accept without question on the view put forward by Stubbs of the relationship between the Clarendon and Northampton assizes. Even though Richardson and Sayles may not have had the last word on the subject, it is unlikely that the earlier theory will be reinstated.
[7] Roger-Benedict, i, 114.
[8] Ibid., i, 116.
[9] Ibid., i, 116–17, 120, 127; Ralph de Diceto, i, 408, 414, 417–20.
[10] Brown, EHR LXXIV, 1959, 249–80.

[11] Ralph de Diceto, i, 415-16.

[12] Vasiliev, *Byzantinischer Zeitschrift*, 29, 1929-30, 233 ff. News of Manuel Comnenus' defeat was probably brought by a second embassy in 1177.

[13] Roger-Benedict, i, 139-54.

[14] Robert of Torigni, 282-3; Rigord, 10-11.

[15] Gervase of Canterbury, i, 293.

[16] Recueil des Historiens, xiii, 683 (Anonymous of Laudun); 'Henry' is of course the young king.

[17] Gerald, Opera, viii, 293.

10: *Absalom*

Sources: Chroniques de St Martial, 60, 190; Gerald, Opera, viii, 188-93; Gervase of Canterbury, i, 295-305; Histoire de Guillaume le Maréchal, i, 3,425-7,174, iii, 44-84; Walter Map, 139-40 (tr. Tupper and Ogle, 178-80); Melrose, 43; Monastic Annals, i, 52 (Tewkesbury); Pound, 43; Ralph de Diceto, ii, 7-20; Recueil des Historiens, xviii, 212-18 (Geoffrey of Vigeois); Rigord, 22-36; Robert of Torigni, 294-308; Roger-Benedict, i, 269-304; Roger Howden, ii, 253-81; Smythe, 78-9; Thomas Agnellus.

Secondary Authorities: Boussard, 533-45; Cartellieri, 37-140, 190-218; Eyton, 237-52; Green, 209-10; Henderson, 45-51; Hodgson, 58-81; Kelly, 203-23; Moore, 25-47; Norgate, England under the Angevins, 219-28: Richard the Lionheart, 39-56; Painter, 46-56; Richard, 202-22; Salzmann, 158-61.

Articles: A. L. Poole, *Deutsches Archiv für Geschichte des Mittelalters*, 2, 1938, 129-48.

[1] Gervase of Canterbury, i, 294; Ralph de Diceto, ii, 7; Boussard, 535-6.

[2] Ralph de Diceto, ii, 12; Roger-Benedict, i, 282-3.

[3] Roger-Benedict, i, 269.

[4] The exactness of Roger Howden's text (Roger-Benedict, i, 278) and dating has been questioned by Richardson and Sayles (439, n. 3) but without any definite conclusion.

[5] Gerald, Opera, viii, 190-3; Gervase of Canterbury, i, 298-9; Ralph de Diceto, ii, 10.

[6] Gerald, Opera, viii, 189-90.

[7] A. L. Poole, Deutsches Archiv für Geschichte des Mittelalters, 2, 1938, 129-38.

[8] Walter Map, 139 (tr. Tupper and Ogle, 178-9).

[9] Histoire de Guillaume le Maréchal, i, 2637-95, iii, 37 (tr. Powicke, *EHR* XXII, 1906, 40).

[10] Histoire de Guillaume le Maréchal, i, 5711-5848, iii, 70-2.

[11] Thomas, 16-17 (author's translation).

[12] Recueil des Historiens, xviii, 212-8 (Geoffrey of Vigeois); Chroniques de St Martial, 60, 190.

[13] William of Newburgh, 233-4 (tr. *EHD*, 360-1); Walter Map, 139 (tr. Tupper and Ogle, 178-9); Thomas Agnellus, 265-7.

[14] Histoire de Guillaume le Maréchal, i, 6572–6984, iii, 80–1.
[15] Thomas, 28–30 (author's translation).
[16] Thomas Agnellus, 267–73.
[17] Roger-Benedict, i, 301.
[18] Histoire de Guillaume le Maréchal, i, 7038–7155, iii, 82–3.
[19] Walter Map, 139 (tr. Tupper and Ogle, 179).

11: *They that take the Sword . . .*

Sources: Gerald, Opera, iv, 368–71, viii, 203–97 (part tr. *EHD*, 382–5), 304–9
(viii, 261, 312–13, tr. Autobiography, 106, 110–11); Gervase of Canterbury,
i, 308–449 (chiefly on Canterbury affairs); Guillaume Lebreton, i, 182–90,
ii, 59–94; Histoire de Guillaume le Maréchal, i, 7302–9432, iii, 85–120;
Holyrood, 170; Melrose, 45–9; Ralph de Diceto, ii, 21–65; Rigord, 40–
96; Robert of Torigni, 309–15 (ends 1186); Roger-Benedict, i, 304–61,
ii, 3–71 (ii, 67–71, tr. *EHD*, 377–9); Roger Howden, ii, 282–367; William
of Newburgh, 234–79 (chs. xiii–xiv, xxiii–xxvi, tr. *EHD*, 364–71).

Secondary Authorities: Boussard, 546–82; Cartellieri, 140–90, 219–315; Eyton,
253–298; Green, 210–224; Henderson, 51–74; Kelly, 224–46; Norgate,
England under the Angevins, ii, 229–72; Richard the Lionheart, 56–90;
Painter, 56–73; Richard, 223–53; Salzmann, 161–74.

Articles: Boussard, *Bibliothèque de l'Ecole des Chartes* CVI, 1945–6, 214–17;
Grundmann, Deutsches Archiv für Geschichte des Mittelalters, 5, 1941–2,
472–80.
Hubert, *Bibliothèque de l'Ecole des Chartes* XCVI, 1935, 285–300.

[1] Roger-Benedict, i, 304–5.
[2] Richardson and Sayles (444–6) suggest that this assize was probably drafted
as early as 1166.
[3] Gervase of Canterbury, i, 313–25.
[4] Gerald, Opera, viii, 200–12; Roger-Benedict, i, 328–33; 335–6, 338;
Ralph de Diceto, ii, 32–3; William of Newburgh, 244–7 (tr. *EHD*, 382).
[5] Pipe Roll 32 Henry II, 1185–6.
[6] Rotuli Normanniae, 110.
[7] Melrose, 45.
[8] Holyrood, 170; Roger-Benedict, i, 351.
[9] Roger-Benedict, i, 350; Ralph de Diceto, ii, 41; Rigord, 20.
[10] Gerald, Opera, viii, 176.
[11] Hubert, *Bibliothèque de l'Ecole des Chartes* XCVI, 1935, 285–300; Rigord,
79–80.
[12] Gerald, Opera, viii, 233.
[13] Roger-Benedict, ii, 30.
[14] Guillaume Lebreton, 189.
[15] Roger-Benedict, ii, 160.

[16] Anonymous of Béthune, quoted in J. Balteau, *Dictionnaire de Biographie Française* (Paris, 1936) 2, 64-5.

[17] The chronology of Henry's last days is perhaps more complex than that of any other period of his life, and has therefore been treated in full in Appendix III.

[18] Gerald, Opera, viii, 296 (tr. *EHD*, 384).

[19] Gerald, Opera, iv, 370-1.

[20] Gerald, Opera, viii, 296 (tr. *EHD*, 384).

[21] Ibid.

[22] Histoire de Guillaume le Maréchal, i, 9113-61.

[23] Histoire de Guillaume le Maréchal, i, 9244-9409; Gerald, Opera, viii, 304-5 (tr. *EHD*, 384).

INDEX